River of Tears

ALEXANDER SEBASTIAN DENT

River of Tears

COUNTRY MUSIC, MEMORY,

AND MODERNITY IN BRAZIL

Duke University Press   Durham and London   2009

Library of Congress Cataloging-in-Publication Data

Dent, Alexander Sebastian.
River of tears : country music, memory, and
modernity in Brazil / Alexander Sebastian Dent.
p. cm.
Includes bibliographical references and index.
ISBN 978-0-8223-4520-6 (cloth : alk. paper)
ISBN 978-0-8223-4537-4 (pbk. : alk. paper)
1. Country music—Brazil—History and criticism.
2. Música sertaneja—Brazil—History and criticism.
3. Country music—Social aspects—Brazil.
4. Música sertaneja—Social aspects—Brazil.
5. Country music—Political aspects—Brazil.
6. Música sertaneja—Political aspects—Brazil.
I. Title.
ML3487.B7D468 2009
781.6420981—dc22   2009013112

An earlier version of chapter 2 appeared as "Country
Brothers: Kinship and Chronotope in Brazilian Rural Public
Culture," Anthropological Quarterly 80, no. 2 (2007): 455–95.

We know the truth, not only through reason, but also through the heart. It is through the latter that we know first principles, and reason, which has no part in it, vainly tries to challenge them.—BLAISE PASCAL, *Pensées*

Contents

Preface

> The task of the translator consists in finding that intended effect [Intention] upon the language into which he is translating which produces in it the echo of the original.
> —WALTER BENJAMIN, "The Task of the Translator"

This book embraces anthropology's commitment to relentless translation, where translation is defined as the movement of a text from one medium into another. My overall goal has been to translate Central-Southern Brazilian rural music into a form in which it can be analyzed. An attached goal has been the development of a theory of performance that is sensitive to the socially and economically neoliberal times we live in. In moving toward these larger goals, countless smaller translations have been necessary, not the least of which has been the conversion of a large number of song lyrics, books, quotations, and conversations from Portuguese into English. I have also had to render music in prose.

The book you are holding contains only the untranslated texts whose Portuguese bears directly on my argument. Those who care to explore what might be thought of as the Portuguese-language "originals" will find them on this book's website: www.riveroftearsbrazil.com. They will also find short musical clips of the songs I cite.

For those already familiar with the Brazilian lyrics from which I quote, you will notice that my English translations do not aim for a literal conversion, complete with rhyming schemes and meter. Instead, calling upon my experience as a writer of lyrics at least as much as my experience as an anthropologist, I have sought to capture the Brazilian sense and feeling of each text for those reading in English.

Acknowledgments

I would like to thank the following for their help and support. Most recently, my colleagues at the George Washington University, Joel Kuipers, Richard Grinker, Catherine Allen, Stephen Lubkeman, Ilana Feldman, Barbara Miller, Robert Shepherd, Jeff Blomstar, and Rob Albro have contributed to an ongoing scholarly discussion, while the rest of the department has provided a supportive and collegial ambiance. Colleagues at other institutions have also engaged in dialogue: Aaron Fox, Ana Maria Ochoa, Anthony Seeger, Bryan McCann, Jason Jackson, Janet Chernela, Daniel Party, Haquira Osakabe, Ivan Vilela, Mauru de Almeida, Jerry Wever, Diane Pecknold, Derek Pardue, Dan Sharp, and Naomi Moniz. At the University of Chicago, my teachers molded my interests, and several of them assisted with early stages of this work: Andrew Apter, John Comaroff, Jean Comaroff, Elizabeth Povinelli, Manuela Carneiro da Cunha, Terence Turner, Philip Bohlman, Dain Borges, Claudio Lomnitz, Marshall Sahlins, John MacAloon, John Kelly, Michael Silverstein, Alan Kolata, Tom Cummins, Susan Gal, James Fernandez, and Moishe Postone. My undergraduate teachers James Boon, John Kelly, Jorge Klor de Alva, and John McPhee shaped my approach to reading, writing, and anthropology in ways that become clearer to me as I complete this project. At Duke University Press, Ken Wissoker has been a patient and rigorous editor.

I am indebted to several musicians. Luiz Faria's patient tutelage expanded my knowledge of my subject, sometimes incrementally, but most often by leaps and bounds. Luiz's friends Sulino, Zico, Liu, and Zalo also played an important role in my education in rural music. Paulo Friere helped with his detailed analysis of the role of nature in *música caipira* practice and by demonstrating a way of combining research, writing, and *viola* playing. Ivan Vilela provided hospitality at his homes in Campinas and also taught me a great deal about viola pedagogy and theory. From Roberto Corrêa I received important viola teaching materials; he has also been an invaluable source of information on production and circulation of rural music. Zé Mulato and Vomli Batista da Silva were extremely generous with their knowledge. Conversations with Pereira da Viola, the personnel of Vento Viola and Braz da Viola, together with members of Braz's Orchestra de Viola Caipira have clarified a great deal.

Fifa, her husband Paulo, and her son Thomás provided one of the best live-music venues I have ever encountered at the Via Roça. Palandi, host of AM radio show *Domingão Sertanejo* in Itapira, was always a gracious host, encouraging me to tape shows, converse with musicians, and ask as many questions as I could muster. Thanks are also due to Antônio de Fonesca and Walter, of the Rádio Clube de Itapira. Turu, Flávio Junqueira, and the personnel of the Professional Bull Riders in São José do Rio Preto, Marcão, Kaká and the staff of the rodeo at Barretos, as well as Beto Lahr of the Americana Rodeo have all been gracious with their time.

In Chicago, a group of colleagues read or discussed parts of the project, among them: Greg Downey, Kaylin Goldstein, Shane Greene, Josh Kaplan, Paul Liffman, Deborah McDougall, Ev Meade, Daniel Rosenblatt, Paul Ross, Daniel Noveck, Jesse Shipley, E. Lee Skjon, Michael Stamm, and Ian Urbina. Anne Ch'ien, without whom the anthropology department at Chicago would not function, has continually assisted. My thanks also go to participants in the Workshop on the Anthropology of Latin America (WALA), the Latin American History Workshop (LAHW), and the Ethnomusicology Workshop (EthNoise). Carole Tiernan and Alvin Palmer lent me their expertise with diagrams and maps. Julia Macedo, Nícia Bonatti, and Ana Lima assisted with transcription and translation. My parents, Julian and Cynthia Dent, were superb editors, reading from their disciplinary perspective in French history. Any clarity herein is due in no small part to them. My wife, Kye Rachel Tiernan, has been a patient companion and exacting editor. My son, Neko, has helped with comic relief in the final stages.

The research and write-up were funded by the Tinker Foundation for the Study of Latin America, the Social Sciences and Humanities Research Council of Canada, the George Washington University Department of Anthropology, the University of Oklahoma Department of Anthropology, the George Washington University Faculty Facilitating Fund, the Institute for Ethnographic Research at the George Washington University, and the Division of the Social Sciences at the University of Chicago. My thanks go to the editor of *Anthropological Quarterly* for permission to reprint sections of chapter 2, which originally appeared in that journal in 2007.

Finally, my heartfelt thanks go to the Bonatti family in Campinas—to Nícia and Ivanil, and their three sons Flávio, Santiago, and Daniel, as well as Nícia's parents Jandira and Joaquín. Their support began the moment I set foot in Brazil and extends to the present day. They are all patient teachers, expert researchers, and self-sacrificing hosts. I also extend a special thanks to the Schumaker family, Roberto, Teca, and Felipe, for providing hospitality, conversation, instruction, and a home away from home in the city of São Paulo.

Introduction

> It was natural that the search for a middle way between aesthetic perception and the exercise of logical thought should find inspiration in music, which has always practiced it.
> —CLAUDE LÉVI-STRAUSS, *The Raw and the Cooked*

This is a book about the musicality of modernity in a minor key. It asserts the centrality of "country" to linear progress, industrialization, and the growth of cities. As far back as the dawn of the Industrial Revolution, modernity has sung about its backwaters (R. Williams 1973). And today, neoliberalism plays an old-fashioned tune that simultaneously denies and facilitates the rupture with the past upon which it depends. Emotionally, spatially, temporally, and economically, the rural makes the city conceivable by stipulating the bygone days in terms of which the present may be celebrated or indicted. This book will argue that important components of this dialogic between forward- and backward-looking have been mediated musically. Ideologies that grant music an ability to mingle philosophical argument with embodiment have shaped the emergent social categories of race, social class, gender, place, and time that modernity calls forth and depends upon.

Understand from the start that country often hides. Country's rare appearance in scholarly circles is part of what makes it country. With a few recent exceptions (Ching 2001; A. Fox 2004; Pecknold 2007), when country *has* shown up in academic work, it has done so in order to reify a romantic "peasant" or propound the "development" of hickishness. But such treatments have revealed little, preserving country's concealment. This is hardly surprising. The way country nurses its tears in the wings in one measure facilitates its taking the stage as modernity's critic, foundation, and fool in the next.

Brazil, the largest nation in Latin America in physical size and population, brings all this into sharp focus. The scale and scope of its engagement with change in the late nineteenth and early twentieth centuries has produced the dramatic contrasts this book will analyze. William Butler Yeats seems to have captured this scale and scope best, though he was talking about the second coming rather than Brazil. For Yeats, the force with which the "gyre" has "widened" has thrown things all that much further from a "center" which "cannot hold" (1996, 187). In Brazil, music has always played a role in such a motion. When that "holding" seems most at risk, a country song is just the thing to keep life from coming apart. Furthermore, Brazil's rural-urban relations force us to question what we think we already know about country. In industrializing England, London, together with other hard-working cities, contrasted with an idyllic "countryside." In the United States, North and South have often stood apart. But in Brazil, the nation's largest and most industrialized city of São Paulo somehow lies in the midst of its country.

Further incongruities in Brazil's country harmonies effect and create Central-Southern Brazilian self-perceptions. To illustrate, in February of 2000, one of my *viola* teachers (the viola is the Brazilian ten-string guitar) enlisted my aid. With the resurgence of rural music that was taking place, he was returning to full-time performing, for which he needed a "realistic" amplified tone. He was looking for a small device to make his viola's vibrations louder, called a pickup, and since I was an acoustic guitar performer and songwriter in Chicago, perhaps I could help. Our initial searches through the city of São Paulo only turned up locally made pickups that sounded tinny and strident, however. He wanted to avoid these at all costs, not simply because their sound-transferring properties were flat, but because he did not want to sound like all the other *violeiros* (viola players) who were using them. After nearly a day of searching, we ended up in a store that advertised American-made acoustic guitars and carried the same amplification I had used in my own instrument, which he had liked. After sound testing the device, my teacher pronounced it perfect. He had found what he had come for. This American product was simply *better* than what Brazil had to offer.

As he celebrated, I struggled, however. I had frankly hoped to find some Brazilian model. It would be inexpensive, sturdy, and the ideal carrier of Central-Southern rural music: a Brazilian pickup mediating an indigenous genre—indigenously. Instead, my teacher was paying dearly for this import. And as he did so, I realized that my study would have to come to grips with such things. Brazilian *rurality*, defined as an ideology and practice that incites an ideal country past over a debased urban present, contained these sorts of contradictions.[1] I somehow *knew* what this moment was supposed to have looked and sounded like. And yet, we were *not* on the porch of a country house as twilight fell, enjoying our all-acoustic finger pickin' after a hard day in the fields. Instead, we were in one of the largest cities in the world, spearheading a revival of traditional Brazilian Central-Southern rural music via the viola by purchasing a pickup manufactured in the United States—all in the context of the staggering popularity of Brazilian commercial country music (*música sertaneja*). These paradoxes led deeper. What role did country play in Brazil's social transformations and in changes in its relations to what it took to be an outside world? How did this rural musicality give shape to political, economic, and communicative domains?

Clarifying these and other questions associated with what I call Brazilian rurality is this book's goal. Throughout, we encounter not only instrumentalists, singers, fans, casual listeners, and critics, but also the way in which the rural music they fashion is produced, circulated, and interpreted. We begin with the foundational distinction between the country and the city, and the way in which that distinction has allowed Brazilians residing in the Central-Southern region (the states of São Paulo, Minas Gerais, Mato Grosso do Sul, Mato Grosso, Paraná, and Goiás)[2] to shape and make sense of their lives. Our story is not one of identity politics *tout court*. Rather, it tells of the way in which rurality enables a series of inhabitable subject-positions, which, in *being* inhabited, facilitate modes of action. Migration from country to city, and from city to city, plays a starring role in all of this, it is true. But it shares the microphone with other tropes.

To spell out this book's problematic more specifically, we will analyze the transformation of the practice of Central-Southern rural musical genres that began in the mid-1980s. As Brazil redemocratized after a period of military dictatorship which stretched from 1964 to 1985, rural music in a variety of forms, including música sertaneja and *música caipira*, began to surge through existing circulatory matrices while it fashioned new ones. Commercial rural musical duos practicing what they called música sertaneja moved from acts important on a limited scale in the Central-Southern region to national and sometimes international best sellers. They inspired one of Brazil's highest grossing films, *Os Dois Filhos de Francisco* (*Francisco's Two Sons*). Transformations of rural music were heralded in other ways, including increased sales of, and radio requests for, música sertaneja (Zan 1995; Souza 1999; ABPD 2001); the rise to prominence of a Brazilian form of rodeo (or Peon's Festival), revolving around rural music and rivaling soccer in terms of tickets purchased (Izique 2000); and high ratings for rurally themed soap operas,[3] one costarring a purportedly "angry" rodeo bull named Bandido (Ripardo 2005; Rondon 2005).[4] Along with this, a revival of folkloric rural music called música caipira, heralded as música sertaneja's ancestor, took shape, particularly in São Paulo State. This was accompanied by an intensification of interest in the consummate instrument of Central-Southern rural music, the *viola caipira* (henceforth referred to merely as the viola). As interest in the viola grew, schools for the instrument sprang up and pedagogical "methods" proliferated in print and on the Internet (Dent 2003). Viola ensembles sprouted and recorded new arrangements of classics deemed traditional.

All the while large numbers of Brazilians in the Central-South were moving to cities, claiming, as they did so, that their Brazil was first and foremost a "rural" nation; "Everyone still has one foot in the country" was the way one rodeo announcer and rural music enthusiast put it to me, summing it all up. I had heard and read this sort of thing before. From the perspective of vocabulary, as descriptors for Brazilian rurality, speakers sometimes employed the Portuguese-language terms *campo* (countryside), *interior* (interior), *sertão* (backcountry), or *roça* (clearing, plantation, or country). At other times they used the English word *cáuntry* (transliterated here, for Portuguese) as a way to signal membership in a "country cosmopolitan"—a transnational set of practices and spaces emerging from Australia, Canada, Mexico, and the United States, the countries whose flags appear beside Brazil's on all Brazilian rodeo posters. These nations all had "countries" of their own, the story went, and as such, they all shared something fundamental with this part of Brazil. Pride in this ruralist translocality was buoyed by the appearance in the Brazilian news media of reports on how the Central-Southern region had saved the nation from financial crisis by dint of farming in the economically difficult late 1990s (Neto and Edward 1999). Central-Southern agricultural products, exported in record quantities to China, the rest of Latin America (particularly to the other members of Mercosul—Argentina, Paraguay, Uruguay), Europe, and also North America, were said to have helped avert the financial troubles that had plagued other countries in the region during the same period. This was what some Central-Southerners meant when they called their agriculture the nation's "green anchor" (Rohter 2004). At the same time, the successes and failures of the Rural Landless Workers' Movement (MST), an organization that sought to occupy unused farmland for use by the rural homeless, were reported in newspapers, on the radio, and in the nightly news. Ensuing conflicts, in which armed landlords frequently retaliated and the MST suffered losses, dramatized the contest over rural space and became a way to think about Brazil's inequalities, set in a rural frame. Such politics and poetics of the backcountry provide the ground on which we must consider the unfolding of rural music in the postauthoritarian period.

At the heart of my study are "practitioners" of música caipira, música sertaneja, and rodeo after 1985, practitioners here taken to refer, minimally, to musicians, fans, listeners, critics, overhearers, and producers; I stress both the casual and the committed. I concentrate on the Central-South (Ferrete 1985; R. N. Corrêa 1989; Freire 1996; Nepomuceno 1999; Sant'Anna 2000; Caipira 2001). In geographical terms, the Central-South comprises the hot and dry interior plateau south of the Northeastern highlands, sometimes called the *sertão*, south of the Amazon forest and river basin, for the most part east of the swamps of the Pantanal, and north of the far southern states. Though late twentieth-century migration has complicated this, the region is musically characterized as entailing a mixture of Indian and Portuguese in the racial type known as *caboclo*. For reasons that will become clear below, this simplification erases, with varying degrees of completeness, complexities such as the presence of significant numbers of people of African, Italian, and German descent. The form of Portuguese spoken and sung is overwhelmingly *caipira*, or hick, even in cities such as Campinas, though in larger urban areas, what might be framed as a softer form of the dialect is often spoken (see chapter 4 for a detailed analysis of *caipirese*). The interior's folklore, speech patterns, and ways of life have been treated in works of social history and fiction by Antônio Cândido (1979) and Guimarães Rosa (1963), respectively. In these works and in other contexts, the term sertão, sometimes reserved for the Northeastern interior, is used to refer to the Central-Southern one, though as we shall see, its valence varies regionally.

The definition of Central-South used by the people discussed in this work pointedly excludes the coastal *samba* state of Rio de Janeiro. It

Map 1. The Central-Southern Region.

consequently stresses "the interior" above all else. In ethnographically tracing the historicities that accompany discussions of this region, we find that arguments for its coherence seek support in evidence as much as five centuries old. One scholar proposes that the region may be thought of as an extension of the old colonial captaincy of São Vicente which was established in the early 1500s by the Portuguese Crown (Sant'Anna 2000, 53). A link between Minas Gerais and São Paulo is also said to date back to the eighteenth century, when mule trains carried gold, diamonds, foodstuffs, and textiles back and forth between them. But perhaps most important, São Paulo purportedly extended its sphere of influence in economic and cultural terms via trade and migration into Minas Gerais and Goiás in the late nineteenth and early twentieth centuries. Railway lines were particularly significant because they connected outlying zones to the state and the city of São Paulo. When the coffee economy collapsed in the late 1920s, those that did not flee to the city of São Paulo frequently moved to others in São Paulo state.

In addition to these lineaments of the region, one frequently hears a cultural-ethnic definition. This is often employed within the domain of regional musical genres, discussions of dialects, and folklore. One violeiro and historian currently residing in Brasília (in the Federal District located in the middle of the state of Goiás) informally explained it to me this way:

> I use the term Central-South in terms of territorial occupation—those people who have música caipira as a kind of identity. [It was] initially influenced by radio programs from São Paulo, and later by radio stations of other cities in the interior. . . . This region stretches across a large piece of Brazil. It is a region where cattle were the chief source of income. Until the middle of the last century, there were large movements of herds, sometimes by refrigerated rail cars—to the city of São Paulo. The regions to the north of São Paulo sent their cattle via Barretos, where the British company ANGLO was the largest buyer. At any rate, these are the kinds of things you collect by living in the region. My father was a farmer in Minas [Gerais], and our family was linked with music and the viola a long way back.

Note, here, the importance of radio, paired with cattle, as technologies of circulation for the conception of the region itself, a subject to which we will return in discussing circulatory matrices of musical rurality in chapter 6. While much of Brazil in the early twentieth century listened to national radio emanating from Rio de Janeiro (McCann 2004, 5), Central-Southerners largely tuned in to the city of São Paulo. Thus locality (the Central-South) and its mediated tradition frame the musical production of self by way of region.

"Country" musicians define their music as "rural," and by this they mean that their lyrics criticize an increasingly inescapable "urban" life characterized by suppressed emotions and an inattentiveness to the past. Using the early twentieth-century countryside as their model, these practitioners long for the wholeness they once had, set in Brazil's rural past. Their music employs a rural "performativity" (detailed in chapter 1) which divides Brazil into a modern urban present and an old-fashioned country past, and then celebrates the virtues of the latter.

This emphasis on the rural does not necessarily mean that rural musicians and fans were born in what we might conventionally think of as the country, that they live in such a space, or even that their rural music is produced and circulates there, though all these things are sometimes true. Though musicians must demonstrate some connection with the Central-Southern interior through birth or residence, many of them may be said to have distinctly "urban" roots. Some may have moved from moderately small Central-Southern cities (population approximately seventy-five thousand) to somewhat larger ones (Campinas, for instance, contains approximately one million), or their parents may have made such moves. But their rural music is produced and circulates in cities. Explaining this apparent paradox of rurality in urban circumstances will occupy a substantial portion of this work. What we discover is that the rurality of some rural music lies not only in references to the countryside and performances in locations explicitly coded as rural. Rural performativity involves making use of space (here, most easily evidenced in a countryside *versus* a city) to frame the fragmentation of the self and the loss of the idyllic past that rural musical practitioners feel urbanization and modernization have wrought. Rural music is imbued with, and brings about, a state of emotional crisis: an emergency of the heart. As a sort of "discourse of the vanishing," defined by Marilyn Ivy as a particular modernity's attempt to erase a past that "hauntingly" returns, the rural does not so much lie, "trembling," at Ivy's "margins" (Ivy 1995, 242). It *wails* at them.

The tremendous growth in the popularity of rural musical genres is no mere coincidence then. It occurs at a particular moment in Brazilian history: the transition from dictatorship in 1985 into a period of intense neoliberal economic and social reform.[5] During this shift, increasing numbers of Brazilians began to use these genres to fashion alternatives to the progress narratives that had been so essential during the dictatorship, especially those associated with urbanization, industrialization, and future-orientation. The backward glance of rural genres that reflect with sadness on the disappearance of "the way things were" was suddenly mobilized with increased vigor to problematize discourses of *brasilidade* (Brazilianness) too readily accepting of progress for its own sake. This mobilization continues as relentlessly forward-looking tropes of social improvement take on new guises of development, institutional reform, and practice. Brazil is frequently described as a place where change may be somewhat slow to come, but when it arrives, it suddenly obliterates all in its path. As a result, in Raymond Williams's words, a country stick is still being used to beat an urban present (R. Williams 1973, 12). And it will be for some time.

Along these lines, rural public culture in Brazil interrogates both homegrown and international versions of brasilidade that have been used to tout Brazil's particular spin on modernity. In particular, it questions brasilidade as defined by soccer (Lever 1999; Meihy 1999; Bellos 2002, 123), carnival (DaMatta 1979), samba (Vianna 1999), and even the mixed martial art and dance genre known as *capoeira* (Assunção 2004; Downey 2005). In its varied contexts of circulation, the rural counters notions of Brazilian national character that revolve around Rio de Janeiro, as well as the Northeastern and strongly Afro-identifying city of Salvador da Bahia, in music, festival, and sport. These Rio- and Northeastern-centric portrayals of brasilidade, many Central-Southerners argue, ignore broader and deeper agricultural roots which are intertwined with manual labor, family, the land, and the past of the Central-South.

This country-critical attempt to move the locus of Brazilian self-identification toward the interior of the Central-South contains a racial component. Fans of rural public culture suggest that the more dominant modes of Brazilian self-imagining grounded in Rio and the Northeast focus too much on the centrality of Africa within the context of Brazil's celebrated racial mixture. By contrast, for rural public culture, the caboclo, the coming together of Indian with Portuguese, embodies the most important form of mixture.[6] For instance, one Central-Southern singer's stage name, Zé Mulato, does not so much call attention to the mixture of black with white, as the term "mulato" customarily might. Rather, it points to the mixture of white and Indian, with some blackness thrown in for good measure. Brazilian explanations of national character frequently rely upon a "mixture of three colors" line of argumentation (M. d. Andrade 1972, 1989; Marcondes 1998; McGowan and Pessanha 1998; Sant'Anna 2000). But whereas conventionally, explanations of Brazilian nationality and identity prioritize African mixture (Vianna 1999; Matory 2004; McCann 2004), often in order to obscure the primacy of whiteness in socioeconomic domains (Hanchard 1998),

Central-Southern public culture, instead, backgrounds Africa.[7] Rural public culture espouses mixture in a slightly different mode, in the form of the caipira (hick or hillbilly) and the *sertanejo* (backlander or cowboy).[8]

The country critique also engages directly with Brazilian gender politics, frequently ratifying gender roles deemed traditional. Laconic men work the fields and dominate sometimes dangerous animals, though they are inevitably torn up inside about their love for women. Expressive women control the home space, men's hearts, and the path to a perfect rural past. Rural musical genres are overwhelmingly practiced by duos, most often of brothers—and this primacy of brother siblingship in musical performance is on the rise (see chapter 2). Women are almost never singers.[9] By way of brotherhood, the music reveals masculine vulnerabilities "on stage" (Shryock 2004a, b) which are customarily kept well hidden, decried by the machismo propounded by other genres of communicative practice. Rural music's torn-up male is the "culturally intimate" side of samba's *malandro*, a wily character who uses his verbal skills for seduction. In this way, rural genres invert two categories shown in many contexts to have long-standing efficacy in Brazil: the house and the street (DaMatta 1979). In his seminal analysis of what he terms the Brazilian "dilemma," Roberto DaMatta suggests that the house is the interior, family-oriented space of personal relationships, whereas the street is the exterior, public, and democratically oriented space of the state, with its laws. The country inversion of this suggestive polarity puts "on show" the delicate manly sensibilities normally reserved for private interactions between a man and a woman. The stoic and reserved male exists in productive tension with the wounded, expressive one, as we will see in chapter 1. Ethnography of gender in Brazil has revealed locations in which other sorts of inversions take place. For instance, sometimes women appropriate aspects of samba's *malandragem*, or wily male manipulation, in order to jockey for social position or obtain momentary control over their male partners (Fonseca 2003). I also reveal the ways in which conventionally female expressive practices, musically mediated, provide Central-Southern males with ways to think about their own emotions and both their power and powerlessness in their relationships with others.

Mainstream modes of brasilidade that have tended to dominate the public sphere often cluster around the concept of change for the better by way of mixture. Manifestations of change-centered forms of brasilidade include: the inherently absorptive nature of Brazil, which was emphasized in the *anthropophagy* (cannibalism) of 1920s modernism (Morse 1996, 20); African-Portuguese miscegenation by way of the sexually predatory Portuguese male and the acquiescing African female that anthropologist Gilberto Freyre (1933) proposed as the heart of Brazilian culture; as well as the *tropicália* musical movement of the late 1960s where musicians proposed to avidly consume cultural practices, thereby making them their own (Dunn 2001; Veloso 2002). All of these approaches to the nation continue to be touted as embodying its heart and soul. Brazil is commonly portrayed as a place with a voracious appetite for rapid modernization. This is evident in proud declarations about the use of laptops for voting (Rohter 2002) or the high number of cellular telephones in the nation (Tigre 2003). And it is frequently reported that Brazil has a relentless future-orientation (Eakin 1998), as evident in the construction of a new ultramodern capital in Brasília (Holston 1989), the tremendous economic growth of the dictatorship's "miracle" years (Skidmore 1988), or frequent references to the nation as a sleeping giant perpetually about to awaken (Janer 2000; Gordon 2001, 38; Horowitz 2003). The country critique takes aim at this progressiveness in a distinct fashion; the "order and progress" that appear on the Brazilian flag are replaced by "emotion and the good old days."

In unraveling the central paradoxes of this critique, the present work addresses itself to two joined concerns. First, it contributes to the ethnography of neoliberalism, characterizing an aspect of Central-Southern Brazilian experience as the nation transitions out of one form of governance and into another: from dictatorship into democracy. Brazilian redemocratization and the neoliberal economic and social policies that have accompanied it have, both in Brazil and abroad, been described by some as radical transformations. In other circles, they are thought to have changed very little. This book shows that this "late liberal" (Povinelli 2002, 3) period, of course, combines both change and continuity. Redemocratization has certainly drawn heavily upon elements of the past in numerous domains, such as aggravating longstanding problems of income distribution, for instance. However, in other areas, important transformations have taken place. For instance, in concert with other parts of the world, Brazilian approaches to "consumption" have shifted (O'Dougherty 2002), as have both the structure of media institutions and the ways public culture circulates (Fox and Waisbord 2002). Analyses of Latin American democracy have shown its grounding in a colonial legacy of monocultures, bureaucratic structures, and clientelistic forms of association (Stepan 1998; Power and Roberts 2000; Cardoso 2001; Avritzer 2002). At the same time, I show that this period is characterized by a transformation in the politics of culture that much of the economically and politically oriented literature on democracy leaves untouched. I interrogate the role of the new politics of culture in the context of the way in which democracy, neoliberalism, and multiculturalism reinforce one another (Canclini 1992; Oliven 1992; Yúdice, Franco, and Flores 1992; Yúdice 1994; Ortiz 1999). I also synthesize the way in which notions of the "popular" shape social possibilities for political expression (G. Williams 2002; Ochoa 2003a, 83–84) and the poetics of memory (Avelar 1999). Finally, I address the way in which contemporary gender identifications are transforming in present-day Latin America (Gutman 2003). Democratization and neoliberalism should be understood as simultaneously political, economic, and communicative processes and practices. Prying these dimensions apart ignores their ontological unity.

Part of my argument is that what Herzfeld has defined as "cultural intimacy" plays an important role in practices of neoliberalism. For Herzfeld, cultural intimacy is the rueful self-recognition that comes with certain practices thought to be crucial to national identity, but which are nonetheless somewhat embarrassing. What distinguishes this from interpersonal intimacy is precisely the public, "on-stage" nature of identification in play. To elaborate further, cultural intimacy is often associated with the idea of a fellowship of the flawed. Greeks break plates and steal goats. The French eat cheese and are romantic. And so forth. In this Brazilian case, the *experience* of neoliberalism on both social and economic levels plays out in the rural musical domain through the embarrassment this music brings. Sometimes this is because it is deemed unseemly for males to wail about the power of love. Sometimes it is because the music is tarred with the brush of imitating that global hegemon, the United States of America. But at other moments, música sertaneja becomes the single truest and most perfect encapsulation of the Brazilian "heart" (*coração*). Across these readings, we shall see the way in which intimacy mediates experiences of neoliberal reform, resulting in the simultaneous production of locality and cosmopolitanism with which the final two chapters of this book are concerned.

In advancing the ethnography of the neoliberal, this work develops a historically specific theory of performance. The two projects advance hand in hand. In this respect, I favor the term "performativity" as employed by Judith Butler over "performance," adhering to Butler's rejection of a prediscursive "subject" inherent to most common notions of "performance." But at this point, my use of performativity parts ways with hers, opting instead for the approach used by Kira Hall (2001), which moves beyond simply asserting that communicative practices such as language actually *do* something, in the sense first elaborated by John Austin (1962) in *How to Do Things with Words*. The kinds of "things" that Austin felt words could "do" were too intimately bound up with highly localized institutions such as western law and religion and with western forms of subjectivity in which an "individual" expresses "intentions" somehow "behind" the meaning of words (Rosaldo 1982). Butler never quite shakes a deeply western preoccupation with intention and referentiality, which is bound up with the late capitalist notions of subjectivity that this book takes apart. My analysis of performativity, instead, delves into the semiotic *ways* communicative practice "does things" cross-culturally. I am particularly concerned with the problem of articulating a coherent theory of performance in the context of multiply determined fields of intergeneric practice. In addressing this problem, I argue for the confluence of ideology, embodiment, and genre—concepts articulated most clearly within linguistic anthropology (Hanks 1987; Bauman and Briggs 1992; Silverstein 1998b)—within the frame of Bourdieuian fields of cultural production (Bourdieu 1993a, b). This book thus aims to establish "performativity" as a coherent theoretical perspective with implications in domains of human interaction beyond the arts and gender. It shows that in order to address the experience of the accountability to audience inherent in all human interaction, participants must make use of structures of voicing grounded in locally instantiated horizons of communicative practice (Hanks 1996). These horizons are crosscut by generic possibilities that carry with them incumbent role-inhabitances.

The following exposition of the book's chapters will elucidate the way in which these concepts unfold, revealing the mutual implication of performativity and the ethnography of neoliberalism. To begin, performativity (chapter 1) places a particular rural chronotope in play (chapter 2) that argues for blood, brotherhood, and the simultaneity of hierarchy and egalitarianism. Participants continually enact song-"texts" within the co(n)text of a broader musical field, itself crosscut by productive tensions of racial, class, and gendered "mixture"; these, in turn, give rise to cultural change (chapter 3). Users of rural music call upon a sense of "what is going on here" in order to orient themselves in performance, which calls for a generically coded historical imagination (chapter 4). Scholarship, journalism, and other sites for the production of this historicity establish the simplicity of the countryside, shutting out rural social complexity in favor of a monolithically "humble" peasant (chapter 5). The way in which participants conceive of their rural communicative interaction takes shape via circulatory matrices of statistical accrual, hydraulics, cattle, and fire (chapter 6). The neoliberal moment in Central-Southern Brazil then bifurcates the field of rural cultural production into a locality (chapter 7), and a country cosmopolitan (chapter 8), both of which must be produced, and both of which are constitutive of the dialogic interplay between tradition and modernity at the root of neoliberal performance.

The means by which I addressed these subjects in the field returns us to "intimacy." The intensely intimate charge this music carries posed a problem and created an opportunity from the start of my fieldwork. The shame surrounding rural musical practice stretches far into the past. When it was first recorded in 1929, música caipira was associated with a kind of São Paulo state-nationalism that disquieted the political and intellectual establishments in the pro-samba national capital of Rio de Janeiro (see chapters 4 and 6 for discussion of Cornélio Pires, the genre's first "producer").[10] Later, when música caipira lost its separatist São Paulo flavor in the 1950s and began to circulate as música sertaneja, an intellectual elite, still buying sertaneja records, although listening to them only in private, began to characterize it as a symbol of the vulgar cosmopolitanism-gone-wrong of migrant workers and their wealthy bosses. As we shall see, such a belief calculatedly elided rural genres' much broader listenership—an elision without which "country" could not, in fact, exist and upon which it still depends. It nonetheless accounts for the intellectual disdain that kept famous rural musical duos from booking high-profile concert halls in big cities such as Rio de Janeiro and São Paulo until the late 1980s. This distaste also prevented the music's presentation as "national" in any context, Brazilian, Latin American, or North American.

My own experience testifies to this, and it imbues my research. From my vantage point in North America, despite my substantial engagement with Brazilian music, I did not know that these rural genres even existed until I arrived in Brazil in 1998. It quickly became clear that they begged for attention, although my hosts nervously trivialized them when I showed interest. In June of 1998, when I first came to the city of Campinas in the state of São Paulo, which is at the heart of the Central-Southern region, the música sertaneja *dupla* (duo) Leandro and Leonardo was in crisis.[11] Leandro had been diagnosed with a rare Askin tumor in his thorax which was growing at a staggering rate. The tragic quality of Leandro and Leonardo's harmonized songs, both in the plaintive timbre of the singing *and* the tone of the heartbroken lyrics, seemed to be playing out in the events that found themselves on the news each day. The calamity the brothers sang of was coming to pass. Leandro was dying and their brotherly union was at risk.

At first it appeared as though doctors might effect a miracle. But despite a few promising interludes, Leandro died a few weeks after the story first broke, and when he did, a large portion of the Central-Southern region went into mourning. Twenty thousand people attended the funeral procession in his hometown of Goiás in Brazil's interior, and at the wake in the city of São Paulo, then-president Fernando Henrique Cardoso sent both his regrets and the vice president. The media channeled the importance of his passing. One television station even had the temerity to stop its World Cup soccer coverage to simulcast the event (after all, other stations would still carry the game), only to watch its ratings spike; in a country that took its soccer so seriously, this was clearly a sign that something significant had taken place. Middle-class newsmagazine *veja*, the Brazilian equivalent of *Newsweek*, explained matter-of-factly that it all had much to do with the brothers' rise from humble tomato pickers a few years before to one of the biggest acts in the land. People *identified* with rags-to-riches, so the tragedy hit hard.

But it seemed clear that there was more at stake than disappointment over a heady success gone wrong and that the sadness related directly to the general characteristics of the genre itself. For about a week, people seemed curious to know how the "gringo-anthropologist"[12] might be responding to this. My hosts, students and professors at the State University of Campinas (UNICAMP), would ask what I thought about the news-media coverage and study my responses with care, searching for I knew not what.

The truth was, I wasn't sure *what* to think. Nothing I knew about Brazil had prepared me for this tearful outpouring over the death of a singer whose genre I had hardly even *heard*. Before my arrival I had listened to plenty of bossa nova, Música Popular Brasileira (MPB), tropi-cália, Olodum, death metal, Northeastern reggae, forró, and even su-perb Brazilian techno. But practitioners of these genres had not made the front page in death. Música sertaneja had, quite definitely, not trav-eled outside Brazil.

The mass grieving over Leandro was not, of course, a complete anom-aly. The funerals of a soccer player (Garrincha)[13] and one Formula One racer (Ayrton Senna—see chapter 8) had drawn spectacular crowds. But what was so striking in the case of Leandro was the way in which the tragedy of the music, and, in ways that were only just becoming clear to me, what was rendered as the tragedy of the disappearance of the countryside itself, seemed to map so well onto the premature demise of the singer. This had not been the case for soccer balls and racing cars. Here, the singing seemed to have empirically proven itself. This point was driven home as Leandro and Leonardo's record company, BMG, released Leandro's performance of his favorite song, complete with lyrical foreshadowings of his demise, penned and recorded long before the tumor's detection. Perhaps this song, and the tragic tone of all the brothers' music, was some kind of prophecy. Or, if not a prediction of the future, it at least seemed to encapsulate the way in which música sertaneja so exquisitely rendered the sadnesses of daily life in present-day Brazil. Whatever the case, the posthumously released tribute record, which included versions of the duo's greatest hits performed by other música sertaneja brother duos, sold like hotcakes. It played on the radio and TV too. Fans speculated on whether Leonardo could decently go on in music, or whether it would be more seemly for him to simply retire to the cattle ranching he and his brother had so come to enjoy. It would certainly be impossible for him to find another partner. So when he did give a first concert to launch his solo career, the only way he preserved the fan base he and his brother had painstakingly built was by saying a tearful prayer for Leandro before beginning and devoting several songs to his memory. Leonardo was, and despite his current success many years later, remains, half of a musical act. Leandro is the ever-present absence that continues to cement his living brother's success.

To be sure, the 1998 crisis of dupla Leandro and Leonardo was per-plexing. The social-scientific paradigms so often foregrounded in ana-lyzing Brazil such as Freyre's big house (Freyre 1933), Holanda's "cor-diality" (Holanda 1995), and DaMatta's house and street (DaMatta 1979), though helpful in some circumstances, did not seem to explain what, borrowing DaMatta's language, sounded like a different "Brazilian dilemma," one surrounding the "country." Euclides da Cunha's classic *Rebellion in the Backlands* (1944) seemed closer to the mark in terms of the way in which late nineteenth-century Rio de Janeiro had reacted with murderous revulsion to a hick millenarian movement in its Northeastern hinterland. But the urban/rural divide encapsulated by da Cunha's Northeastern sertão (or backlands) did not seem to correspond with the sertão that was the constant indexical ground of música sertaneja (where "sertaneja" means *of* the sertão). Rather, a different set of contrasting categories seemed to be in play, categories that were in one sense more local to the Central-South, but which nonetheless seemed poised to lay claim to a national audience.

Adding to the complexity of the initial framing of this problem was the frequency and forcefulness of opinions voiced to me at every turn on the subject of Leandro's funeral, rural music, and country singers, dead or alive. Once I started to ask about rural music, I discovered that *everyone* had an opinion and *none* were neutral. Some thought that música sertaneja was the *only* Brazilian music that really spoke to and from the heart. Others found it saccharine, or Americanized and urbanized (these two somehow blurred), representing cultural imperialism at worst and Brazilian subservience at best. Some said it was the child of more traditional música caipira, others, that it had entirely divested itself of its musical parent. It was "truly modern" while being Brazilian in the same moment. Or it was backsliding, bastardized, and irreparably *other*. This classifying went on, and it was some time before such opinions started to coalesce around patterns I could recognize (see chapter 4).

What became apparent was that all these opinions took performance seriously; their animators had a clear notion of the importance of song, sport, TV, dance, and food to social production and reproduction. Nowhere was there any doubt that rural public culture was fundamentally *significant*, whether wonderful or ghastly. And these indigenous approaches to performativity were only partly concerned with identity politics, which had long been the torch song of scholarship on the subject. The opinions given to me set forth a larger range of ways in which musical practice was permitted to signify. Somehow, mysteriously for me at the time, the heart, the past, gender, race, social class, and space all clung tightly together, forming a knot.

Naturally, for a gringo to propose to untangle that knot presented difficulties that only transformed into opportunities later on. A series of Brazilian academics had done important work on música sertaneja, I was told, and this work was often taken as gospel by scholars, students, and laypeople entreating me to swear off the subject. But many of the works mentioned in these warnings struck me as partaking of precisely the same rural poetics that characterized the songs and rodeos ostensibly being analyzed. Both the songs, and the scholarly books, articles, and stories about them, longed for the past in what looked like identical ways. Furthermore, these analyses not only failed to take the embarrassment that was such an important part of discussions of this music into consideration as material to think with. They seemed very much to fuel that embarrassment by scolding the inappropriateness of male expressiveness or the "commodification" of commercial genres in tones redolent of Adorno's anti-"jazz" screeds (Adorno 1938, 1989). This seemed like trying to explain a phenomenon either by simply pointing to it or by scolding it. More recent work, in failing to address the tensions in the field of rural musical production that motivate change, though helpful with details, did little to address the dynamics of rural performativity (Reily 1992; Carvalho 1993; Freire 1996). I therefore persisted in attempting to unravel what appeared to me to be a postauthoritarian Central-Southern dilemma. To extend a question once famously cannibalized by modernist poet Oswald de Andrade, "Tupi, or not Tupi" became "to be country, or to be city?"

Layers of Generic Finalization

Before embarking on an analysis of what música sertaneja and música caipira share in chapters 1 and 2, and how they differ in chapters 3 and 4, some preliminaries are in order.

Música sertaneja may be thought of as an ornately produced ensemble music of electronically enhanced string instruments, keyboards and drum kits. Performers wear blue jeans and American ten-gallon hats, or tight-fitting designer clothes in black, white, or gray synthetic fabrics. Songs are performed in a variety of contexts including the expensive concert halls of São Paulo and Rio de Janeiro. Locations also include rodeos, where música sertaneja plays constantly in the background (see the opening of chapter 4), and in the well-attended stage productions that follow the rodeo events. Several prime-time television shows are devoted to it. Duplas Zezé di Camargo and Luciano, Chitãozinho and Xororó, and Leandro and Leonardo have been particularly important. These three duplas refer to themselves collectively as The Friends, or Amigos, and began to meet annually for a group concert in 1996. Tremendously successful attendance (one hundred thousand people) and sales of the live recordings (one million copies) led to continuation of this practice, despite (perhaps especially *because* of) Leandro's death in June of 1998. Música sertaneja practiced by the "Amigos" and their like circulates extensively on the radio. In my chief field site of Campinas, for example, one FM radio station, Rádio Laser, devoted itself entirely to it. In the small town of Itapira, another field site, the Rádio Clube de Itapira's AM and FM radio stations devoted several hourly programs to música sertaneja. It sells a tremendous number of records at licit shops. Expressed as a percentage of the national total of CD sales, this amounts to between 11 percent and 13 percent (ABPD 2001; IFPI 2001). It also accounts for a large percentage of the content available for sale at illegal record stands selling pirated CDs. From my observations in Campinas and in the city of São Paulo, rural genres probably amount to close to 20 percent of these illicit sales.

The genre's constituency is extremely broad, in that música sertaneja in the Central-South is currently as much an upper-class music as it is a working-class one.[14] The continually circulating notion that the music is consumed only by the lower classes comprises a crucial component of the generic policing that cultural intimacy requires, a notion which we will explore in more detail below. This idea also makes up an important aspect of the music's self-presentation as working class. However, despite this, the genre's performers and fans are recruited across class lines (Carvalho 1991).

In terms of education, most música sertaneja performers have finished high school and may have completed some university. Their musical training frequently mixes formal with informal instruction. Most received teaching from their parents or purchased books of songs containing chord charts from magazine stands and bookstores. Many have limited training in reading and writing music, and if they are not familiar with actual notation, they can use chord charts. Zezé di Camargo provides an example of the kind of musical background música sertaneja performers possess. He received accordion lessons from his parents and played for ten years, learning to read music, and providing the accompaniment for family parties. Maurício, of Maurício and Mauri, on the other hand, received more formal training. He learned jazz and rock bass, and then played in dupla Chitãozinho and Xororó's band for ten years before embarking on his own career. Another musician and scholar of música sertaneja, Welson Tremura, recounts that many of his friends who now back up Chitãozinho and Xororó played jazz and classical music before embarking on professional careers in commercial rural music.

Central-Southern rural genres collectively must be read within the context of a broad "turn" to the rural that valorizes the country past. However, caipira and sertaneja address themselves to this valorization in ways that sometimes differ. With respect to música sertaneja, performers hope to update what they view as outmoded música caipira via electronic instruments, an emphasis on love, smooth singing, Standard Portuguese, and designer clothes. It is in this sense that they wish to be stylistically "modern." The career of Chitãozinho and Xororó, sometimes referred to as "The Brazilian Kids" (*os meninos do Brasil*), illustrates several aspects of música sertaneja. The pair began singing música caipira together at circuses and on television programs in the 1960s and gained considerable attention on television toward the end of the decade. In 1969, one of these shows' producers awarded them their current stage names, which were derived from the title of a famous folkloric rural song about two birds,[15] and provided the pair with the production expertise and financial backing that helped launch them into the national spotlight.

From the beginning of their career, they demonstrated a desire to modernize the sound and imagery of the música caipira they had practiced in their youth, a process they began somewhat slowly with their first recordings in the early 1970s, introducing electric guitars, drums, and electric bass, and singing increasingly about love. This newer format reached its zenith on their record of 1982, in which the song "A Strand of Hair" helped the record sell one million copies and strengthened a trend in música sertaneja. Their music was framed by melancholy, regret, and grief over a love that was intense and conflicted.

Since the success of "A Strand of Hair," the dupla has continued to incorporate electronic instrumentation and, increasingly, generic features of Nashville country music (they actually recorded an album in Tennessee in 1998), such as the pedal-steel guitar and the twanging sound of the Fender Telecaster electric guitar. Chitãozinho and Xororó are currently one of the best-selling acts in the nation, their song "Alô" topping the charts in 2001. They have recorded in Spanish for the rest of the Latin American market under the names José and Durval (producers assumed that their Brazilian names would be too difficult for Spanish ears and mouths) and have played shows with North American country star Billy Ray Cyrus.

They are aware of the criticisms leveled at them by nationalists and by practitioners who hold rigidly to música caipira. Xororó guardedly explains:

> It doesn't work anymore—singing música sertaneja for some public that just doesn't exist—that lights its houses with kerosene lamps. We love talking about the lasso, about the dirt—that stuff is beautiful—but on most farms they already have VCRs, microwaves, and satellite dishes. Today's caipira surfs the Internet and buys stuff on the phone with credit cards. He wants everything that technology has to offer, and our music wants to reach him. There, in the middle of the frontier-state of Goiás, in Tocantins, the guy's selling his cattle by the pound in American dollars! (quoted in Nepomuceno 1999, 418)

Note that not only is Brazil's currency the *real* and not the dollar, but Brazil uses the metric system, so that selling in dollars by the pound doubly removes the farmers Xororó claims to describe from their ostensible embeddedness in the Central-Southern backcountry, placing them into direct contact with the United States. Such remarks indicate that practitioners of música sertaneja feel that their music simply mirrors what is actually going on in the backcountry; in effect, the backcountry from which música caipira ostensibly once sprang has changed. According to Xororó, the change in the music reflects changes in technology. The new caipira can surf the Internet, so why shouldn't that caipira demand more advanced production standards in his music? People who still practice música caipira address a "public" that no longer exists, Xororó argues.

But audiences for música caipira,[16] to whom we now turn, do, in fact, exist. And they also feel that these kinds of modernizing changes are taking place in rural Brazil, although they do not wish to accept and mirror them in musical style. Quite the opposite: caipiras hope that their music will help to keep things the way they were before what they deem to be an exclusively financial orientation arrived to destroy brasilidade. The performance and consumption of rural music deemed *folk-*

lórica (folkloric), regional (regional), or raíz (roots)—which is to say all música caipira—is categorically framed by nostalgia. However, where música sertaneja bemoans the disappearance of a past love, or a life in the countryside, música caipira places more emphasis on the disappearance of man's embeddedness in "nature" by way of wind, water, fire, and earth. Música caipira also frames its practice with nostalgia for the culture from which an originary caipira music is believed to have sprung. In effect, the fact that this music is thought to have originated in the context of precapitalist caipira sociality becomes both the justification and the inspiration for current practice. Practitioners hope that through their music, many aspects of rural society may be revived and Brazil's cultural independence preserved (see chapter 7).

Many current "caipiras" once practiced what they called música sertaneja. The need felt by this group of once-sertanejos to switch their descriptor back to caipira is one of the distinguishing features of the traditional revival of the mid-1980s that coincides with música sertaneja's explosion in popularity. Acceptance by folkloric types of the label música sertaneja ended in the mid-1980s, when duplas increasingly began to modernize both their look and their sound in the ways described above. Perhaps the most famous música caipira duo of all time, brothers Tonico and Tinoco, which I analyze in chapter 2, best illustrates this progression.[17] Their career spanned more than forty years, beginning in 1943 and ending with the death of Tonico in the mid-1990s. It was marked by their prolific output which, though marketed as música sertaneja at the time, maintained most of the generic features now referred to as música caipira.

Despite the fact that its death knell had been sounded long ago by scholars like José de Souza Martins (1975) and Waldenyr Caldas (1977, 1987), the term "música caipira" began to be used more and more in the 1990s, as a particular group of performers of rural music, including Zé Mulato and Cassiano and another famous roots duo, Pena Branca and Xavatinho, wished to set themselves off from the megastars of música sertaneja. This group felt that the multiheaded beast that música sertaneja had become obscured the true meaning of what música caipira once was, and what, with the correct impetus, it could become again: a Central-Southern rural genre that was profoundly local.

Currently, música caipira points to rural Central-Southern Brazil specifically. It originates there, is performed in dupla, and harmonized in parallel thirds. Its instrumentation differs substantially from that of música sertaneja in that it is accompanied by viola and classical guitar and pointedly lacks electronic enhancement or production. When playing live, performers almost always limit themselves to these two instruments. Occasionally muted acoustic bass and some form of hand drum may be used as a rhythm section. Thematically, música caipira revolves around four nodes: country life and nature; sadness as metaphorically encountered in nature; troubles in love, set in the countryside and sometimes coming to a violent end; and, in a fashion that is both comic and tragic, the way local or national politics ignores the common man. Practitioners of música caipira aim to revive the past, evoke nature, and move the traditions of the Central-South "forward."

Música de viola is a more erudite form of Central-Southern music, the performers of which ally themselves strongly with performers of música caipira. These ten-string guitar players, a group of musicians who largely began their study of music as guitar players and then switched to the viola, practice a music that mingles original pieces composed with natural or folkloric themes and renditions of the traditional música caipira repertoire. They focus on technique, and all of them possess superb command of their instruments and are able to execute difficult picking patterns. Many of them forefront the viola in their performance, though they also sing at times. They circulate CDs with carefully researched songs and cover notes, create methods for teaching viola which are circulated on the Internet and in print, and have even opened schools for teaching viola. One of them, Ivan Vilela, is now a professor of viola caipira at the University of São Paulo.

Performers of música caipira considered in this work tend to value only folkloric rural music that circulates little on the radio, though there are a few crossover figures who call upon rural themes, but receive substantial airplay on stations and TV programs featuring Música Popular Brasileira. Most of them have sufficient musical education to be able to read and, in many cases, write music, though there are notable exceptions. Their recordings circulate on a small scale, in local shops close to where they live; in fact, many distribute their recordings themselves, often using the Internet. The labels on which their recordings are released are almost always independent. Increasingly, they are creating their own labels on which to release their material. Their sales are small, that is, in the thousands of copies per record.

This introduction to the rural music of the Central-South in the post-authoritarian period provides a foundation for the discussion, analysis, and comparison of the genres which begins in chapter 1. I conclude with some remarks on methodology.

The Ethnography of Public Culture

One of the central concerns of this project is the ethnography of public culture. Given the nature of its modes of address, the size, shape, and duration of the communities it calls into being, and the multiplicity of practices associated with its production and reception, public culture poses special challenges to ethnography. These have been answered in various ways by Askew (2002), Spitulnik (2002), Abu-Lughod (2002), Mazzarella (2003), Mankekar (2001), and Turner (2002), among others. Within the domain of music, the most useful approach considers the mutual implication of musical and social structures, an approach found in Weidman (2006), Fox (2004), Feld (1989), Stokes (1992), Seeger (1987), Erlmann (1996), Saul (2005), and Bohlman (1992). Throughout, it is important to understand that musical "texts" are oriented toward continually shifting "publics," refracted through processes of mediation that also fail to hold still. These processes of multiple embeddedness require a thorough understanding of how particular users are calling upon public culture in differing situations. This returns us to the importance of ethnography as a method; the only way to know what public cultural texts mean is to investigate the way they are actually used in social life. This approach shaped the research upon which this book is based.

This project draws on a period of fieldwork stretching from 1998 to the present, conducted in the state of São Paulo, Brazil, and centering in the city of Campinas (population approximately one million).[18] I concentrated on a city because, as I have noted, rural musical genres are largely, though not exclusively, produced and circulated in cities. In Campinas I lived with a family that had originally come from the interior of the state. The mother and father of this family were grandchildren of Italian immigrants to Brazil in the early twentieth century, precisely the kind of people that might have bought Brazil's earliest rural musical recordings. In Campinas, I researched musicians, their fans, and the contexts of rural musical performance. Part of this approach involved learning to play the ten-string guitar, or viola. Campinas proved ideal because of its centrality to the revival of interest in música caipira and the explosion of popularity of música sertaneja in evidence there. Three prominent ten-string guitar experts (violeiros) resided in the city, frequently playing at a performance space on the outskirts of town. The owner of this restaurant, whom I will describe in chapter 7, was aggressively developing this space by offering an increasing number of shows by well-known rural musicians. Campinas was also useful because the famous romantic and commercially successful rural musical dupla Chitãozinho and Xororó spent part of its year there, and indeed, Xororó was an acquaintance of one of my host's eleven brothers, who had bought the singer's old house. Chitãozinho and Xororó had opened several barbecue restaurants in 1999 that contained memorabilia of Central-Southern rural music. Campinas itself, with several large and prestigious universities and an expanding technology sector in its suburbs, had numerous performance spaces, record stores, and large kiosks selling C D s by bus stations. It evidenced a great deal of interest in rural genres, manifested by concerts and radio stations devoted to them. It was also close to two of Brazil's largest rodeos, Jaguariuna and Americana, which provided some of the most important performance spaces for rural genres.

Campinas was equidistant from other locations in which I undertook research. I frequently visited the city of São Paulo for shows, conversations, and visits to rural-themed bars. I also traveled to three smaller interior cities, Itapira (population 61,000), Mogi Guaçu (population 115,000), and Mogi Mirim (population 75,000), where my Campinas host-family had grown up and my host-family's mother's father had worked in telecommunications for many years. The latter's contacts opened the way for my Sunday research in live radio. In addition, I traveled for particular events or meetings to Ribeirão Preto, São José dos Campos, and São José do Rio Preto.

Throughout my research, I strove to address questions about values and the integration of institutions, actors, and genres within a field of cultural production. With a view to determining the broader contours of the Brazilian field of musical production, I pursued information about forms of Brazilian popular music other than simply the rural. My sense that fields of production contained genres, musicians, producers, and listeners that defined themselves, and were defined, *relationally*, according to affinities and contrasts, was reinforced by the statements I collected and the actions I observed. In effect, I felt I could say little about rural genres without understanding at least something of urban ones since they were often compared.

To delineate aspects of the field of production, I sought interviews

Map 2. The State of São Paulo.

with listeners, musicians, songwriters, journalists, record-company owners, radio hosts, and club and studio owners: in short, those people one would most often associate with music. However, in my attempt to determine aspects of the field of production that might not normally be thought to be part of it, I also sought informal encounters with music wherever I could, including domains that might normally be considered extramusical. What radio station did the construction workers building the wall next door turn to? (It was Rádio Laser, a local música sertaneja station.) What songs blared from downtown furniture storefronts? (It was música sertaneja.) What did they play over the PA at shopping malls, and how did those selections shape commercial space? All of these kinds of data contributed to my sense of "the field."

Not long after arriving in Campinas, I began regular lessons with a ten-string guitar player, José,[19] who will appear prominently in chapter 5. I did this for several reasons. First, my musician friends repeatedly told me that the viola was the "country" instrument, the opposite of an easily controllable and predictable modern instrument, such as my own acoustic guitar. Playing the viola required understanding principles they held dear. When they espoused the potential of the instrument to transform consciousness, they sounded like Pierre Bourdieu speaking on *habitus*. I, in no sense, hoped to use the viola as a smooth conduit for "unmediated" truths of the country critique. Indeed, I believed that the country critique, like any other critique, was, by its very nature, relentlessly mediated. I nonetheless hoped to become familiar with its mechanics, techniques of practice, and theories for performance. Following the ideas of Sudnow (1978) a classical piano player turned jazz musician, I wished to learn at least some of the "ways of the hand."

However, my commitment to learn to play had deeper roots. Many musical ethnographies I had read had valiantly attempted to preserve the musical integrity of their subject. However, as I read these texts, the moments where their authors seemed most engaged with their material were those in which the music seemed to be reduced to other domains of social life. Music was *in fact* about migration, class, poverty, race, gender, generation—indeed, almost anything *but* music. It was an *idiom*—in other words, a way of saying something that was *really* about something *else*. And even if these reductions were accompanied by many others, making for a multidimensional sound-print, their approaches nonetheless enacted a thoroughgoing translation of music into other social domains.

Musical practitioners themselves often explicitly call upon economic, political, geographical, and social metaphors to explain what they do. However, methodologically, I wished momentarily to avoid the reduction of music to other realms of social life at least in one part of my research. My sense was that those with whom I spoke would suggest that there was something about what they were doing that they would not be able to tell me in a question-and-answer format (see, also, Fox 2004; Weidman 2006). This was correct. On a few occasions, a moment's discovery about how to hold my hands altered much of my thinking on how to project my "heart." For fear of invoking Joycian epiphanies of the sort described in *Portrait of the Artist as a Young Man* (Joyce 1997, 131): I would play, make some mistake, and José would bark at me. And while often, in those moments, I just felt dumb, at others, I thawed and shifted (see also Feld 1989, 164). For instance, once, frustrated with what he characterized as my mechanical approach, my teacher grumbled that the viola was an instrument that was "sentimental *by nature*" and that if I could not grasp this simple fact, I was hopeless. Another time, he informed me that a particular passage ought to sound like "sobbing." And another time, I was told that the instrument could not be mastered and practiced, but needed to be "seduced."

I am still far from being a competent violeiro, but those moments showed me a great deal about what I might have to do to *become* one. They also communicated much about rural performativity that I had not been able to extricate through questions and observation; the viola was the locus of emotion in performance, and the mechanics of repetition alone would not teach this. Rather, one had to develop one's sense of Central-Southern nature (trees, birds, fishes), and one's heart (coração). What I learned in these lessons shapes the ethnographic treatment of rural music that we will now begin.

1

What Counts as "Country"?

RURAL PERFORMATIVITY IN THE TWENTIETH CENTURY

The "Jeca theme" from a song called "The Sadness of Armadillo Joe" seeds our examination of rural genres and allows us to lay out rurality's approach to subjectivity. This theme reworks itself in Central-Southern rural "variations" (Lévi-Strauss 1969) throughout the twentieth century. The Jeca theme and variations' most important attribute is that the singing, playing, and listening subject separates a debased urban present from an idealized rural past and then *uses* that rural past as a means to reprimand the present. This sounds simple enough.

However, the dynamics of this reprimand are not without complication for several reasons. First, it is only one part of Joe that longs for a time in which he was whole, "off in those hills." In the present, the protagonist is both geographically and temporally cut off from the moment in which he felt intact. In a fragmented "now," the singer is divided, living partially, longing for completion back then, off *there*. At the beginning of the twentieth century, rural song-texts grieved for the impossibility of a return to there and then by way of imagery from nature, sometimes joining this with the impossibility of returning to a romantic love that had gone wrong. By the end of the century, romantic love comes to play an increasingly important role, as the space in these songs once occupied by cows, birds, fish, and rivers fills with man's unbridled passions. This chapter nonetheless argues that throughout this period, the pith of musically instantiated rurality remains consistent.

The Jeca Theme

This continuity can be seen from an analysis of the Jeca theme, together with its histories. Reading these histories, in turn, reveals the way in which rurality relates the past to the present. So, to begin: On May 24, 1918, sometime dentist, police scribe, and music-store owner Angelino de Oliveira premiered the song in question. It would become one of the most famous rural songs in the history of Brazilian music—a tune current ten-string guitar player, music critic, and novelist Paulo Freire calls the Central-Southern rural "hymn and most representative song" (Freire 1996, 15).[1] In "The Sadness of Armadillo Joe" ("Tristezas do Jeca"—also translatable simply as "Jeca's Sadness"), Oliveira set out to write candidly of the difficult conditions of the hillbilly without being maudlin. In Oliveira's view, the basic point was that the song's protagonist had been forced to move away from where he was born.

In the song, Jeca misses the place he still thinks of as home, where nature does the nurturing. He wants to go back.

> I was born off in those hills
> In a hut, cradled by the ground.

At the same time as Jeca wants to return, however, he knows full well that he cannot. Jeca's absorption in his grief dominates the song and the mood it establishes. As with all Central-Southern rural musical song-texts, the protagonist cries, musically, because he finds himself involuntarily separated from something he once lived close to, in this case, nature and home, joined. Jeca displays his past proximity to a natural home through a description of the house of his youth. The moonlight comes through openings in the roof. The ground "cradles" sleepers. One awakens, not to an alarm clock or to sounds from some bustling street, but to the song of birds that the porous structure invites inside:

> Our simple house so full of holes,
> And lit by moonlight.
> And when dawn came,
> There, in the forest, the songbirds
> Started the morning's sounds.

Back in the good old days, Jeca's house did not maintain strict boundaries between man and nature, but allowed its residents to live practically out-of-doors. Each day, Jeca went to sleep and woke up in a home that was of the forest.

But those days are gone. And Jeca's resultant sadness relates both to the passage of time and to his movement in physical space. Jeca is older now and has had to leave those distant hills along with his youth. And it is not only time and space that provide the metrics for this movement, but also Jeca's incumbent sense of self. As mentioned, in the present, part of him still resides off in those hills where he was once whole, while the other half lives here, in a diminished now. As he bemoans his inability to return to those hills, he simultaneously longs for the countryside, the past, and a sense of completeness predicated in part upon ignorance of the outside world; that forest was all he knew. In this pining, he's aiming for an unreachable target, one that is inaccessible, not only because the past is closed to him, but because to return to childish years would mean relinquishing the present. The present is, necessarily, a loss, but one that must be held on to because to go back is a loss also. Jeca cannot return, not only because the past has passed, but also because the past is a childish place, and he must now live in a grown-up world. So, despite its not being a manly thing to do, Jeca weeps. He weeps because he *cannot* go back, because he *should* not go back, and because he nonetheless *wants* to go back. Add to this the fact that Jeca is unable to govern his emotions because his countryness makes him a more "natural," and hence more emotional, man, and you have a perfect storm of tears.

Oliveira felt that most contemporaneous rural music approached Jeca's sadness simply by rendering some rural domestic disaster in lyrics. But for Oliveira, the laundry lists of calamities these tunes contained failed to capture the underlying grief of rural experience. He wished instead to render the rural protagonist's deep-seated melancholy. Jeca's *feelings* were not only the result of drought, hunger, poverty, or his cheatin' love. These events were surely capable of catalyzing Jeca's grief, but they did not *encompass* it. The recitation of difficult occurrences did little to explain what Jeca felt in his innermost self, whereas Oliveira hoped his song would do precisely that. "Jeca's Sadness" therefore contains no events whatsoever, instead proffering an abstract cosmology of Jeca. Indeed, the lack of specificity of reference to the past is part of the point of this song, and part of the point of Brazilian rurality itself. This is not a tune filled with specific references which place Jeca's past precisely. Rather, the song evokes a sense of the past that is rigorously nonspecific, and in that nonspecificity, it evokes a past that is easily appropriable. That the past to which Jeca points may be said never to have existed is part of the point.

Throughout, music plays a crucial role in Jeca's state of mind and in his ability to conjure bygone days that are simultaneously from no-where and everywhere. For Oliveira's Jeca, singing and playing provide both an occasion and conveyance for his deep-seated melancholy. The sadness of having once been embraced by nature and then forced to leave it finds unique expression in song. Jeca, who uses his *viola* to sing his "longing," tells us:

> I can't sing no more.
> Because when Jeca sings
> You wanna cry.
> And the tears you cry then
> Slowly flow away—
> Like water, t' the sea.[2]

As in all Central-Southern rural music, Oliveira fuses singing and play-ing the viola with grief itself. The singing and playing of the song both channel the performer's grief and elicit grief in kind in those who hear it; Jeca's melody makes him cry, and listeners cry while listening. The song thus simultaneously mediates bodily and intellectual, individual and social aspects of grief (see Leavitt 1996, 531). This makes maintain-ing musical coherence throughout the song more difficult. Jeca is so sad that the song only just manages to stay on track; grief threatens to overwhelm him and send the music into the domain of mere weeping.

Sonically channeling the grief of both performer and audience does not dissipate that grief, sending it to a kind of emotional "ground" like an errant electrical charge. Rather, the physical manifestation of inner sadness in the form of the hick's tears integrates him with nature once again. Singing and playing, and their incumbent tearfulness, embed Jeca in cyclical hydraulic processes. The tears listeners and singers cry in response to the song form rivers, leading, eventually, to the ocean. One day, they'll fall again as rain. At the same time as water emerges from eyes, each note from the song forms a tear. So the music drips like water, as falling tears play the melody of the song. The countryside and its natural attributes map the emotional topography, or musically in-stantiated "structure of feeling," in which grief temporarily reinte-grates those who perform and listen to rural music with nature and with their pasts. "Structure of feeling" here conveys the link between a way of shaping and responding to individual experience on the one hand, and a certain mode of cultural production writ large on the other

(R. Williams 1977, 128–35). And as Raymond Williams noted, the opposition between the country and the city provides a vocabulary for a set of "historical ideas" that do not necessarily reference a specific time and place. This structure of feeling reveals the way in which an "experience finds material which gives body to the thoughts" (R. Williams 1973, 291).

Rural music historian and *violeiro* Paulo Freire's historical book on rural music, in which he praises and historicizes "Jeca's Sadness," draws its title from the first line of the song. *I Was Born off in Those Hills* (Freire 1996) seeks to fix Brazilian rurality's past by ascribing a seed-like quality to this tune, describing its momentum—the way it carries emotional force across time and space. For Freire, it is the conveyance of sadness in the song that promises, albeit temporarily, to allow listeners and singers to touch their long-lost homes. The song builds a bridge, but it calls attention to the fact that it builds a bridge that it must soon tear down. Musicality thus mediates time and space, fusing fragmented portions of subjectivity together, as it signals the very impermanence of that fusion. Freire's analysis of the song in print (as we shall see below, he provides other details onstage) begins with the night of its first rendition. After Oliveira played it for friends at his local bar in Botucatu,[3] we read that there was silence. Apparently the song did not fit into an immediately recognizable pattern of listener response. People seemed, at first, unsure of what they had heard and required a few moments to understand their own reactions. Only after a few seconds did their silence turn to deafening applause. In the course of the evening, those present requested the song six more times. In Freire's telling, from its first rendition, "Jeca's Sadness" carried in its very melody and words the ability to generate a desire for its repetition. The audience felt compelled to keep feeling sad *again*. The hurt was so *good*.

Part of this pleasurable pain emerges from Jeca's appeals to his audience through the symbols of the *caipira*, the viola, and the song itself:

> With this viola
> I sing, and cry, truthfully
> And each tune is like a piece of longing.

And this sadness and longing carry with them a sense of powerlessness. The narrator seems trapped. As Jeca would have it:

I want to tell you
Of my suffering and my pain.
I am like the songbird,
Who can only sing of sadness
From his branch.

Fully expressing this powerlessness contributed to the song's force. But somehow confessing the sense of being trapped, which lies at the center of Jeca's predicament, made the song comforting. And this is another important element of Jeca's theme. For its audience on that night in Botucatu, the song had a simultaneously soothing and saddening effect, one that not only perfectly captured Jeca's sense of imprisonment (Freire 1996, 22), but also elicited that same feeling in listeners. They *became* Jeca, together.

The effects of the song were not limited to Oliveira's bar-friends in Botucatu, Freire's story goes. Freire continues with tales in which Oliveira's singing and crying hick transcended both geopolitical boundaries and, on one occasion at least, violence. One year after its premiere in 1919, Freire writes, only somewhat tongue in cheek, the police ordered the pit orchestra to play the song during a riot at a theater in the small interior town of Barretos, São Paulo. The rioters stopped in their tracks, and when the music ended, they quietly left the theater. Even when it was arranged for orchestra and thus stripped of its originary rural instrumentation and singing styles, Jeca's sadness still evoked the essence of Brazil abroad. In the 1930s, for example, one particularly homesick Brazilian journalist reportedly stepped off a train in a hamlet in Russia and was amazed to hear Jeca's sonic tears emerging from a bar (Freire 1996). He would later recount that that sound had transported him home, melting the ice and snow. More widespread evidence of the song's significance lies in its having been used by radio stations in Germany, Holland, and the United Kingdom to begin transmissions concerning Brazil in the years before the Second World War. In this way, Freire establishes the extent to which this rural song perfectly hit the target of Central-Southern rural grief in such a way that listeners across time and space could not help but recognize it as embodying Brazil itself.

But who was Jeca? Why was he so sad? And how did this song so perfectly capture his plight? At the moment in which Oliveira composed his tune, "Jeca" was the stereotypical name for a Central-Southern hillbilly, the "Joe Sixpack" of São Paulo's interior in the early twentieth century. And the caipira was contested terrain in early twentieth-century Brazil. Some had it that he was a painful reminder of how far there was left to go before arriving at First World status (Lobato 1998). Others had him as a tragic-comic genius whose simplicity allowed him to see more clearly than his ostensibly sophisticated but overconfident urban counterparts (Pires 1927, 1985). What is clear is that then, as now, the rural subject was a site where the transformations of Brazilian society could be interpreted and enacted by way of notions of country and city. Contrasting perspectives on Jeca went along with differing understandings of the former's relation to the latter and with prescriptions for how that relation, and along with it, Brazil's future, ought to be handled. Should the countryside modernize and all traces of the past be done away with, in particular, degenerate hillbillies? Or should city-dwellers learn a thing or two from their country cousins about how to do things the old-fashioned way, appreciating hick wisdom and preserving the backcountry in the bargain? Part and parcel of this back-and-forth involved commentary on modes of materially conceived production. Should small family farms be preserved, or should industrialization and wholesale monocrop agriculture take over? Could the two modes coexist?

As Freire's history of rural music reveals, the practice of Central-Southern rural musical genres has carried the legacy of the issues raised by "The Sadness of Armadillo Joe" through the remainder of the twentieth century and into the twenty-first, configuring them in different ways according to transforming historical needs. Rural genres have been used to interpret and act upon the changing relations between the country and the city, to affect modes of social and economic production, and to fashion categories of gender, social class, and race. Pining for the past, as evidenced in this seminal song written by Oliveira and historicized by Freire, recurs in modulated forms throughout the twentieth century, providing continuity to Central-Southern rural musical practice. In this sense, rural genres, operating by way of rural performativity, may be thought of as the playing of a theme, "Sad Old Armadillo Joe," and variations. The process, unfolding as music must, in real time, clarifies the way that practices and beliefs both continue and change. According to Lévi-Strauss (1969, 66–78; 1973, 250), a theme and variations involve the repetition, modified, of a discrete musical idea, where repetitions continuously generate an emergent structure with new possibilities and textures at each statement. In the same way, Central-Southern singers and listeners repeat a grief-stricken longing for the past set in the countryside throughout the twentieth century. Thus, a rueful sadness and longing, reconfigured at different moments, becomes the recurring element in this rural musical practice.

When Freire performs the song live, he fashions its power to move his listeners in the present. On June 22, 2006 in the SESC (Serviço Social do Comércio—Commerce Social Services) "Cultural Space" in Campinas,[4] for instance, Paulo prefaced the tune with a musically accompanied story of Oliveira needing to move himself and his family to another town for work. Arriving at the train station of his new home, depressed and wet from rain, the Oliveira of Freire's yarn is delighted to find the station manager humming "Jeca's Sadness." The station manager replies to Oliveira's leading question about "who wrote that song" with the fact that he doesn't precisely know, but that whoever it was, he was clearly a "good caboclo" (a union of Portuguese with Indian, here indexing the racial mixture of Central-Southern rurality, as we shall see in more detail below). This anonymity pleases Oliveira. That the station manager doesn't know who wrote the song underscores its accurate summary of rural grief; the tune's appeal has nothing to do with the reputation of the songwriter and everything to do with its pure and simple effect. A "good caboclo" should be anonymous. His lack of fame has thus allowed the song to take on a life of its own, circulating naturally, like water, wind, or fire. After completing his story, Freire begins the tune without pausing, and the entire audience, primed by the narrative, bursts into song. As they sing, many wistfully stare off into the distance, shaking their heads, tearing up a little; though these gestures are not choreographed, and they aren't performed by all listeners at the same moment, for the many who manifest their emotional engagement with the song in this way, the gestures look as though they form an identification with the song:

> In these special verses
> My pretty one, my love
> I want to sing, for you, my suffering and pain.

Those present know every word, and they sing the piece so loudly that they drown out Freire, his amplified viola, his brother's electric bass guitar, and the percussionist. In that moment, framed by my reading of

Freire's history of the song, it was possible for me to imagine the song's having had a similar effect on Oliveira's friends in Botucatu back in the early twentieth century. This, of course, was precisely the result that Freire desired.

We have seen the way the recurring theme evident in "Sad Old Armadillo Joe" continues to unfold in and through rural music. The remainder of this chapter analyzes this theme from different vantage points. I focus on how gender, space, and time fuse in musical performance with important consistencies throughout the twentieth century and into the twenty-first. I also place Jeca's variations into the context of a Central-Southern "turn" to the countryside. But in order to accomplish this, I must first elaborate on "rural performativity," addressing its embarrassments.

Two Brazils, One Ruefully Proud

> But, if there is only one culture and only one nationality of which Brazilians are so proud, that single culture has two aspects, or even better, two completely different levels. Brazilians are divided into two systems of social and economic organization—different levels with different methods for living. These two societies did not evolve to the same rhythm and have not reached the same phase; they are not separated by differences of nature, but by differences of *age*.
> —JACQUES LAMBERT, *Os Dois Brasis* (*The Two Brazils*)

Rural performativity begins by separating country from city, and then uses this dichotomy to fashion and comment upon other social dichotomies. This section's epigram, by French scholar and contemporary of Lévi-Strauss's, Jacques Lambert, provides a glimpse of such dichotomous thinking. Therein Lambert proposes that Brazil should be thought of as split into two societies that differ in the stage at which they find themselves: a Brazil past *together with* a Brazil present. Elsewhere in the text, he makes it clear that this past "aspect" is to be found in the countryside, while the more current one occurs in the city.

Such dichotomizing practices have held sway in both informal and scholarly contexts in Latin America for some time as a way of accounting for the interdigitation of modern and antiquated, prosperous and poor, foreign and local. And within such contexts, the rural is often portrayed as backward, or in some sense lacking something that the city has. Pejorative connotations of the country in relation to the city stretch back much further than Lambert.[5] In the nineteenth century, for instance, Argentinean Domingo Sarmiento's *Facundo: Or, Civilization and Barbarism*, published in 1845, argued that the "country" barbarism of local strongmen had destroyed the limited urbanity Buenos Aires's elites had managed to import from Europe (Sarmiento 1998, 54, 61).

A nearly contemporaneous Brazilian reworking of this notion found expression in journalist Euclides da Cunha's great historical essay *Rebellion in the Backlands*, first published in 1904, in which the Northeastern countryside psychologically and physically retarded its inhabitants (da Cunha 1944). Da Cunha described the way in which a colony of anti-federalist Christian zealots living in a backwater called Canudos were brutally stamped out by federal troops in 1897. The work presented a distinct Northeastern interior, almost medieval in aspect, in contrast with an urban south aspiring to federalism, standardization, and modernity. Da Cunha's take on the polarity contains more nuance than Sarmiento's since da Cunha's urban armies and their commanders were far from perfect. Indeed they were decadent, whoring after aspects of European social thought that da Cunha felt were unsuited to Brazilian reality. For da Cunha, the urbanizing south tragically failed to understand the *sertão*. For this reason, instead of treating the backlanders like invalids, which da Cunha argues it ought to have done, the urban south criminalized and killed them. But note the power dynamic still in play across this polarity despite the criticism of the city. The countryside is the sick child and the city is the older bully that *ought* to know better. For da Cunha, fear that the countryside might pull the nation back into the past threatens urban progress. This sensibility remains. Today, the countryside continues to haunt the horizons of da Cunha's debased urban modernity, in part by way of his book's inclusion in the Brazilian literary canon.

A similar country-city polarity is often employed to explain Brazil's relation to other nations. For instance, urban-rural dichotomies frequently ground explanations for why Latin American countries fail to progress like the United States or Europe, and in such cases, Latin America becomes "country" to the United States' or Europe's "city." Note in this regard, neoliberal champion and Brazilian ex-president Fernando Henrique Cardoso's reprimand of Brazil as a nation of hillbillies in an interview granted to a Spanish newspaper in 1996, *during* his presidency: "Since I lived outside Brazil for many years, I became conscious of this: Brazilians are caipiras knowing nothing of the other side [Europe, North America] and when they do, they're seduced. This is the problem with Brazil" (Sabino 1996). Cardoso's statement, which even his unswerving supporters deemed an unfortunate slip, reveals the enduring power of urban-rural dichotomies to explain center-periphery relations in Latin America, as well as the rawness such dichotomies may elicit. For Cardoso, Brazil becomes the countryside, and its citizens are isolated hayseeds, either lacking knowledge of the city (Europe and North America, in this case), or being wowed by it. What Brazilian qua country people lack is the seasoned capacity for *judgment*. It is as though the world outside, the urban one, has the power to cause some kind of addiction precisely because the countryside's residents are so insular. The world outside contains shiny trinkets, and country people can't tell that trinkets lack substantial value because they've simply never seen them before. Recall Jeca's isolation in those hills.

There have, of course, been some critiques of positing the existence of "two Brazils." Some of these note that such polarized models oversimplify, while others draw attention to the way in which the two poles are not antagonistic, but in fact coconstitutive (for example, Alves 1997; Lima 1999). But despite such critiques, recent scholars and laypersons continue to use bifurcating models to account for stark social contrasts between Brazil and the rest of the world, and within Brazil itself (Maxwell 1999; Sawaya et al. 2003; Shirley 1971). In these, the countryside is figured as the backward, the forgotten, and the stuck.[6] To use DaMatta's phrase, the distinction between country and city is a Brazilian "dilemma."

The power of explaining social relations within and without Brazil by means of such polarities would have come as no surprise to Raymond Williams, of course. His analysis of these contrastive categories suggested that such spatiotemporal paradigms and their emotional entailments characterized modernity itself (R. Williams 1973, 82). Centers required their peripheries, and vice versa. But one thing that is apparent through this short analysis of the use of country-city polarities to explain forms of social difference in Brazil is that the distinction clearly concerns much more than just space, conceived simplistically. Indeed, rural performativity does not ask that its spatiality be taken literally. Rather than thinking of the urban and the rural simply as forms of space that emerge from some ostensibly underlying means of economic production and are then merely *pondered* in conversation, literature, or song, such an analysis reveals that users of these categories chronotopically *fashion* such spaces in conversation, on stage, in books, and in interviews, to cite just a few contexts. In other words, Brazilians *sing* the countryside into existence just as much as they plough it, consolidate it, make it more efficient, *live* in it, or preserve it. Following Jean and John Comaroff's analysis of a madman's use of rurality to come to terms with social change in South Africa in the 1980s (J. L. Comaroff and J. Comaroff 1992, 159), rural performativity offers its users a contrastive model for both interpreting and acting upon the Brazilian social order's late twentieth-century transformations. In this case, that transformation involves Brazil's modernization and concomitant urbanization, together with its emergence from military dictatorship into an ostensibly redemptive, but unfortunately fallen, age of democratic neoliberalism.

Here is where country's multiple drifts emerge most clearly, and where a coherent understanding of performativity is required in order to chart those drifts. We have so far seen that rural performativity relies upon the separation of a country from a city. It then establishes "country" in a privatively marked relation to the city,[7] wherein the country represents a kind of lack. But a shift occurs. Because as Jeca's theme reveals, much Brazilian rural music *celebrates* the rural. Armadillo Joe's idyllic past would seem to contrast starkly with the pejorative characterizations we have just considered. But rather than a contrast, it in fact offers a relation. Brazilian rurality's positive valuation of the countryside only makes sense in relation to the sort of negative readings we have just examined. The celebratory nature of rural performativity continually addresses itself directly *to* such pejorative valences. The unpleasant aspects of country—its embarrassments—continually create the conditions of possibility for Brazilian rurality. The countryside is that place to which those who celebrate it say they *shouldn't* want to return, and yet, they *do*. Thus, discourses of rurality first inhabit, and once they have inhabited, only *then* counteract, rurality's complications.

This multiply determined subject-position finds itself put to use in a wide variety of situations in which rurality may be brought to bear. For instance, it is often applied in narrating what are framed as personal "experiences." As embarrassing as it is to wail about it in public, Jeca longs to return to a place, a time, and a sense of personal wholeness that can be realized only "off in those hills." One need not have moved very far from one's place of birth, and one need not have had one's heart broken by love, to feel the tragic pull of a Brazilian country song. I frequently discovered that Jeca's sadness explained some aspect of the life of people who had simply moved from one place to another in the Central-South, however small the distance. Take, for instance, the case of Antônio, with whom I regularly consulted in the course of my weekly visits to Itapira. His account of how he had come to live there suddenly sounded like singing one day. His story enacted the kind of polarizing involved in rural performativity with respect to the stark divide between an ideal there and a debased here, couched in some embarrassment over wanting to return to "there."

Antônio (a pseudonym) was in his eighties when I last spoke to him, experiencing heart problems that kept him tied to the comfortable chair in his apartment, and grief-stricken over the death of his wife two years before. Since we had known each other a long time, he felt as though he could show me an intimate and emotional part of himself. "Last night," he reported, "I thought my time had come for certain, and I cried. I cried a lot." He then described a state much like Jeca's, in which he was utterly absorbed in his tears, unable to pull himself out of the abject state, divided between a self that must continue with his life as it was, and one that ardently hoped to return to things as they had been. This confessional grief over his imminent death and the loss of his wife segued into discussion of his youth, off in those hills. In a reflective mode, he reported that he had been born and raised in the interior São Paulo town of Mogi Mirim, just twenty minutes away. But not long after he married, the telephone company for which he was working informed him that they were expanding their operations into the nearby town of Itapira and that they needed someone who could work without direct supervision for extended periods. He had shown himself to be just such a man in Mogi Mirim, so they now needed him to move to Itapira with his young wife to open up this new frontier.

At the time, he really did not want to go. But they offered him an increase in salary, so he agreed on the condition that he could return to Mogi Mirim in six months. The company accepted this condition, and he moved to Itapira to begin his work establishing phone service there—installing lines. On the weekends he and his wife would take the short trip "home" to be with his family. In six months the company contacted him and asked him to stay on, but he reminded them of their commitment. They responded by raising his salary, which was a strong incentive to a young man with a new family, and he continued in

Itapira. Another six months passed, at which time he definitively stated: "I want to return to my homeland." This line, which appears in many rural songs, surprised me; it was as though he had sung the phrase rather than speaking it. In Itapira, Antônio was a short distance from the town of his birth. Was he not already in his homeland? The answer, apparently, was no, at least within the context of our discussion that day. The phone company raised his salary again, somewhat more this time, and once again he stayed. This process continued at expanding intervals for the next ten years or so, at which time he felt somewhat established in Itapira, and his longing to return to Mogi Mirim had diminished a bit, though he continued to feel as though Mogi Mirim was really where his heart lay.

What emerged from this story was the strength of his desire to return to a place that he considered home despite the fact that he seemed, according to my reckoning at least, hardly to have left it. Much like the protagonist of every rural song, what struck me was his way of speaking of his sadness, like Jeca, who wants to go back to those hills. Since so many people in the Central-South have moved at least a short distance, most often for work, Jeca's sadness seemed to apply, potentially, to almost everyone. But what is important to notice in the case of Antônio is that this movement, however small, became laminated together with the loss of his beloved wife and what felt like his own approaching death, according to a country framework. He was therefore able to make sense of his losses bundled together.

Simply moving from one location is far from the only occasion in which the rural comes into play as a way of decoding personal or collective experience. One of the fundamental attributes of a country critique relies on a distinct form of performativity—a commentary upon, and transformation of, social life by way of a particular brand of textuality (Hanks 1989). Since poetics provides a foundation for thinking about performance, I will begin with poetics, and then move to performativity. An explanation of the relationship between indexicality and metaindexicality will follow. The chapter ends with an analysis of Jeca's theme in a postauthoritarian mold.

Poetics, Performativity, and Meta-Indexicality

Poetics has received substantial treatment within anthropology, both linguistic (Bauman and Briggs 1990; A. Fox 1994, 2004; Hymes 2001;

Kuipers 1990) and more broadly sociocultural (J. L. Comaroff and J. Comaroff 1992; Herzfeld 1985; Trouillot 1991). Herzfeld takes care to dispel the misunderstanding of poetics *as* "poetry" by dwelling on the way in which it focuses on "the message" for its own sake (Herzfeld 1985, 10; 1996, 147). However, our current purposes demand more than this. What we require is an understanding of the fluidity of the poetic by which categories such as time, space, subjectivity, race, gender, and social class are put into action in practicing and interpreting rural textuality. How, we must wonder, does this array of social categories become laminated into something like rurality?

Much work on poetics partakes of Roman Jakobson's famous pronouncement on what he calls poetic function (Jakobson 1960, 358). Set in the context of five other functions of communicative events (conative, phatic, referential, metalingual, and emotive) in turn mapped onto five *components* of communicative events addressed by the aforementioned functions (respectively, addressee, connection, context, code, and addresser), Jakobson suggests that the sixth function, the poetic function, turns the paradigmatic and the syntagmatic in upon one another. The kind of parallelism to be found in verse—where patterns map *across* phrases in the form, for example, of unified meter, or of rhyme—projects equivalence from what Jakobson termed the axis of selection (the paradigmatic, in a Saussurian mold) to the axis of combination (the syntagmatic). In other words, on, for instance, a lexical level, poetry made the choice of what word might occupy a particular spot within a sentence, which might be simply a paradigmatic concern in less poetically dense contexts, into a syntagmatic choice. Under poetic functionality, the paradigmatically constituted group of possibly usable lexical items comes to be defined in part by whether or not that word *combines* properly in the ongoing, poetically dense, and syntagmatically unfolding structure.

To demonstrate this somewhat abstract point more concretely, consider the following instance of poetics at work, derived from poetry purely for the sake of convenience.[8] Let us pretend we were present at the inception of sonnet number twenty-nine by William Shakespeare. He began this sonnet, of rhyming scheme *abab cdcd ebeb ff* with the following: "when in disgrace with fortune and men's eyes / I all alone beweep my outcast state, / And trouble deaf Heaven with my bootless ——." Let us assume for the moment that this blank suggests that Shakespeare did not know quite how to proceed; he was unsure of what word should finish this phrase. However, say that he had decided that he wished to convey the notion of a vocalization of grief at the end of this third line. He had to find a lexical item that appropriately completed this section of his emerging, metricalized text. Certain parameters both constrained and facilitated our bard's choice. He should select lexical items to fill that blank that were appropriate to his decision to write of grief: sobs, stricken shouts, crying grunts, whimpers, sad sighs, and so forth. All these comprised a paradigmatically coherent set of possibilities. But the choice of what word to use was not *merely* constrained and facilitated by the kind of paradigmatic concerns that he would face outside of the construction of a sonnet, were he completing a sentence for quotidian speech, for instance. Rather, he was operating *within* the confines of a particular poetic form (recall, *abab, cdcd, ebeb, ff*). Thus, the space at the end of his as-if as-yet incomplete line also had pronounced syntagmatic claims upon it because whatever he chose needed both to make sense as a lexical unit that might complete this sentence and also had to rhyme with "eyes." All of this made the choice of "cries" both eminently sensible and poetically appropriate. Having made this choice, this poetic text suggested a kind of affinity between eyes and cries (as Shakespeare also suggested within the first stanza between "state" and "fate") that its construction and interpretation called into being, and continues to call into being at each act of reading, recitation, quotation, and scholarly tomfoolery.

To further define poetics in order to arrive at a fuller conception of performativity: Michael Silverstein elaborates on Jakobson's concept of poetic function in a way that clarifies it in terms of utterances more broadly, not just poetically dense ones. Note the importance of lamination for poetics, evident here in Silverstein's discussion of "layers." Poetic utterances are

> construct utterances with unit lengths measured out, in as many layers as you want, so that units in relatively similar (or regularly computable) positions in some higher structural layer have some special metaphorical pseudo-definitional (or an antidefinitional) relationship, which in effect suggests categorial identity (or oppositeness). (Silverstein 1981b, 5)

Silverstein uses the Bakhtinian definition of "utterance" (Bakhtin 1986) in order to emphasize the diversity of domains of communicative practice with which poetics engages. Also important is that poetics need not be perceived as an all-or-nothing concept, whereby a text is either poetic or it is not. Rather, as Bauman and Briggs (1990) have argued,

Table 1. Features of Country vs. City.

Space	Country	City
Gender	Female	Male
Time	Past	Future
Human Development	Nature	Nurture
Geopolitics	Brazil	North America and Europe
Orientation to Change	Old-fashioned	Modern
Orientation to Subjectivity	Emotional, copiously expressive	Rational, controlled
Race	Caboclo	African/White
Interaction with the Nonhuman	Animal	Machine
Social Relations	Brotherhood— kinship	Anonymity—voluntary association
Social Class	Working class (peon – peão)	Upper class

poetics must be framed according to degree, where certain moments of communicative practice may be framed as maximally poetic, while others may be less so. This is to some extent consistent with Jakobson's insight that each communicative event involves the aforementioned zones (addressee, addresser, message, code, etc.), though each event emphasizes one or more of these zones more than others. With respect to the form of musical performance under scrutiny here, poetic function combines, by way of musical textuality, features indexically linked to aspects of everyday life ("units" in Silverstein's usage) into a delimited taxonomy. This combination takes place not merely in the social space directly indexed by country versus city. Table 1 lists just a few of the kinds of features recruited by the production and reception of rural song texts in Brazil.

The process whereby the rural poetic function calls these various categories into dialogue with one another is what Silverstein means by "definition"; concepts are relevant within a given stretch of communicative practice by way of performativity. Put another way, the poetic combinations within a given text both constitute and comment upon the social world (we will see numerous examples of this below). The poetic function both flags and fashions the rules of social life (A. Fox 1992). As we can see from table 1, within Brazilian rural performativity the spatial category of the country simultaneously comments upon and brings forth, for instance, history, gender, emotion, social class, race, place, and nature. This is, in part, the nature of indexicality; it is that pointing *to*, inherent to all human behavior, whereby pointing *to* involves both presupposition and entailment (Hanks 2001).

However, attention to the way in which poetics focuses on the message for its own sake risks losing sight of a crucial feature of this musical communicative practice: that it is oriented toward an audience of some kind which is in some position to evaluate the effectiveness of that very attention to the message (Bauman and Briggs 1990). In other words, whether poetic texts are addressed to single speakers (even to the speaker who happens to be constructing them) or to broader, differently periodized "publics" (Warner 2002), there is both an anticipation on the part of their author that they will be received, together with an act of reception. In unison, these generate *meaning*. Both production *and* reception focus on the structure of the message for its own sake. Thus, the concept of performativity places poetics into a more explicitly shared domain by acknowledging that not *only* does poetic textual practice "set" to the message (in the sense of "attend to" the message that is discussed by Herzfeld 1997). But in addition, a set to the message is crucial to the understanding of what constitutes a "public" (Warner 2002)—the way a message's meaning gets established *across* interactional space.

To understand the ways in which this mapping across interactional space takes place within Brazilian rural music, it is useful to draw a distinction between indexicality and meta-indexicality. Since all human sign-related behavior works through the pointing-to known as indexicality, and indexicality involves both presupposition and entailment in each communicative act, all sign use (and hence, social life) both draws upon some preexisting communicative system (language, for instance) and fashions that system in the same moment. Performativity serves to highlight the centrality to communicative practice of indexicality by drawing attention to it. It thus involves a double pointing-to. To draw upon John Austin's classic "performatives" as an illustration, the statement "I hereby pronounce you man and wife" is not only indexical in terms of its pointing to a man and a wife, though these indexicals are certainly present within the statement. This Austinian performative also points to the particular act of pointing-to. It draws attention to some "I" that indexes "man" and "wife," the context of the act, and its expected outcome. In this pointing-to the pointing-tos, the classic performative is profoundly meta-indexical.

This helps to explain some of the aspects of Brazilian musical rurality discussed above. We have already explored the way in which rurality addresses the possible negative connotations of the countryside by contradicting them, mobilizing the rural for positive ends that fly in the face of its deprecation. We have also seen the ways that any employment of the rural in Brazil simultaneously signals, not just space, but also, at least, time, as well as gender, race, social class, and so on, depending on the instance of use. In other words, these various ideas become meta-indexically available in moments of communicative practice marked as rural. Furthermore, we have seen the way in which a divide between the country and the city also involves a divide in subjectivity between emotional and rational components of the self. By this rationale, rurality as a category of subjectivity would seem to lie at the heart of communicatively shaped approaches to the self within modernity.

As noted in our analysis of Jeca, rurality divides subjectivity along temporal lines, in terms of the way in which the rural subject longs to be "back then" while knowing that he cannot return there, nor should he want to. But how does rural music naturalize a divide between rationality and emotion? The economics of "passion" in Brazilian rural contexts elucidates this.

Emotion: A Rural (Re)Turn

The countryness of rural genres must be understood within the context of a broad Central-Southern "turn" to the rural, which many participants classify as a *return*. One of the crucial components of this is a vast increase in the popularity of rodeo, where performance of both live and prerecorded rural musical genres sets the event's ritual frame.

A series of magazines and web sites devoted to rodeo and the connection between rodeo and rural music has sprung up in the last ten years.[9] According to some estimates, attendance at the nation's largest rodeo,

Barretos, in the state of São Paulo, exceeded 1.5 million in 2000, a figure that has steadily increased since then.[10] The National Rodeo Federation (A Federação Nacional do Rodeio Completo—or FNRC), an organization created in 1996 to support the "development of rodeo as a sport" (FNRC 1999), was finally successful in 1999. At the Brazilian National Rodeo Championship in November of that year, the minister of sport pronounced rodeo, with its eight events, to be an official Brazilian sport and promised to introduce legislation in Congress to solidify this announcement (FNRC 1999). The very next year, they felt their nationalization of the sport had been well founded since, in 2000, Brazilians purchased 24 million rodeo tickets. To the ostensible surprise of everyone in the news media, the total was equivalent to the number of tickets sold for professional soccer matches in the same year.

In a purely financial vein, the gross income from Barretos in 1996 was US$120 million, much more than the US$45 million generated by Carnival in Rio that year (Izique 2000). In the São Paulo town of Americana, their rodeo makes US$15 million and accounts for 10 percent of the region's annual income (Izique 2000). Such figures seem remarkable since Embratur (the Brazilian Tourism Office) offers no financial aid or advertising support to rodeo, although they heavily fund carnivals. Yet 1,200 rodeos acknowledged by the FNRC blanket the nation. Moreover, this number of official events fails to include the countless informal ones that have sprung up in urban and rural environments alike.

Those performing or listening to rural musical genres, as well as those attending or competing in rodeos, offer a variety of reasons for turning to rodeo and things "country." One rodeo producer explains it this way:

> In a country like Brazil, where society has its origins in a rural life, rodeo fills a hole in our current lifestyle. Today, the magic of rodeo is catching, among people in small *and* large cities, and it's leading to increasing tourism, as well as economic, social, and cultural activity. It is providing dreams, and happiness. Rodeo is a kind of cultural revolution. (Júnior 2000, 22)

Thus, we see that this growth of rurality may be framed as a *re*-turn to the rural; Brazil had tried to forget its countryness by yearning for progress and urbanity during the dictatorship years. The dictatorship brought explosive economic growth. But economic progress and the modern do not necessarily define Brazilians as people, many suggest. Rather,

Central-Southerners frequently make different claims about Brazilian-ness (brasilidade); they choose to take pride in being hicks, addressing, as they do so, associated negative connotations.

The "emotion" involved in rural performativity was one of the central characteristics that many spoke of at rodeos, concerts, and interviews. They pointed to a rush of adrenaline, adventure, and passion in both rodeo and rural music. Many reported that it was emotional for them to see someone dominate a fearsome animal by staying on its back for eight full seconds. Comparisons to soccer were frequently made, such that rodeo was thought to offer more excitement. In soccer, the story went, only one or two goals are scored per game, and "tied" games frequently occur. In bull riding on the other hand, there are many matches throughout the evening, and there are no ties, one enthusiast explained. In eight seconds, either the bull or the rider has won. Furthermore, the risks are great. When a bull rider falls, he gets more than a yellow card. He may be gored or trampled, adding even more excitement. The bull rider takes risks that the soccer player would never dream of; the wound caused by the horn of an angry steer cannot be compared with a twisted ankle. The risks of the bull rider's being injured by the bull help to generate "emotion."

The rural is frequently framed as an approach to the emotional in another sense. Rather than exercising the strict control over emotions thought to be required by a modern, urban way of life, a country mode suggests giving free rein to feelings within prescribed contexts—almost always musical ones. Indeed, música sertaneja and rodeo are described as eliciting "emotional" states of mind involving grief, love, pain, laughter, and joy. For example, the advertisement for the música sertaneja compilation of songs devoted to Leandro stated, simply, "You WILL become emotional." But what might be meant by emotion, here?

Rural Epistemology

To capture the essence of what counts as country, we must inquire into a country epistemology that emerges in performance—a way of knowing by doing. In one particular show, brothers Zé Mulato and Cassiano introduce their song "Tear" with a question: "Why do people cry? And why do they *need* to cry?" The song that follows is a *toada*, a slow, plaintive song form in a minor key that treats issues of sadness, grieving, and loss.[11] Here, the *dupla* produces a kind of functional explanation whereby the longing for loves of the past builds up in the heart like water behind a dam. Tears are the way that pressure is released, and failing to give vent to one's emotions threatens damage—the bursting of the dam.

> *When I wake up, all raw*
> *With my eyes all full of tears,*
> *It's just that longing in my chest*
> *Filling up—making a dam.*
> *And that tear is the drainpipe*
> *That empties out the sadness.*
> *If you don't cry, that dam*
> *Will burst, for certain.*
> *So every tear that falls*
> *Is our self-defense. (Zé Mulato and Cassiano 1991)[12]*

Another cause for the buildup of emotional pressure is reason itself. Reason attempts to curb sentiment, but sentiment's buildup cannot be avoided, and tears provide the escape valve:

> *Reason is the blockade*
> *That makes up real life:*
> *A barrier that calls a halt*
> *To the sentimental side.*
> *And in this filling and emptying*
> *That is our day-to-day,*
> *Passion is that constant pain,*
> *That hurts as much as it grows on us. (Ibid.)*

Several other features characterize this topology of sentiment. First, individuals must experience both pain and joy; you can't have one without the other. Second, history becomes an emotional narrative. In this song, tears represent the events of the past moving through one, and crying becomes a way of acknowledging that history's happenings form a portion of identity. Though adherence to one's past might be conceived of as somewhat shameful, the song argues that one must embrace it:

> *Longing's what fills up*
> *A passionate heart.*
> *The open valley empties, like the tide—*
> *The past leaking out.*

The loves that come and go
Nestling in memory—
If a man has no past,
He deserves no history. . . .
That's why I'm not shy
About confessing my sorrow.

This last quotation reveals another important element of the music, which is that the male singer must not be shy about confessing his feelings publicly. Note that his need to state this lack of shyness belies itself. As Jeca has already shown us, and we shall see in more detail below, that males should publicly confess their ability and desire to cry provides one of the fundamental inversions through which rural performativity enacts its country critique.

Jeca's theme is in evidence here, and in other locations within the context of rural music. Often, the music's subject matter explores the ways in which the contradictions of love establish its "natural" reality. Many rural songs in the postauthoritarian moment argue that someone who is in love exists in a constant state of tension, oscillating between affection and dislike. Consider, in this respect, Leandro and Leonardo's first hit, "Contradictions" (Contradições):

We embrace, bite, and complain
After, we've come apart, crying—we kiss
And discover how much we still love each other
They're contradictions of a love without reason,
I deny it, and deny it again, but I know I need it.
(Leandro and Leonardo 1985)

What is important in this sort of meditation on love is that "true" love contains precisely these sorts of contradictions; though one might wish for a kind of love without this back and forth, it wouldn't feel genuine. Love is opposed to rationality. Its contradictions can't be solved. It is "without reason." A similar structure characterizes another famous early Leandro and Leonardo song, "Between Slaps and Kisses" (Entre Tapas e Beijos):

Today, we're happily together
Tomorrow, I don't want to see you
Separating, and coming back

We go through life between slaps and kisses. . . .
And that's how I'll live
Suffering and wanting
This unhealthy love—
But if I'm without her
My world, without her
Is also empty.[13] *(Leandro and Leonardo 1999)*

These impassioned male narrators are nothing alone; without their women, their worlds are "empty." Love therefore has an obsessive component. It is inescapable, despite its difficulties. It is a ticket on the train to heaven and hell, it seems, but these narrators would not do without it, nor could they, despite the extent to which doing without it might make them more "healthy."

The point is that love exerts a fundamental power over the individual by arresting rational processes and making the male speaker less than sane. Note Zezé di Camargo's and Luciano's song "It's Love" (É o Amor), which rocketed them to success in 1991:

You are my sweet love
My happiness
My fairytale
My fantasy
The peace that I need to survive
I'm your lover—my soul's transparent
A raving lunatic, inconsequential
A case that's tough to understand.
It's love that messes with my head and makes me
This way
That makes me think of you and forget myself
That makes me forget that life is for living
It's love that arrives
Like a bull's-eye, at my heart
That bowls over the strong base of my passion
And that makes me understand that life is
Nothing without you. (Zezé di Camargo and Luciano 1991)

This narrator confesses utter absorption—that all of his thoughts and energy are tied up with thinking about his woman. He is mad, inattentive to matters of daily life. He lacks control. And, without her, he is "nothing." Like Jeca, who becomes utterly absorbed in his weeping, this narrator is stuck.

Jeca's loss of his natural homeland maps onto the loss of the natural love of a woman in the postauthoritarian moment. Many rural songs focus on love in the past, love lost, broken hearts, unrequited love, and cheating women. This grief-stricken tone is at the center of "A Strand of Hair" (Fio de Cabelo) sung by Chitãozinho and Xororó (1982). The song sets the scene in the same sort of broad terms Jeca employed, suggesting that when a man loves a woman with whom he does not live, "anything helps us remember: / An old piece of her clothes / Means a lot." The narrator continues to explore the sorts of objects or sensations that might cue his memory, and as he does so, it becomes clear that he is grieving, and that "not living with the woman that you love" is essentially a euphemism for permanent separation. He is haunted by

> That little scent of her—
> She once kept in a bottle on the dresser,
> Showing that the room was once the scene
> Of a passionate affair.

Gradually, the song builds in intensity until we reach the fundamental object that painfully transports him back to the happy union:

> And today made me sadder still.
> I found a little piece of her—
> A hair on my jacket.
> I remembered all that passed between us:
> The vivid love,
> That long strand of her hair,
> Once stuck in our sweat.

In Marcel Proust's famous essay on the power of memory (Proust 1981), the narrator is suddenly filled with his past when he tastes a piece of madeleine dipped in tea. But here, in this rural song text, instead of a delicate, tea-soaked cookie, the protagonist's memory is touched off by a hair from his lover's head, now stuck to his jacket. The song expresses emotions sonically. It is sung in the slow 3/4 time of the *guarânia* song-form, and the voices of the brothers suggest pain; the tone is plaintive, the subject matter anguished, and the melody lurches into its highest register when they are singing about the hair itself.

At the same time as these songs underscore the continuity of Jeca's theme and variations, they also represent the way in which that theme transforms over the course of the twentieth century. The songs in evidence here are important from the perspective of the history of the genre. They were the first big hits for now megastars Leandro and Leonardo, Zezé di Camargo and Luciano, and Chitãozinho and Xororó, the last of which is considered to be the first dupla to take música sertaneja to a massively commercial scale. The songs also occupy special places in formal and informal histories of the dramatic increase in the popularity of música sertaneja; fans and musicians refer to them when asked about classic examples of rural music. They thus represent significant phases of the translation of Jeca's theme into the late twentieth-century context. These songs have an important continuity with Jeca's theme because they include dichotomizing practice, an emphasis on grief, obsessive mulling over of the past, and an insistence on the present importance of loss. Memory is not just a recommendation in rural genres; it is an all-encompassing downward spiral. However, these songs also reveal the way in which natural imagery and longing for home are more and more displaced by longing for lost love. We will address this transformation in subsequent chapters.

In the meantime, we should review the path so far. In this chapter, I have argued that we can best understand the oppositions of which rurality is constructed by means of the concept of performativity. Performativity also allows us to analyze the way in which this dichotomizing practice transforms and comments upon social change in Central-Southern Brazil. An important aspect of this is that the tone the performers take in each case runs against conventional expectations for the relationship between gender and the public expression of sadness in Brazil. For example, men should be stoic about problems in love. They must not be like Jeca, completely shattered over the loss of home. Nor must they be like the narrators of the songs that appear later in the chapter, which is to say, overly expressive about the loss of love. Other musical genres more closely associated with acceptable forms of Brazilian national culture govern male expressivity quite differently. Note an example of male expressiveness in samba. Though samba sometimes bemoans the loss of a woman, it frequently maintains an upbeat tempo and tone as it does so. Furthermore, in the lyrics, it frequently allows for the possibility that the lost woman has been re-placed. Take, for example, Paulinho da Viola's "Where Pain Makes No Sense" (Onde a dor não tem razão), in which the narrator has finally turned his life around:

> The shadows of a past love are finally gone
> My heart's no longer the shelter of lost loves.
> It's a calmer lake, where pain makes no sense
> In it, the seed of a new love grew
> Free from all that rancor, a flower opened
> I come to reopen the windows of life
> And to sing this happiness like never before.

He ends by noting that he has finally "pulled" the "thorn" of past painful loves from his chest.[14] Taking such a redemptive posture would be impossible within música sertaneja, where the woman's departure remains an open wound and ongoing state. Cueing off this feature of the music, detractors of música sertaneja cast doubt on its masculinity. Listeners nevertheless believe that this plaintiveness is profoundly mas-culine. The emphasis on love as the central feature of the singers' lives and the particular construction of gendered relations set within a coun-try frame form part of an argument that rural music is inherently more "natural" than other ways of representing gender. Indeed, it is the only honest way. The country is the place where the vulnerable portion of maleness can be revealed. As we shall see in the next chapter, this intimate revelation of masculine tenderness becomes one of the funda-mental means through which Brazilian country music enacts its his-torical inversions.

In the meantime, in support of these contentions about Jeca's theme and its twentieth-century variations and by way of further illustrating rural performativity, I end this chapter with my experience of a Sunday in Itapira. I was walking through a newly built neighborhood on the outskirts of town where a park had been built beside orderly rows of reddish houses that stretched off into the distance. In the park, beside the swingsets and slides, a permanent bandstand had been built, and there, a group playing romantic música sertaneja was the focal point of a party to celebrate both the completion of the new neighborhood's houses and its park. I was on my way to a broadcast of my regular música caipira Sunday show that would take place that day at an improvised bandstand within a neighborhood in Itapira I had not yet visited. Thinking for a moment that what I saw might be the radio show, I paused, and as I did so, something caught my ear.

"I hear people say, all the time, that música sertaneja is not masculine," the lead singer said, introducing the next song—"that guys shouldn't stand up here on stage and whine about their women. That it isn't manly. But I don't agree. What could possibly be more manly than standing up here, in front of everybody, and laying bare my soul— telling my woman how much I love her? I ask you, men, what could be more manly than loving your woman?" It was Valentine's Day, the singer went on to say, or Lover's Day, as it is called in Brazil (*Dia dos Namorados*), and he was going to sing another country-inflected love song, as confessional and obsessive as Jeca's theme. How indeed that song might have been "manly" will occupy the next chapter.

2

Country Brothers

KINSHIP AS CHRONOTOPE

> I was born in a shack
> At the bank of the creek.
> I grew up on the farm
> Of Senhor Vescia Simon.
> I was never apart
> From my beloved brother
> We were accustomed to this—
> We were raised by working cattle
> Herding bulls out on the highways.
> —GINO AND GENO,
> Cowboy Brothers

Whereas the last chapter tackled the question of what counts as country by way of Jeca's theme and variations, this chapter analyzes the brother form in which the theme and variations are played. We address the way in which brotherhood establishes rurality, mediating space, time, and person by way of a particular approach to kinship. The migration of brothers from country to city provides a way of framing social change and cultural reproduction. Despite the fact that rural-to-urban migration may or may not play a role in the lives of current rural music listeners and musicians, it continues to shape the way the music fashions the split subjectivity so essential to Brazilian rural performativity.

Forgetful Brazilians:
A Scolding

When Pena Branca won the Latin Grammy for best "roots" record in 2001, he seemed more despondent than pleased, and questions by reporters as to precisely why seemed to make him worse. His musical career had been grounded in nearly forty years of performing with his brother, Xavatinho, in the brother *dupla* form that characterizes both *música caipira* and *música sertaneja*. But Xavatinho had passed away two years before, forcing Pena Branca to use friends and acquaintances on the winning record (*Hick Seed*) for the parts his brother would otherwise have sung.

Pena Branca reported at Grammy time that it was not as though Xavatinho was utterly gone from the record for those who cared to listen carefully. *Hick Seed*'s moments of "greatest beauty" were those in which his brother's presence filtered into the very sound of the instruments. And there were more explicit reminders too. On one of the record's tracks, Pena Branca sings an arrangement of a hymn:

> *It doesn't matter where you're coming from, my brother*
> *Our house will be yours, my heart will be yours*
> *You'll drink our wine, and eat our bread.*[1] *(Pena Branca 2000)*

But despite such present absences, by arriving after Xavatinho's death, the Grammy was a day late and a dollar short for Pena Branca, feting what could never be his best work simply because it was sonically incomplete.[2] And fans of rural music should have *realized* this. They should have understood that any happiness Pena Branca felt over his award was tempered by an equivalent grief that his brother wasn't there to celebrate too. But instead of acknowledging this fact, the fans, along with everyone else, seemed to have let Xavatinho slip their minds. The uproar over Brazilian rural music's long-awaited arrival on an international stage had done its work: "Brazilians are just like that," Pena Branca explained, regretfully. "They forget."

Those conversant with Central-Southern rural music recognized that this scolding of the nation grew out of the intense attachment to the country past that the music continuously enacts—in part by way of the brother form itself. And in addition to explicitly scolding, Pena Branca's statement echoed these musical genres in another important sense. Though it bemoaned the elision of the death of his brother in the press, his statement shared the plaintive tone that practitioners often consider to be the central feature of these songs: grief, conveyed in parallel harmony,[3] by a pair of twinned male voices.

But could Pena Branca not have sought a more localized target, stating, for instance, that it was "people in the music business" who forget, or perhaps, "music fans"? Why scold Brazil as a whole? Taking a cue from the singer's sad tone together with his rebuke, we may break Pena Branca's grief into two connected questions that should be asked of rural music itself. First, according to Central-Southern rural musical genres' performers and listeners, what, precisely, *do* Brazilians forget? Second, how do rural musical genres, with their emphasis on brotherhood and publicly expressed masculine grief, set in the countryside, help them remember?

The answer to both questions resides, in part, in brotherhood itself. Pena Branca meant to imply that Brazilians forget the past broadly speaking. And he also felt that Brazilians forget the importance of consanguineous kinship as a way of organizing musical performance. But this is not just *any* consanguineous relationship. We are dealing with brothers here, and part of the reason why is that this music addresses the fact that what gets concealed, and hence, forgotten, in the course of daily affairs, is the vulnerable side of masculinity, so often hidden by a layer of tight-lipped machismo, perhaps even chauvinism (Herzfeld 2007, 318). So, a genre that forefronts brotherhood stands to reinculcate the politics of consanguineous kinship while also addressing itself to masculine expressiveness. Male siblingship thus plays a defining role in the notion of "country" inherent in Brazilian genres of rural public culture. It has become increasingly important over the course of the twentieth century. Despite the fact that some currently practicing duplas are merely "partners" rather than brothers born of the same parents, these pairs still cast their *cáuntry* in the mold of brotherhood. Chronotopically uniting the past (time) and the countryside (space) by way of kinship, the rural provides one of the central means through which to criticize a degraded present in light of an idealized past.

In the last chapter we analyzed how rural performativity calibrates social life by recruiting specific polarities into communicative practice, making them available for possible inhabitance. In this chapter, we build upon this by examining the way in which participants frame the "blood" of brotherhood through alternating poses, both on- and offstage: a hierarchical pose, emphasizing separateness, difference, and individuality, and an egalitarian pose, emphasizing togetherness, similarity, and unity. The alternation between these poses addresses the split subjectivity so central to rural music. It also argues for the prediscursivity of blood relations.[4] By prediscursivity, here, I refer to that which is thought not to be open to rational discussion, and hence to that which is thought to exist outside the realm of the symbolic.[5] "You don't pick your brother," one musician told me once. "He's just *born* your brother." Furthermore, according to rural music practitioners, it is nature that bequeaths how brothers' voices attune to each other (egalitarian), and, at the same time, the way brothers are born unequal (hierarchical). These poses require little negotiation, duplas report, because the relations they both reveal and inculcate are simply "natural." Thus, what is taken to be the simple social fact of brotherhood incites what are thought to be old-fashioned forms of hierarchy and relating.

Addressing the reliance of this imaginative turn to the rural on male siblingship promises to underscore the continued efficacy of kinship for understanding social relations and cultural production in varied domains (Comaroff 1987, 54; DaMatta 1979, 63–68; note the oft-overlooked Freudian substrate of Habermas 1991, 43–51; Turner 1979, 149). In addition to its more conventionally anthropological associations with descent, social roles, and group structure, I take kinship to be a historical practice for generating social relationships that, to use Nancy Munn's phrase, attends to the "co-constitution of time and space in activity" (Munn 1992, 97).[6] The "activity," in this case, is the performance of rural musical genres themselves, as well as all social activities in which public cultural rurality plays some role. Focusing on kinship yields a way of understanding the argument which this music makes about the role of blood in history. But it does so in a broader domain than music. In the singing of it, rural music reaches out not just to the categories comprised in family and romance, but to fields such as commerce, politics, gender, race, and class.

In a period of increasing dissatisfaction with neoliberal economic and social reform (Sader 2006), and sometimes even disillusionment with democratization itself, rural public culture casts change-focused self-imaginings as destructive, offering, as a counterargument, the more "natural" sociality inherent in the consanguineous relations of a country past. One song in particular brings these social relations into focus: the classic "Chico Mineiro." Recorded in 1946, the opening of brother-dupla Tonico and Tinoco's famous rendition is spoken rather than sung, and in this prefatory declamation, the narrator tells us of his life as the boss of a cattle-herding troupe in Brazil's interior. On his herding trips he is accompanied by his courageous friend, the *viola* player and cowboy Chico Mineiro, lauded here as a "good *caboclo*"

(Tonico and Tinoco 1968). The consummate "sadness" of Chico's viola playing supports the narrator's judgment that Chico is both the best musician and the best cowboy. Determination and emotional expressivity intertwine:

> *Every time that I remember*
> *my friend Chico Mineiro—*
> *The trips that we took*
> *on which he was my companion—*
> *I feel a sadness,*
> *And I wanna cry—*
> *Remembering those times,*
> *That'll never return.*
> *Despite me bein' the boss,*
> *I held, in my heart,*
> *That Chico Mineiro was my friend,*
> *a good caboclo, determined—*
> *His viola playing was the saddest,*
> *and he was the best o' the cowboys.*[7]

The singing that follows this spoken text ushers in the song's central event. Chico is killed at a Saint's day party one night, causing the boss and narrator to withdraw from cattle herding and go into extended mourning:

> *The party was a good one,*
> *but we should not have gone.*
> *Chico was shot*
> *by an unknown man.*
> *I quit buying cattle.*
> *They killed my companion—*
> *put an end to the sound of his viola—*
> *they put an end to Chico Mineiro.*

Despite the fact that this murder represents the song's focal happening, few words describe it, and we receive the saddest news of all in the last line. The protagonist discovers Chico's birth certificate, and with it, comes to know that his employee and fast friend was in fact his blood brother:

> After that tragedy,
> I was even more bowled over.
> I'd never known the truth about our friendship,
> because we two were actually united.
> When I saw his birth certificate,
> my heart was cut in two:
> I came to know that Chico Mineiro
> was my legitimate brother.

This discovery in the very last bars of the tune suggests that the social roles associated with economic life (the boss-employee relation) have interfered with the simple truth of brotherhood. This "cuts" the narrator's heart "in two." This is not to say that economics has trumped blood entirely. Indeed, the message of the song would seem to be that brotherhood will out regardless of circumstance; the two have clearly been closer than a normal employer and employee would be, a fact the narrator is able retroactively to attribute to his kinship with Chico. But despite the fact that Chico's death is awful, the fundamental tragedy of the song is that the two were never able to bring their brotherhood to conscious and public levels, despite the fact that they seemed almost to have known about it.[8] They were friends, certainly, but the full extent of their connection went unrealized because other forms of association interfered; they could be only fast friends, never brothers. The sadness of the song, then, is that in death, the narrator discovers that his relationship with Chico was less intense and meaningful than it ought to have been.

Kinship as Country Epistemology and Sociology

> Time becomes, in effect, palpable and visible [audible?]; the
> chronotope makes narrative events concrete, makes them
> take on flesh, causes blood to flow in their veins.
> —MIKHAIL BAKHTIN, "Forms of Time and the
> Chronotope in the Novel"

Within the Brazilian understanding of the rural, male siblingship naturalizes the relationship between space (the countryside, sertão, campo, interior, or roça) and time. Time, here, indexes a not-so-distant past, childhood, the bygone days of life in the country as observed from the vantage point of a diminished existence in the city, and an era of true and realized romantic love. Space is the not-here in which these past events took place, locations distant enough to feel only just out of reach. In bringing these two domains together, kinship "causes blood to flow" in the "veins" of Brazilian "country."

Kathleen Stewart (1996, 93) and Aaron Fox (2004, 81) have both suggested that the lineaments of "country" in the United States might be specified by means of Bakhtin's chronotope. As with many of Bakhtin's concepts, however, in order to make use of the chronotope for analytical purposes, we must consider his suggestive treatment of literature and extrapolate it into the domain of genred forms of production whose modes of textuality differ from those of the novel. For the purposes of this analysis, I suggest that the chronotope provides a means of specifying both "the ratio and nature" of "the temporal and spatial categories" (Holquist and Emerson 1981, 425) in a given form of cultural production, in this case, the rural.

However, more needs to be said for the chronotope to assist with explaining how time and space mingle in certain forms of textuality. Note that Bakhtin's use of the chronotope did more than briefly map modes of text production in which some explicit time-space component exists. Indeed, what form of textuality does *not* deal in time and space? Rather, he brings it to bear more precisely as a metric for literature: a means of *evaluating* genres. For example, he employs the concept to analyze Greek Romance, which he defines as "an adventure chronotope" characterized by "a *technical, abstract connection between space and time,* by the *reversibility* of moments in a temporal sequence, and by their *interchangeability* in space" (Bakhtin 1981, 100, his italics). This enactment of the concept reveals that the chronotope guides the way to specifying not simply the copresence of time and space (a given, as stated), but the nature of the relationship between them.

Bakhtin also suggests that the chronotope elucidates the handling of the concept of personhood (Bakhtin 1981, 85) within a given genre. Ethnographers have picked up on this. In his exploration of the concept of the chronotope, David Lipset (2004, 209), via Eric Auerbach's examination of the *Odyssey*, argues that Odysseus is not radically changed by the encounters that move him through the work. Odysseus proceeds from one event to another almost as though they were modular.[9] Brazilian rural genres, by contrast, rely upon a pronounced vector, finding deal past in a nonurban Central-Southern rural space. For this n, the chronotopic properties of Brazilian rural public culture come much closer to what Bakhtin described as the "idyll," where "the real organic time of idyllic life is opposed to the frivolous fragmented time of city life" (Bakhtin 1981, 228). Brazilian rurality proposes that in the countryside, the past as an idealized rural space cancels the need for the detailed consideration of social relations that is required in the city, instead calling for a simpler scanning of social surfaces. Bakhtin (1981, 147) also recognizes as a chronotopic aspect of certain forms of textual production that they execute a "*historical inversion*" (his italics). According to this inversion, certain social ideals, in this case, for instance, brother siblingship, are located in the past: "a thing that could and in fact must only be realized exclusively in the *future* is here portrayed as something out of the *past*, . . . a thing that is in its essence a purpose, an obligation" (Bakhtin 1981, 147). The relationship between two brothers singing in dupla enjoins listeners to relate in a certain way to others and to adopt a concomitant reading of objects and actions. In sum, the chronotopic properties of the Central-Southern Brazilian rural fashion a country sociology and epistemology.

With respect to the way in which rurality impacts subjectivity, the experience of migrating from the country to the city suggests a certain direction and magnitude of individual transformation. Quite unlike unchanging Odysseus, the experience of migration profoundly alters the singing voice of música caipira and música sertaneja, a singing voice which is, recall, actually two voices *heard* and *sung* as one. Brother siblingship, in performance, provides the means to manage the breaks that modern life requires. I will return to kinship's mediating function within the rural chronotope and the way it gives rise to a country sociology and epistemology by way of the in-concert story about bathing a pig and adorning it with a necktie. But first, a short treatment of Central-Southern brotherhood is in order.

Heading Out Together

Thus all the social roles which are articulated by an ideology of substance necessarily associated with body and blood (as in the case with the domain of kinship) must be created and acted out in and through the house in the Brazilian case.
—ROBERTO DAMATTA, *Carnivals, Rogues, and Heroes*

A brief archaeology of brotherhood in the Central-South begins with economically prominent sugarcane plantation families in the state of São Paulo in the eighteenth and nineteenth centuries (Bacellar 1997, 15).[10] Brothers who hoped to extend their family influence and obtain property of their own might accept a loan from their father, combine this with some of their own income, and, paired, strike out (Bacellar 1991, 64). This brother-mediated extension of family influence seems to have played a role in paving the way for the transformation of the interior of São Paulo from the production of sugarcane in the late eighteenth century to the all-important monocrop of coffee that would prove so vital to the unfolding of Brazilian history in the twentieth (Fausto 1994; Skidmore 1967).

The departure of brothers was partly rooted in inheritance patterns. One detailed study of the town of Santana de Parnaíba, in São Paulo state, which ends in the nineteenth century, reveals that land was often willed, not to sons, but to daughters. This practice differed markedly from the practice in Portugal during this period, but in any case, in this region, it was sons-in-law who took control of family fortunes by way of their marriage to daughters (Metcalf 2005, 116). Thus patriarchs pushed sons out and pulled sons-in-law in. Sons would therefore leave home to seek fortune and marriage, often settling at some distance from their consanguine kin. In the eighteenth century, many migrating sons went to distant gold mines in Cuiabá and Goiás (Nazzari 1991, 44–46). In the words of one social historian:

> As a family custom, deeply ingrained in planter families since the earliest days of settlement, the migration of sons helped to solve the inevitable decline in a family's prosperity base as it became subdivided among more and more descendants each generation. (Metcalf 2005, 112)

This strategy sought to maintain past accomplishments and to establish growth opportunities for years to come: "fathers sent their sons out into the frontier to plan for the future; they recruited their sons-in-law to protect what the family already had" (Metcalf 2005, 113).

Moving forward in time, analysis of families of the Northeast of Brazil between 1890 and 1930 suggests that when the country-city relations that had governed economic and social life up to that point began to change as cities expanded and their functions diversified, "family connections had to be extended on a much wider plane than before, often by means of complementary tandems of brothers" (Lewin 1979, 289). There were two somewhat different patterns by which brother collaboration took shape. First, siblings often benefited by close coop-eration with each other after parcels of parental land that had once been joined were willed to them separately. Through collaboration, these smaller parcels of land could still operate as though they composed a larger whole (Lewin 1979, 288). Second, echoing older practices of traveling to gold mines or simply to appropriate new lands in the inte-rior, brothers began to cast off toward cities to establish careers that would accrue emergent forms of value. These teams of brothers, paired by role as *coronéis* (colonels, or strongmen) and *doutôres* (doctors, law-yers, or simply lettered men), "coordinated family affairs at several levels of officeholding" (Lewin 1979, 288). The institution of brother-hood then, was one of the methods by which some families extended their influence over a larger geographical and social area within the context of a rapidly transforming society (Lewin 1979, 292). Brother-hood provided a kind of bridge through which families held on to or increased social and economic capital via migration and emerging occupations.

These patterns from the interior of the state of São Paulo in the seventeenth and eighteenth centuries as well as from the Northeastern region in the early twentieth century overlap with the much lower-status context of hillbilly migration to the city of São Paulo through the latter half of the twentieth century. Somewhat like the wealthier sugar families described in earlier cases, the hillbillies employed migration as a means of survival (Cândido 1979, 222). At the beginning of the twen-tieth century, *caipiras* migrated continually because the technique of slash-and-burn agriculture, learned from the Indians, necessitated new soil every few years.

The late-twentieth-century explosion of migration to the Central-Southern region, São Paulo in particular, may still be thought of as partaking of the long-standing strategy for maintaining social equi-librium in Central-Southern life. Once again, this process often has a masculine beginning. It is deemed easier for brothers to establish themselves before sisters, and eventually parents, follow (Durham 1984, 123).[11] In a study of migrants to the city of São Paulo, sociologist Eunice Durham reveals that two important facts of social life in the interior impelled men to migrate in the 1980s. Both echo the problems faced by wealthier planter families in previous centuries. First, as land became scarce, peasant families had to maintain the integrity of family plots at inheritance (Durham 1984, 63). Also, some sons simply grew tired of continuing to work family lands at the behest of their father, whose patriarchal authority may have been burdensome. In circumstances in which their servitude yielded little for brothers, who often had their own plots to worry about in addition to those of their parents, many chose to simply move to the city (Durham 1984, 114).

The experience of leaving the interior for the city with your brother reveals itself clearly in the life histories of current duplas. The reasons they cite for leaving home to seek their fortune sound very much like the accounts of brother migration from the nineteenth and twentieth centuries we just examined. For example, the brothers from the prominent dupla Liu and Leu spent their youth picking coffee in the interior of São Paulo. As we shall see in further detail below, their older brothers, Zico and Zeca, were already a best-selling dupla living in São Paulo when their father sent them away, stating that there was simply no opportunity for them there: "there's no point in you two staying in the countryside," Liu recalls his father sitting them down to say one day.[12] They moved to the city of São Paulo in 1957 and took jobs as clerks at the Swiss Mercantile Bank before their talent as singers was spotted. Soon they won a competition in the city of São Paulo and went on to radio performances and fame.

A more recent dupla of brothers shares a similar experience. Leandro and Leonardo grew up working on a tomato farm in the backcountry of Goiás. As they reached adolescence, they began practicing their singing and argued to their parents that music seemed more promising than tomatoes. In a biography released shortly after Leandro's death, the scene is described this way: "We need to try our luck, mom," Leandro proposed one day. "There's nothing here. Dad knows it's true. There's no future in the work we're doing" (Santos 1999, 45).[13] They depart together because they believe that they will be able to support each other emotionally while keeping expenses low and pooling their money. Leandro started by selling clothing, and Leonardo worked in a drugstore in Goiás, the capital of the interior state of Goiânia, until their singing captured public attention. They eventually achieved tremendous success, selling more records than any dupla before them.

As early as the eighteenth century then, brother siblingship provided a conduit through which social relations flowed during periods of change in Central-Southern Brazil. In the twentieth century, these brothers have the sense that they are escaping diminished opportunities in a countryside which once sufficed to meet family needs. But though they leave "home," the experience, far from utterly rupturing family bonds, channels social change by way of kinship. Consequently, these processes of migration to cities in the Central-South have not broken families apart so much as reconfigured them (Durham 1984, 128–29; Galizoni 2000).

The experience of migration provides a substrate for thinking about brotherhood, but the strength of the bond between brothers does not always revolve around movement and music. To consider brotherhood "offstage" in the sites where I worked, take the example of two brothers who collaborate via their small town's radio station in Itapira. Flávio and Paulo (pseudonyms) traded roles. While one was elected local *deputado*, the other managed the affairs of the radio station. Then, the one who had managed the station campaigned for political office, and when he won, the brother who had been in politics stepped into media for a time. The complementarity and alternation of their roles made their family a formidable political presence. In another instance, two brothers who had been successful rodeo cowboys started a rodeo school in a small town in the state of Mato Grosso do Sul. One had won considerable acclaim as a bull rider while the other had been national champion in a Brazilian style of bronco riding. The two came together in teaching, recruiting, and managing the school. In these and other domains, I heard the same refrain. Yes—one fights with one's brother, just as one could be expected to fight with anyone. But with your brother, I was told time and again, in domains musical and otherwise, you have no *choice* but to come back together. Thus, the argument is not that brotherhood is free of conflict, surely a naïve contention, but rather, that brotherhood regiments conflict in a safe fashion, and that regimentation makes the relationship much more likely to last.

Brother Hegemony

My argument in this chapter is that in the late twentieth and early twenty-first centuries, the brother form increasingly shapes Brazilian rural music. However, not all duplas are composed of brothers. An archaeology of brother pairs that seeks to elucidate the current hegemony of the dupla form in rural genres requires treatment of these cases, addressing how they relate to brother siblingship. This requires a brief look at música caipira from its moment of commercialization in the late 1920s.

The kind of singing that Cornélio Pires drew upon to make what are universally spoken of as the first commercial recordings of música caipira (Caldas 1977, 1987; Dent 2003; J. d. S. Martins 1975; Tinhorão 1986) was deeply rooted in informal Catholic and secular rural singing of the interior of the Central-South. Major contexts of circulation for this kind of paired-voice, parallel-third, tight-harmony singing, accompanied by guitar and viola, included churches, where families often sang together, *folia de reis*, which are annual Christmas processions in honor of the magi,[14] and *Festas Juninhas*, the yearly June Festivals in honor of St. John, St. Anthony, and St. Peter.[15] The duplas that animated these musical contexts were the sort that Pires brought to the city of São Paulo for the performance at McKenzie University in 1910, which was aimed at a middle-class audience. And it was these kinds of pairs that he first recorded for Columbia Records in 1929 (Ferrete 1985).

The success of Pires's initial recordings launched a commercial genre and led to the development of a series of much-recorded duplas. We will revisit Pires's early recordings below, but for the moment, we should note that some of these duplas were not brothers. Moreover, some of the early duplas which many rural musical fans still consider to be of extremely high caliber with respect to the blending of their voices, a central criterion by which duplas are judged, as we shall see in a moment, were merely *companheiros*, or friends. Among the most famous were Zé Carreiro and Carreirinho,[16] Raul Torres and Florêncio, and Raul Torres and João Pacífico. Later non-brother examples worthy of note included Milionário and José Rico, Pedro Bento and Zé da Estrada, and Tião Carreiro and Pardinho.

However, oral histories of rural genres posit that these duplas are the exception simply because, lacking brotherhood, the majority of non-brother duplas did not last. The absence of kinship and life experience of brotherhood results in fights which pairs cannot reconcile. After conflicts, members of many non-brother duplas paired up with other musicians. Raul Torres is a prominent example of this, as is Tião Carreiro, who had legendary battles with his partner Pardinho, only to reconcile later. Torres and Tião both played with a series of partners. The battles that split non-sibling duplas are often over jealousies arising from hierarchical roles in the dupla, where one member feels insufficiently valued by the other. This frequently surfaces over finances and causes permanent ruptures. As one *violeiro* explained, echoing a statement a brother team had made to me in a nonmusical context (the running of a construction company): "with your brother, you can fight over money, but it always resolves itself eventually. It's just *easier* with your brother, because there's nowhere to run to. There's just no way to stay mad at your brother forever." Note that it is not that there is no way to *get* mad at your brother. Rural musical performers simply believe that brother siblingship provides much the best way to reliably manage the inevitable conflict that comes from the inequalities inherent in social life broadly speaking, and in the dupla form specifically. Family is inescapable, whereas simple friendship may not be strong enough to contain the tensions of collaboration, in music or in anything else. Thus practitioners cite the tremendous difficulties associated with staying together through thick and thin as the main reason for the current hegemony of brothers.

Duplas feel that fights between brothers are easier to resolve. More important, fewer fights occur because brothers are "naturally" aware of how to relate to each other. Recounting their musical histories, brother duplas frequently state that they "were born to sing." Their ability to handle hierarchy with respect to each other is given by a mixture of birth and the training they receive growing up together. Thus, unlike friends who decide to sing together, brothers are believed to have both a biological predisposition to fight less and a lengthy education in how to handle it when they do.

Tonico and Tinoco, the singers of Chico Mineiro, discussed above, illustrate how male siblingship organizes performance of rural musical genres. The perfection of the match of their voices has garnered them the status of greatness among fans, who often describe them as the dupla "closest to Brazil's heart" (Nepomuceno 1999, 303). They also sang in a higher pitch than many previously noteworthy duplas, and more forcefully. They claimed that this force was the result of learning to project their voices without a microphone. They were still one of the most popular duplas in the Central-South when Tonico passed away in 1994. Their staying power led to a solidification of rural musical style, such that the high and plaintive twinning of the two voices delivered loudly became more important than it had previously been.

Several prominent duplas that followed Tonico and Tinoco solidified the prominence of brother singing as a principle of harmony and adopted Tonico and Tinoco's style of higher-pitched singing. They include the aforementioned Zico and Zeca and Liu and Leu. Like Tonico and Tinoco, Liu and Zico tell stories about their first performances in which the well-tuned quality of their voices, believed to be the result of their brotherly connection, renders the crowd "paralyzed . . . silent" to use Liu's phrase. And to further reinforce that this twinning of voices emerges from "nature" rather than training (Tonico and Tinoco were described as sounding like "two songbirds" by an early fan, a metaphor carried forward by Chitãozinho and Xororó, who are named for two birds), these duos often emphasize that their first performance was preceded by minimal practice; the voices of the two brothers simply become one, and the crowd is bowled over.

The strength of brotherhood provides convincing testimony as to why rural music in Brazil increasingly relies on teams of brothers. In the 1940s, 1950s, and into the 1960s, there were popular rural music trios where the third member was often an accordionist. But this format has all but disappeared. Nowadays, both in commercial and folkloric rural genres, the brother form has taken over almost completely. At present, a large number of young brother teams is attempting to make it on the Central-Southern music scene at rodeos and dance halls.[17] Doubtless, this is fueled by the fact that the three duplas credited with spearheading the "boom" of música sertaneja (Chitãozinho and Xororó, Leandro and Leonardo, and Zezé di Camargo and Luciano) all consist of brothers.

Other more strictly musical principles contribute to the increasing momentum of brotherhood. In the same way that "language ideologies" pull language change in prescribed directions because speakers believe in the seamless relationship between language use and concepts such as identity and intention, the ideology of "paired" voices in the dupla has pulled the form toward brother siblingship. We will discuss the importance of ideologies more in the next chapter, but for the moment, suffice it to say that the principle of perfection in vocal blending and the absolute togetherness of the voices increasingly relies on the perceived inherited origin of the physical vocal apparatus itself: the vocal cords. This coming together of two voices in hierarchy and equality may be thought of according to a notion of the "grain" of the voice as developed by Greg Downey (2005) in the different context of hearing the central rhythmic instrument used in Brazilian capoeira: the berimbau.[18] Downey argues that the capoeira practitioner hears the sounds of the berimbau in terms of the instrument's physical properties, which he understands from having played it. Understanding the sound-producing object's properties and being able to hear it thus become phenomenologically intertwined. In a similar vein, correctly hearing rural musical genres relies on a sense that the listener has of the shared physical substance of the two mingled lines of the brothers' singing voices. Thus sonic brotherhood occupies the apex of the dupla form because an increasing emphasis on *hearing* the blending of the two voices as a biological fact pulls it in that direction.

The success of the few current duplas that are not necessarily brothers does not invalidate the importance of male siblingship. This is because even these teams of companheiros aim at the perfection of twinned voices most easily achieved through brotherhood. And their success is measured in terms of proximity to male siblingship in sound. Partners who are *not* brothers, in their press kits, emphasize the extent to which they are in tune (*afinados*), something brothers never do. Non-brother partnerships must strive for a kind of classificatory kinship, then.

The only currently successful dupla that might seem to contradict the primacy of brotherhood in rural musical practice is the team of Sandy and Júnior, a sister and brother currently enjoying considerable success. But family ties, and especially brotherhood, still shape the way they are heard. They are the children of Xororó, half of brother dupla Chitãozinho and Xororó. Fans continually refer to the importance of the family ties of the pair, which also extend to their uncle, famous rural musical instrumentalist Zé do Rancho. To the limited extent that Sandy and Júnior's singing may be perceived to exist within a dupla mold, that singing takes place very much under the umbrella of their father's performance with his brother, Chitãozinho. Despite this, media and fan discussion of the pair does not treat them as it treats other duplas, whose members are referred to together. Instead, critics focus almost exclusively on Sandy (the older female sibling), portraying Júnior (the younger male) as a kind of talentless sideshow. Much ink has been spilled on when Sandy will finally leave her brother. Fans and media commentators thus hardly seem to consider these two as practitioners of rural genres at all. They are a brother and sister singing together, not a dupla.

Despite the presence of a very few prominent sister duos in the 1950s, and one husband-and-wife team in the 1950s and 1960s,[19] neither música caipira nor música sertaneja seem likely to be sung by females again anytime soon. There are several reasons for this. First, as we have seen from the narratives of brothers moving from the countryside to the city, brother siblingship in this musical format partakes of a special form of social production—often revolving around Central-Southern modes of relating to nature such as mining, farming, and cattle ranching. Even when it is not ex–coffee pickers, ex–cattle ranchers, and ex–tomato farmers that become brother duplas, it is nonetheless male labor, once rooted in the countryside, but which must move to the city, that provides the framework for interpreting rural musical performance. Brothers who do not actually have an agricultural background, and there are many, emphasize the recent migration of their parents or the importance of family farms still owned by grandparents, uncles, or brothers. Some prominent duplas invest in cattle farms the moment that they have the funds to do so, a fact that is reported, not in the "entertainment" section of newspapers, but in the "agricultural" pages (Sebastião 1999).

So far as heading out together is concerned, then, brotherhood as the centerpiece of rural musical genres entails specific chronotopic properties. These include the spatializing and temporalizing of kinship itself according to a particular notion of personhood which, in turn, is rooted in the experience of migration as loss. Unlike constant Odysseus, the brother form in rural genres indexes a necessary experience of dividing the self. Male siblingship recommends an approach to handling self-fragmentation, in the same moment as it argues for the very permanence of that fragmentation. And rural genres have come to represent masculinity in a distinct and split mode. The masculine domination of the bull rider over the angry bull, currently so popular in Brazil's enormous rodeos, operates as a kind of opposite pole to the extremely expressive, torn-up self of the music that accompanies rodeos (música sertaneja). Many bull riders I spoke to framed their laconic exterior as a cover for their emotional interior, as represented best by the music. Thus, their split subjectivity involved a fragile interior state that they did not show to the world, shielding it with a tough exterior. But most important, the Bakhtinian "historical inversion" discussed above relies on the culturally intimate revelation of expressive masculinity. To simplify: the gender inversion facilitates the historical one, an inversion to which we must now turn in more detail.

Alternating Poses

The dupla form moves between two poses in the act of performance; both are thought of as inherent to the relations between male siblings.

In one pose, brothers underscore the fact that the dupla requires clearly delineated dominant and subservient roles. In the other, they stress that they are on an equal footing, mainly through the fact that, in the moment of singing, they must be heard as one voice.[20]

We begin with the importance of hierarchy. As stated above, brothers harmonize with each other, often through the entire course of the song. This takes place in prescribed intervals—parallel thirds and sixths, for the most part. One brother sings the lower part, the other, the higher. Depending on the dupla, the melody may lie with the higher or lower voice. Hierarchy is established by who carries the melody because it is so important to song structure. And whatever singing role a dupla member takes he retains for life. This is to say that once you sing the melody, whether in the higher or lower voice, this is your role. It does not vary from song to song, from performance to performance, from year to year.

There are other important distinctions between brothers' roles, for instance, in instrumentation. In commercial rural music, one brother often plays the guitar while the other, more instrumentally passive, sits by, sings, and watches. In cases where one brother suddenly picks up an instrument on stage, the brisk introduction of the musical instrument itself serves to focus the performance onto the instrumentalist. The distinction of role by instrument is even more pronounced in the case of folkloric rural music, where the performers continually refer to the viola, which is clearly dominant. We will consider the differentiation of brotherly roles according to instrumentation when we consider locality in chapter 7 and the country cosmopolitan in chapter 8, but I note for the moment that in each dupla, one brother is clearly more instrumentally adept.[21]

Rural musical performers frequently perform material written by others. However, in most cases, the dupla generates at least some of its own material, and it is usually one of the brothers, sometimes in collaboration with another writer or lyricist, who produces the majority of it. Many of these songwriting performers also produce material for other performers. For instance, Zé Mulato has written numerous songs for other duplas, and Zezé di Camargo has produced songs for numerous Brazilian genres. Songwriting prowess most often extends to another duty—that of telling stories onstage. In the context of folkloric performance, these tales can last up to forty-five minutes. Stories told by one brother also comprise an aspect of the commercial stage-banter repertoire, though they are frequently short and sometimes just jokes. In any case, one of the brothers clearly establishes himself onstage as the one who may change the course of the show from its established routine by inserting a story, shuffling the order of songs, or responding to an audience request. This unequal relationship often means that the brother who is not in the leadership role takes on menial tasks. In one concert at the Palácio in São Paulo, Luciano, very much the second to Zezé di Camargo, came out onstage to "train" the audience for the live video the record company was about to shoot. He emerged long before the actual show and coached us on lyrics and motions. This sort of cheerleading work was beneath Luciano's brother Zezé, the star, the writer, and the carrier of the melody.

Organizing the activities of the dupla provides further testimony to the distinction between brothers' duties. Many duplas cannot afford a manager, so one brother books shows, collects payment, and makes important artistic decisions about record labels, venues, and repertoire. Often, he consults his brother, but frequently, logistical decisions lie much more with one than with the other. These tasks most often fall to the brother who leads onstage. Significantly, hierarchically differentiated tasks and responsibilities do not always fall into uniform clusters, that is, writing the songs, singing the melody, playing the viola, and handling logistics are not always performed by the same person. Sometimes, the two brothers divide duties. And the prioritizing here does not necessarily correspond to age. Sometimes the younger member of the dupla takes a dominant role in one or all of these areas. However, audiences generally regard the brother who controls the flow of the performance onstage as the more dominant of the two. Hierarchical distinctions between dupla members may be summarized in the following way (see table 2). We can see from this chart that the roles of the brothers reveal the dominance of one role over the other.

By contrast, the fundamental way in which the egalitarianism of brother siblingship takes shape is in the fusion of singing voices. As is the case in American country music (A. Fox 2004, 301), the singing "voice" is Brazilian rural music's most important attribute. If one of the two brothers is a superb viola or guitar player in addition to being a great singer who blends well with his brother, then so much the better. But strong musicianship and a propensity for witty crowd banter are not requirements for success or esteem. Instead, performers consider the singing to be paramount; in fact, several duplas do not play instruments at all.

To elaborate on the importance of melded voices, good duplas stay in

Table 2. Brother Roles in the Dupla.

Leader—*mestre* (master)	Follower—*contramestre* (foreman)
Melody	Harmony
Viola (or, in música sertaneja, guitar or other instrument such as piano)	Guitar (or, in música sertaneja, no instrument at all)
Songwriter	Performer
Manager and decision maker	Dupla member and decision ratifier
Storyteller and song-list organizer	Polite listener and supporter

tune with each other no matter what happens musically. The truly great pairs are able to compensate for each other, even when one singer goes slightly out of tune. In such circumstances, as one performer told me, "the other should follow," preserving the unity of the fused voices. In marked contrast with most other musical genres involving harmony, practitioners deem the togetherness of the two voices more significant than whether the overall effect remains in tune with the key of the piece as stated in the song's opening—though hopefully being out of tune should not occur too often. The point is that because brothers think and perceive in similar ways, they are believed to be able to sense each other's voices and respond to them without reflection or practice. This musical form thus relies on a kind of phenomenology of brotherhood.

In another important way, the unity of voices in the dupla differs from much musical harmony, where musical structure calls attention to a multiplicity of voices singing together. In other genres, harmony is used differently. For example, performers may introduce it at specific moments of the piece for the purpose of contrast; fixed harmony is not a constant feature. For example, a lead singer might sing verses solo, and a "backup" singer or singers might enter during the chorus. Or, if harmony remains constant, the intervals by which the harmonizing voices relate to one another often vary over the course of the work. Thus, even in a classical western choral performance, where togetherness and the blending of individuality into the whole are also paramount, tenors, for example, are not always separated from baritones by a fixed interval of, say, a third. Rather, their distance from other voices changes; they may even sing below the baritones at times.

These examples illustrate that while togetherness, blending, and pitch are significant in other forms of harmony singing, harmony in Brazilian rural genres differs in two ways. First, in Brazilian rural music the entire performance is harmonized.[22] Second, the interval that separates the voices is always a third or a sixth. Thus the constancy and fixity of rural musical harmonization set it apart from other genres. As already noted, a great dupla is one in which the two voices are indistinguishable at the moment of singing.

Within the egalitarian pose, the brother who carries the melody is not perceived as in some sense being *accompanied* by the brother who performs harmony. Indeed, the melodic part cannot exist without the harmony to give it shape, almost as a glass gives shape to water. They belong, naturally, together. A concrete example illustrates this point. In August, 2004, I interviewed two brothers of two duplas, Zico and Zeca, and Liu and Leu, all four of whom are brothers to each other. On this occasion, only Liu and Zico were present. As it happened, Zico and Liu fulfilled complementary roles when singing with their other brothers Zeca and Leu, and so, despite being "mismatched," as they put it, they were able to sing together for my benefit. This situation was distinct. Here were two brothers, both members of famous duplas, whose other half was missing, but whose present brother happened to match the musical role of the absent other. Thus, Zico and his brother Liu performed for me in a way they deemed competent. But they described the resulting performance as vastly inferior to what would have taken place if the complete duplas had been present. Zico, described by many as the finest melodic high-register voice (*primeiro*) in rural music, was described to me as requiring his brother Zeca to "rein him in." Liu couldn't quite do it; Zeca could. Thus simply being brothers does not suffice. Rather, *particular* pairs of brothers are thought to be better matched in terms of the way in which their interlocking harmony and melody parts facilitate each other.

In a perfectly blended dupla, one should not even be able to determine which voice carries the melody and which the harmony, I was frequently told. A further case supports the way in which the singing roles of two brothers facilitate each other in such a way as to illustrate that you can't have one without the other. In his youth, Zezé di Camargo (Mirosmar José de Camargo, offstage) performed with his younger brother, Emival. However, Emival was killed in a car accident when the two were still adolescents, leaving Zezé to attempt a solo career. He moved to São Paulo and began writing songs, recording an album. Many of his compositions were tremendously successful, garnering hits for other duplas such as Leandro and Leonardo. But Zezé's solo record was a failure. Clearly this did not stem from his compositional abilities because his songs had been hits for others. Zezé's difficulties as a solo artist became clearer when his much-younger brother, Luciano (Welson David de Camargo, offstage), decided to join him. With his new brother partner, Zezé's song "É o Amor" (This is Love) reached the top of radio playlists in their home state of Goiás and soon rocketed them to national sales records. By himself, Zezé's melody singing and songwriting could not succeed. He required the harmonizing support of his brother.

Apart from the sonic reasons associated with the blending of voices, duplas make use of other important means of establishing the equality and sharing of substance deemed natural to brothers. The first is visual. Many duplas in folkloric rural music carry a matching guitar and viola. Zé Mulato and Cassiano are just one of many current examples of this. In their case, both instruments have precisely the same colored wood tops, sides, necks, and bridges, as well as identical curvature and tuning machines. Their names are emblazoned on each instrument in identical script. The instruments have clearly been made for them as a matching pair. My ten-string guitar teacher explained the importance of the uniformity of the instruments to me by referring to the fundamental importance of blended voices; the instruments should *match* the in-tune quality of the singing voices, without, of course, taking their place. They should be made from the wood of the same trees ideally, much as the vocal apparatus of brothers is made of the same natural substance because of their blood relationship.

In both música caipira and música sertaneja, brothers reinforce their visual likeness through dress. Zé Mulato and Cassiano, for example, wear the same baggy white pants, blue and white checkered shirts, and brimmed felt hats. They coordinate pattern and color carefully for shows. Folkloric duos commonly don such attire. It is their intention that the outfit should resemble what a caipira could have worn in the 1920s. Commercial brother-duplas also make use of sartorial equality, though in a slightly different mode. They sometimes wear clothes that are cut of single-color synthetic fabrics, which are shiny and often tight-fitting, as with Zezé di Camargo and Luciano. Other duplas choose to wear the same style of blue jeans, checkered shirts, and may wear cowboy hats, as do Chitãozinho and Xororó, and as Leandro and Leonardo did in the past. The main point is that clothing emphasizes sameness without clearly defined hierarchy. And note that instruments and dress, as just discussed, are not aimed at communicating membership in a family; this is not an instance of marking family difference by, for instance, having all members of the Camargo family appear in red, the Durval family in blue. Rather, these visual cues simply point to the fact that the *brothers* are alike.

Dupla resemblance is not limited to dress. Physically, they often simply *look* like brothers, and they attend to personal grooming in ways that stress this. For example, Zé Mulato and Cassiano are both in their early forties, and *caboclo* (a racial-spatial descriptor they proudly apply to themselves in performance). Zé is somewhat taller and broader than Cassiano, but their essential shape and comportment are all but identical. They have the same fleshy ball at the ends of their noses, the same dark brown eyes, and the same way of smiling. Both have bushy black hair and eyebrows, and well-trimmed mustaches. Their physical resemblance is hardly surprising, of course, but they have done everything they can by personal grooming and dress to emphasize it. Similarly, Chitãozinho and Xororó and Zezé di Camargo and Luciano have identical haircuts as well as matching dress.

To conclude this examination of the combination of hierarchical and egalitarian components of the dupla form, we should consider the way duplas are named. Between the 1950s and the 1980s it was common for duplas to name themselves as though they were twins. Liu and Leu, Zico and Zeca, Zilo and Zalo, and Tonico and Tinoco are four examples, though there are countless others. The idea here is that some phonetic components repeat themselves, while others do not. In recent days, this twinning of names has not continued to the same extent, with duplas sometimes choosing to put together two first names that may or may not be their real names. Examples of this phenomenon include Edson and Hudson, and Alisson and Alessandro. But note that even in these cases, some phonological feature of the two names often matches ("dson" in the first case, "Al" in the second) thereby giving the names a shared substrate.

If we look at both the hierarchical and the egalitarian poses which brothers adopt, it seems clear that neither is dominant. Rather, they exist in tension with one another. All are subsumed within the sibling relationship. Therefore, the way in which the blending of the two voices functions, together with the distribution of hierarchical responsibilities, is thought to be a consequence of birth and growing up together. This is not subject to negotiation.

Postauthoritarian Musicalities of Space-Time

In his treatment of the rapid increase in the popularity of "death metal" in the working-class neighborhoods of the city of Belo Horizonte, in the state of Minas Gerais, Idelber Avelar (2001) details the music's approach to the fusion of time and space. The increase in popularity of Brazilian death metal coincides with the rapid rise in the circulation of rural public culture in Brazil, namely, the postauthoritarian period. And both rural musical genres and death metal prioritize the relationship between time and space. For instance, one of the central purposes of death metal is the eradication of the relevance of the past as rooted in the Brazilian landscape, which obliterates the possibility of a future. Here, the imminent apocalypse of the present is figured by the importance of repetition, indexed by the way in which all instruments rhythmically and melodically double one another rather than playing the interlocked and differing parts most common in popular music, especially in Brazil. The apocalypse removes the listeners and performers from the Brazilian landscape, moving them to a transformed and destroyed space of ruins, crushed under the weight of judgment (Avelar 2001). From a chronotopic perspective, metal's space is that of the apocalypse itself: a ruined present with all expectations foreclosed.

Brazilian rural musical genres also criticize redemocratization by presenting modernity as a corrupting rather than a progressive influence. But while both death metal and rural genres intently focus on the musicality of space-time, rural musical genres take an entirely different approach to the past, which metal eradicates, and with it, the landscape itself. Rural genres enact this critique by inverting the conventional expectations for gendered communicative practice, so that normally laconic males become tremendously expressive. Furthermore, instead of the obliteration of history and land, rural genres propose the absolute necessity of recollecting oneself as rural, culled from an ideal past, rich with the blood of brothers. The bond of brothers and their musically enacted presentation of hierarchy and egalitarianism are believed to be subsumed within the natural accident of birth. This is the pre-discursive space of siblingship that naturalizes the relationship between time and space within the Brazilian rural chronotope. One can't change nature, nor should one try, and this, emphatically, extends to human relations as well. Indeed, in its chronotopic properties, these rural genres may be thought of in terms of Benjaminian "messianic" time, which is "filled by the presence of the now" (Benjamin 1968, 261). And as Judith Irvine (2004, 107) argues in her treatment of the role of temporality within language ideologies, the comparison of culturally and historically located moments reveals that temporalities, configured differently, of course, tend to exist in opposed pairs. The current case supports this conjecture, so that rural genres oppose their idea of messianic time, in which modernization becomes a corrupting influence, to that of mainstream Brazilian culture's notions of historical, or linear time, where the present is the result of ineluctable progress. Rural genres question the inevitability of progress at every turn precisely through the lamination of time and space that kinship executes. The result is a proposal for how to read objects and people: a country epistemology and sociology.

Moments of a particular música caipira show exemplify this country epistemology and sociology. In the middle of this performance, Zé Mulato pauses to tell the story of the brothers' old record company's attempts to "modernize" them by having them do away with their caipira accent. But Zé explains that such a transformation could never work. Modernizing their music is like bathing and dressing a pig, he tells us. What you have at the end is just a clean pig; you have failed to change its essence. You are what you are, Zé informs us, and in addition to being brothers, we are rural people who have to sing rural music.

By telling this story Zé Mulato delineates a theory about the relationship of objects to their appearances and people to each other, in the countryside. Whereas in the city, objects might not be as they appear (one might see a pig asking to be thought of as something else, for example) or an individual might be half one way and half another, in the countryside, things are what they purport to be. In the introduction to a song later in the evening, the audience is told that "you can't be half caipira, just like you can't half believe in God. . . . If you're caipira, you're caipira." Later still, in "Caipira in a tie," which Zé Mulato wrote when he was working as a security guard in Brazil's capital, Brasília, the brothers further reinforce their argument about country appearances. One day Zé caught sight of himself in the mirror as he was heading to work and thought to himself, "how ridiculous to see a caipira in a tie." In this case, the tie belied the personality of its wearer, and in the course of the song the speaker takes it off and quits the job. If one's roots are rural, a move to the city is an uprooting, to be sure. But crucially, it is an uprooting from time, space, and kinship at the same time, all of which the practice of the Central-Southern rural music stands to reinstantiate. To return, then, to Pena Branca's reprimand—Brazilians forget the past, kinship, and the countryside. And through the chronotope performed in rural public culture, which relies on the alternation between hierarchical and egalitarian aspects of male siblingship, they stand to remember.

~ઌ~ 3

Mixture, Sadness, and Intimacy
in the Brazilian Musical Field

> In the final days of the Empire, at last, and in the first days
> of the Republic, with the *modinha* already moving from the
> piano of the salons to the guitar of the street-corners, with the
> *maxixe*, with samba, with the formation and coming-togeth-
> er of the *choro* ensembles and the evolution of the *toadas* and
> the rural dances, popular music grew and defined itself with
> incredible speed—abruptly becoming the strongest and most
> beautiful characterization of our race.
> —MÁRIO DE ANDRADE, *Aspects of Brazilian Music*

> Only Cannibalism unites us. Socially. Economically.
>   Philosophically.
> I am only interested in what's not mine. The law of men.
>   The law of the cannibal.
> —OSWALD DE ANDRADE, *The Brazil-Wood Manifesto*

Brazilian Musicalities

In the last two chapters we have discussed Brazilian rurality's division
of the world into a debased urban present and an ideal rural past, its
promulgation of a split subject, and its distinct chronotopic properties
framed by brother kinship. We have seen the way in which *dupla* singing alternates between hierarchy and egalitarianism while propound-
ing a country epistemology, where knowledge is mediated through the
heart, not the mind. Rural music also problematizes tireless future-
orientation in part by inverting conventional expectations for maleness,
thus generating its high degree of intimacy.

Like all Brazilian music, commercial and folkloric rural genres call
upon a durable Brazilian musical ideology which developed over the

course of the twentieth century, but was first consolidated during Getúlio Vargas's two early presidencies (1930–36 and 1937–45). This chapter will investigate that ideology, exploring the importance of "genre"
for fields of cultural production, a task that will continue into chapter 4.
Finally, we will consider how rurality approaches social "mixture," so
central to Brazilian cultural production, by way of sadness.

Ideology is here understood in the sense advanced within linguistic
anthropology, and not in terms of the mystification or distortion so
often associated with traditional Marxist analyses (Woolard and Schieffelin 1994, 57). In this aural case, ideology involves the conscious understanding of how music functions as a communicative practice and
the sense of what social purposes that communicative practice fulfills.
Following Jean and John Comaroff, I hold that messages associated
with the ideological "must be communicable" (J. Comaroff and J. L.
Comaroff 1991, 30). Brazilian musical ideology comprises a set of accessible assumptions about the way in which music's nature, structure,
and use link to the Brazilian social order. Central to this framing of
ideology is the fact that certain features of musical structure are more
available to userly reflection than others, that is, they fall within each
user's "limits of awareness" (Silverstein 1981a). Precisely as is the case
with language ideologies, those features of communicative practice to
which users are most attuned carry the normative weight of ideological
constructions. These features analogically pattern other aspects of social life, bringing them into alignment with musicality.[1]

One of the pillars of Brazilian musicality is the idea that music involves mixtures of all sorts, in particular, race, language, time, space,
and class. Musical ideology translates these minglings in terms of various aspects of musical structure. Features of Brazilian music that participants call upon in framing aspects of *social* mixture include the
following: 1) instruments; 2) singing "voices"; 3) melody, rhythm, and
harmony; and 4) spoken and sung language. In Brazil, music's users
are conscious of the way in which these elements are laminated together into the compact space of what are termed "popular" songs, and
they then extrapolate these mixtures that occur within such songs to
those that occur in social domains.[2] For instance, racial mixture, to
choose one example from our list, may be spoken of in terms of the way
certain kinds of rhythms and melodies come together: typically, melodies from Portugal and rhythms from Africa. But it is significant that
much of this coming together takes shape through tropes of sexuality.

In Brazil, music *seduces* elements which might not normally co-occur into contact with one another. Brazilians speak of themselves as "eaters" of other cultures, keeping in mind that the verb to "eat" (*comer*) also means to "have sex with" in the sense of penetrating. Below, we will see the way in which these tropes of sexual exchange are refracted through what I term "mutationism," as well as through cannibalism, *tropicália*, and miscegenation.

Because of the way in which aspects of musical structure ideologically carry the weight of social structure, and vice versa, scrutiny of Brazilian musical ideology reveals how musical and social structures map onto each other. Music offers a kind of rationalization for social life, as aspects of social life come to make musical sense. Musicians and listeners come to consciousness of how music functions and then impose that understanding not just on future musical practice—making the structure of music use more uniform—but also onto less explicitly musical processes and procedures. Recall the increasing hegemony of brother harmony discussed in the last chapter as an example of this process at work. Rationalization enacted through musical ideology thus describes the way in which participants in music making impose musical meanings on broader spectra of phenomena (Silverstein 1979).

So far in this book we have discussed the fact that rural genres challenge hegemonic arguments for what it means to be Brazilian that were consolidated during the Vargas years and reworked and reused through the dictatorship (1964–85). For instance, rurality contests the notion that Brazil is exclusively the land of soccer, samba, and carnival. However, the practices of rural musicians and their audiences also borrow heavily from elements of the dominant Brazilian musical ideology that supports such notions. In other words, at the very same time as they articulate a musically, and hence socially, bifurcated nation (country/city), users of rural genres agree—on television, on the radio, in newspapers, on street corners, and standing around enjoying a quick hit of coffee—that Brazilians are "musical" people, a belief that forms the centerpiece of understandings of Brazil as the land of samba and carnival. Rural musical practitioners thus agree with proponents of these long-standing tropes of coherence that Brazilians are prone to spontaneous outbursts of song, that they are good dancers, and that they are able to sing along tunefully with expert recall of words heard just once. Such notions often form the backbone of contrastive statements such as Brazilians are musical, whereas Americans and Europeans are not. Here, music becomes an idiom for the establishment of Brazil's place in the world system, as well as for sociability itself, because it occasions the mingling not just of minds, but of bodies. Once again, music "seduces" one into sociability (Veloso 2002, 7) by moving one into contact with others and getting inside body and mind in one fluid motion. In Brazilian rural music, as in other musical genres, music hits you in the head and the heart at once.

One of the most significant aspects of this Brazilian musical ideology is that it elevates music over other forms of public culture as fundamental to Brazilian self-understanding and self-projection. Speakers often root this characteristic in Brazilian history, to the effect that Brazil developed a close relationship to music in its days of limited literacy, when people could engage more easily with it than they could with poetry, painting, or drama—all art forms apparently requiring more training in how to "read." This privileging of music in turn has a history that emphasizes particular forms of mediation. Historian Bryan McCann, describing the role of radio in the formation of Brazilian society between 1930 and 1954, suggests that during this period, a group of people who were able increasingly to conceive of themselves as "listeners" through their engagement with radio began to view their choice of musical genres as a kind of participation in civic affairs. He refers to this as "popular citizenship" (McCann 2004, 12). Musical ideology thus carries with it an approach to belonging, as well as a way of conceiving how individual activity accrues to broader structures. In this way, music becomes the easiest channel for a locally defined expressivity that builds up over time, like coral.

Music in Brazil, therefore, is intrinsically political, as its users believe that it provides one of the primary channels through which social reproduction takes place. The volume of discussion surrounding musicalities of various sorts should therefore come as no surprise. Take the prototypical case of samba in connection with carnival. Samba music becomes the ritual frame through which carnival might suspend differences of gender, race, and social class, invert conventional hierarchies (DaMatta 1982, 1984), or perhaps create opportunities for "resistance" to Brazilian society as dominated and dominating (Browning 1996; DaMatta 1979). In effect, the role of music in what is often spoken of as this most Brazilian of national rituals can scarcely be overstated. Hence, it makes sense that a public outcry over the commercialization of carnival in its home space of Rio de Janeiro should begin with discontent over samba music, extending only later into broader upset about trans-national domination. Critics of the carnival held in 2003 objected to the substitution of a samba-like genre called *pagode* (a commercialized and sped-up samba that bears little resemblance to the rural genre of the same name that we will consider below), with its electronic instrumentation. They also decried what they perceived to be a concomitant lack of creativity in lyrics, in contrast with the verbally astute traditional, acoustic samba. So the quality of the instrumentation directly relates to the verbal acuity of the lyricist, here. These critics claim that, whereas in the past, the rhythm of carnival music compelled dancers to participate, now, pagode merely alienates them. Pagode does not get people to move the way the more culturally authentic sambas once did, the story goes. Thus, when the correct music absents itself, the prescribed rituals may not occur.

As if the absence of dancing weren't enough, further proof of the musically induced poverty of the carnival of 2003 apparently lies in sales. Where once the compilation of carnival hits could be expected to gross two million, barely two hundred thousand copies sold in 2003 (Rohter 2003). The intrusion of what are deemed non-Brazilian elements is blamed for this. As one member of a Rio samba school (one of the complex institutions responsible for organizing processions during the festivities)[3] complained, no one even knows the words to the songs in this day and age. This precludes the right kind of participation and dilutes or defuses the ritual. If dancers, singers, instrumentalists, and observers are not seduced by the music, and are thus unable to take part within the ritual frame, then there is no carnival, no samba, and, it is feared, eventually, there will be no Brazil. You can't be seduced if you don't know the words and can't feel the beats (conjoined processes). Note, in all of this, the way in which the various layers collaborate (minimally, rhythm, instrumentation, melody, and song texts), in turn implicating the singing voice. These musical elements *mix*. Understand from this description not merely the fact that music is deemed important, but that various elements must come together.

The notion of music as a fundamental register of social life that undergirds Brazilian sociability has a distinguished genealogy. As with so many domains of Brazilian social thought, we begin with anthropologist Gilberto Freyre. In his *Order and Progress* (first published in 1959), Freyre extended ideas he had begun to develop in earlier works published in 1933 and 1936. He found that music provided a way for Brazilians to transcend boundaries of social class; music was, in his words, "the form most congenial to aristocrat and plebian alike for the expression of their Luso-American spirit" (Freyre 1986, 67). Later in the same work, Freyre notes that during the late nineteenth century there was a unique union of music with "the Brazilian social order" (Freyre 1986, 77).

In contrast to other dominant social scientific paradigms in circulation at the time of Freyre's publication of *The Masters and the Slaves* (1933), Freyre argued that Brazil's racial intermixing was not a sign of its backwardness in relation to whiter Europe. Brazilian and European critics had characterized Brazil as backward because of its racial mixing. Freyre turned this on its head and used it to argue instead for Brazilian vitality. In fact Freyre transformed racial mixture into that which was both most Brazilian and most progressive on a global scale. He suggested that an apparently distinctively Brazilian mixture achieved through fruitful cross-fertilization accounted for a growing Brazilian superiority with respect to other nations. Music was to be one of the major modalities in which this mixture was to be played out, particularly the urban samba of contemporaneous Rio de Janeiro (Vianna 1999). Samba both presupposed and entailed mixture, it was said. Moreover, expression of this Brazilian musical ideology provides one of the significant sites at which national ideologies of race mixture continue to be articulated. Those seeking to account for the distinctiveness of Brazilian music tout the importance of a confluence of "three races." Rhythm and dance are most often thought to come from Africans and to a lesser extent, indigenous peoples, while, in a predictably racialized topos, instrumentation, melody, and language all hail from the Portuguese, for example.

Other takes on the paradigms of Brazilian musicality-as-mixture emerge from an analysis of the two unrelated Andrades quoted in this chapter's epigraphs: Oswald and Mário. Both were at pains to establish what was specific to Brazil in the early twentieth century. Oswald was the poet and essayist who wrote the *Brazil-Wood Manifesto* (published in 1928)—sometimes also called the Cannibal Manifesto—a poem in which he proposed that what distinguished Brazil from other nations was its propensity for absorbing other people and practices. He suggested that the way in which Brazil's first indigenous inhabitants ate their enemies provided a template for current Brazilian social action. The implication was that twentieth-century Brazilians were also eaters of others because they voraciously consumed cultures. Oswald de Andrade's promiscuous racial culinary praxis became the flag for the Brazilian modernist movement that exploded onto the national scene with São Paulo's Modern Art Week in 1922.

Oswald de Andrade's namesake, Mário, though somewhat less flamboyant in his textual strategy, was no less important to Brazilian modernism. Mário was a musician and sought to elaborate a Brazilian musical philosophy, in part by exhaustively cataloguing Brazilian genres. He spent a great deal of time traveling the backcountry, observing music, describing it, and recording it. As the epigraph shows, he articulated the notion that music both represented, and brought into reality, the mixture of races that made Brazil stand apart from other nations. Though his treatment of music was much more detailed than that of Freyre, it nonetheless dovetailed with Freyre's in its broad strokes.

Rural music shares important aspects of this musical ideology by focusing on the politics of mixture as mediated by sound. In the case of musical rurality, this entails the coming together of, at least, landscapes, historical periods, and genders, in the context of a hardship inevitably imposed by what gets referred to as "nature." But before exploring this distinct approach to Brazilian musical ideology, it is essential to understand the way in which a penchant for musical mingling provides the central axis around which the field of musical production revolves. Along these lines, position-takings with respect to mixture as indexed by sound create dialogical tensions within the field. This happens because not all mixture is necessarily the same. Some of it aims "high," while other minglings may be characterized as decidedly "intimate," in Herzfeld's sense of a "fellowship of the flawed" (Herzfeld 1996, 28). In order to understand the difference between high and intimate mixture, we must delineate the contours of the musical field of cultural production. This begins with an examination of the way in which, broadly speaking, Brazilian music's users think about genre.

The Rural Field as Generic Activity

The concept of a "field of cultural production" supplies a way to think about the forces performativity brings into dialogue with one another. Bourdieu employs it to consider how nineteenth-century French literature and painting were implicated in the transformation of French society (Bourdieu 1993a, 1993b). More than simply giving a social history of a particular practice, however, use of the concept of fields allows one to trace out the way in which that practice participates in, and represents, mutually reinforcing components of social life. This fundamental attribute of fields of cultural production leads to another. Considering "fields" moves us away from the notion that transformations result primarily from "creativity" and/or "genius," a perspective that shortcuts social change by placing the responsibility for it solely at the feet of particular individuals divorced from their environments.[4] Instead, fields of cultural production elucidate practice as part of a dialogue between individuals, institutions, and practices set in broader social milieus.

I take the field of musical production in Brazil to include, at the minimum, the following actors: radio listeners, record company artist-and-repertoire workers ("A and R guys" who initiate recording contracts between performers and labels), recording engineers, songwriters, record companies, instrumentalists, singers, record-company executives, scholars, critics, recording-studio owners, politicians, journalists, and fan-club members, among others. Several institutions are also important, among them, television stations, record companies, governmental organs responsible for "culture," banks, beer companies, and concert halls. Within the field, practices and pieces are produced and interpreted. This requires circulation. As Michael Warner (2002) argues in the case of "publics," fields should not be conceived of as composed solely of durable objects—concatenations of "audiences" made up of individuals somehow fixed in time and space. Fields, just like the publics which in part compose them, are at times constituted by mere attention (Warner 2002), and therefore continually shift in ways that are nonetheless open to ethnographic investigation.

Generically structured activity provides interpretive and creative resources within the context of fields. Actors, institutions, and practices within the field of musical production both explicitly and implicitly use genre for a variety of tasks, among them, the role recruitment and inhabitance so often glossed as "identity formation," and the coconstitution of time and space. Often, stances within the field are momentary. Music's users almost invariably inhabit a variety of position-takings with respect to genres and their associated practices. For example, those with a penchant for the traditional may well listen to commercial country. Only in rare cases do listeners *only* listen to one given type of music, having no truck with others.

Understanding the role of genre in orienting participant movements is essential to comprehending the field of musical production. The remainder of this chapter will be devoted to considering the indigenous explication of genre and its relation to the broader musical ideology that positions genres in relation to one another. This treatment of genre will remain at a level of position-takings, which is to say that we will focus on interrelatedness. The next chapter continues the treatment of genre in order to establish its role in the constitution of rural subjectivities.

Practitioners within the Brazilian musical field ascribe positions to genres according to at least the following attributes: space (urban and rural), time (modern and traditional), locality (regional, national, and international), race (black, white, and Indian), gender (male and female), social status (high to low), and emotional affect (sad or celebratory). Genres also have chronotopic properties that mediate between various inflections of time and space (as explored in chapter 2). Furthermore, as we shall see, this mixture of possibilities for positioning in turn gives shape to the tension between practices touted as "national," versus other practices deemed "culturally intimate," and hence embarrassing (Herzfeld 1996, 4).

Renegotiations of the position of a particular genre, song, or artist within the field take place continually. For example, with respect to the rural, Chitãozinho and Xororó, sometimes imitative of American country (Dent 2003), sought recognition from those who esteem Brazilian traditions by recording an album of classic songs from the established repertoire of Brazilian rural music (*Classics from the Back-Country*—1996).[5] Instead of their usual blend of newly composed pieces, sprinkled with versions of recent Latin and North American country hits, they guided themselves in making this record according to their sense of the traditional Central-Southern rural repertoire. They knew this repertoire well from the days when they performed at local circuses, before they had experienced national success by "modernizing" themselves. By recording these "classics," this duo sought to shift its position out of the ultrapopular and romantic domain of the musical field and toward a traditional pole. This represented an attempt to move from their customarily "intimate" domain into one where their practice might please fans of the traditional.

Genres fulfill and define various tasks within the musical field. As Negus (1999) has shown in his study of the recording industry in the United States and England, genres shape the way songwriters compose, the sorts of venues in which a band may or may not play, which record companies are likely to take an interest in a body of material, and the way in which that material will be recorded and circulated. Negus suggests that performers and fans escape genre with difficulty. Even for performers striving to transcend its boundaries by seeking their own novel sound, genre's primary importance has a way of reasserting itself in the course of transacting what might be termed business. For example, the organizers of the rodeo at Americana hoped to expand the audience of ticket buyers by including musical genres other than the customary commercial country in the post-event shows. On one evening, for instance, the youth-rock group Babado Novo filled the stadium with a young crowd dressed in urban baggy jeans and oversized nylon shirts. Even on nights such as these, however, the organizers sought to maintain the theme of the rodeo as revolving around country music by having "traditional" *música sertaneja* playing off to the side of the main arena at all times. They were also adamant that they had booked the best-attended evenings of the rodeo, which were Fridays, Saturdays, and Sundays, with commercial country music. "Our *foundation is still música sertaneja*," one of the press agents informed me matter-of-factly, "though we're trying to offer something for everyone."

Genres are made and unmade in places as mundane as record stores, where categorizing performers and records facilitates shopping, restocking, and buying. These categorizations are frequently fluid. For example, with respect to the way in which genre melds notions of geography and tradition, traditional rural music (*música caipira*) frequently appears in record stores as a subset of what is called, simply, "regional music" (*música regional*). This generic categorization dates back at least to the early twentieth century (see chapter 4), but the term "regional" is used today to demarcate a series of mostly (though not exclusively) rural genres from various parts of Brazil that attend to tradition as the most significant feature by which they should be judged. Música caipira points to the Central-South; *choro*, an improvised instrumental music mingling strings with woodwinds, to urban Rio; *música nordestina*, to the interior of Northeastern states such as Bahia; Gaúcho music, to the South; *forró*, an accordion-driven music, growing in popularity among the middle class of the Central-South, hails from the Northeast. Those browsing in record stores will find these locations marked by way of this generic categorization, set off in terms of an explicit attention to something called "tradition."

Genres are also defined by musical criticism offered by fans and performers in informal contexts, as well as by the music press. Critics often comment upon a song based on its membership in a genre or transgression of the boundaries of a genre it purports to uphold. Such and such a dupla are not "really" singers of música sertaneja, I heard time and again with reference to Sandy and Júnior, for instance. In a slightly different vein, one of my ten-string guitar teachers, taking on the role of critic, bitterly attacked the current state of the rural musical field. He claimed that practitioners of revivalist *viola* music (*música de viola*) had stolen aspects of what he felt was "true" rural music and had melded it with completely noncharacteristic elements of jazz and classical. He inveighed against those who began as guitar players in classical or jazz scenes and only much later took up the viola. His bitterness was reinforced by the ease with which some of these players obtained radio time and booked shows, whereas he had much more difficulty. "Those of us who still play *real* rural music are stuck on the outside and can't find a way to get in [to the market]," he complained. Another example of divisions over "the real thing" occurred within a radio station I attended for research. The Rádio Clube de Itapira offers rural music in two distinct ways. The two men who host these two shows hold competing ideas about how to represent "real" rural music, and their listeners debate the virtues of each. One of them "*only* works with duplas that have a recording." The other runs a live show in which any dupla is free to appear and perform a song on the radio. The former accuses the latter of lacking "standards." The latter accuses the former of going against the core of rural music, which is allowing all comers to sing and draw pleasure from that singing. In ways such as this, criticism, journalistic, informal, and at the level of quotidian affairs, relies upon and ratifies the boundaries of genre.

Genres play an important role in radio broadcasting. They provide the organizing principle for Brazil's AM and FM radio playlists, and frequently, for stations as a whole. For example, as in the United States, radio stations in larger Brazilian cities often devote themselves entirely to rural music, rock, pop (a "light" rock with soft percussion and smooth instrumentation), or, in Brazil, MPB (Brazilian Popular Music —a hybrid genre mingling traditional elements with rock—see below). In Campinas, for example, Rádio Morena plays mostly MPB, some regional genres, and a touch of jazz, whereas Rádio Laser plays música sertaneja, some romantic pop, and a smattering of *música caipira*. In smaller cities and towns, instead of devoting themselves entirely to one genre, single stations like the Rádio Clube de Itapira play a wide variety of music by dividing programming into specific hours devoted solely to one genre in which the disc jockey plays entirely Música Popular Brasileira (MPB), for instance, or all música sertaneja for a demarcated hour. Similarly, television channels offering a variety of programs from sports to news will present hour-long programs of videos and music, often based on a particular genre. Inezita Barroso's folkloric rural musical program Viola, Minha Viola, on state-sponsored TV-Cultura, for example, exclusively revolves around traditional Brazilian rural musical genres, while MTV Brasil offers a mixture of rock, rap, and MPB. Brazilian variety shows, which broadcast for as much as three hours on Sundays, showcase music by genre; some of them focus on música sertaneja.

In addition to these contexts, genre also plays a role in certain public rituals. These include rodeo in the case of rural genres, or carnival in the case of samba and trio eléctrico. Both rodeo and carnival thus rely on music for their framing and enactment; music shapes the progression of events, the movement of bodies, and the flow of time. Música caipira animates folklorically oriented June Festivals (Festas Juninhas) and Three Kings processions (Folia de Reis) (see the detailed ethnography of Reily 2002). Listeners also organize their musical tastes by orienting what they characterize as their "mood" according to genre, opting for danceable samba when they feel animated, or rural genres when they wish to linger on their feelings. And note that the flexibility inherent in most current listening practices in Brazil problematizes strict allegiance to any one genre, thus requiring rethinking pat equations of genre with identity. Few fans or musicians I encountered in the Central-South claimed exclusive allegiance to only one genre. One physical education teacher and trainer of bulldogging participants for rodeos listened overwhelmingly to rural music, although his tastes spanned the popular and the folkloric. However, most people I questioned on their tastes by genre sampled much more widely. Genres, and the position-takings associated with them, tended to be perceived much more as currents that might be stepped into and out of than as markers of inalienable self.

This brief discussion of the institutions, actors, and practices that collaborate to provide a sense of genre reveals the multisited nature of fields of cultural production. In addition to thinking of fields as multi-

sited zones of activity, we may think of them also as oriented by fundamental values (Chernoff, 1979; Graeber, 2001; Turner, 1984). This returns us to the subject of mixture, because much of the field of Brazilian
musical production deems mixture to be strongly positive. How mixture is handled, however, varies from genre to genre. Within the ambit
of the musical field, we therefore turn to the way in which rural genres
approach mixture, providing a sense of how they position themselves in
relation to other genres in the field. First, we consider the union of
mixture and sadness. Next, we consider the repercussions of this union
for generic position-takings.

Mixture as Sadness, and as Historicity

> In a radiant land, there lives a sad people.
> —PAULO PRADO, *Portrait of Brazil: An Essay on Brazilian Sadness*

Practitioners of Central-Southern rural genres reinforce the Brazilian
musical ideology with which this chapter opened by privileging music
over other expressive practices. For instance, in the words of one rural
music enthusiast and scholar, traditional rural music represents "one
of the most relevant expressions of a radically Brazilian art and culture"
(Sant'Anna 2000, 25). However, rural genres inflect mixture in different
ways from other musical genres. First, they emphasize a different racial
geography from that found in mainstream Brazilian musical production. Rural musical histories customarily begin with a shift away from
Freyrian African-Portuguese contact in Salvador, or creative *mestiçagem*
in the hillside slums of Rio de Janeiro, toward the early contact between
Portuguese Catholics and Indians in the Central-Southern region.

For instance, Captain Swindled (Capitão Furtado, the stage name of
Ariovaldo Pires, Cornélio's nephew, whom we shall meet in more detail
below) suggests that rural music, indeed, Brazilian music as a whole,
resulted from the Jesuit attempt to convert the Indians, not through
preaching, or even catechism, but through song. Note that the Brazilian
musical ideology in evidence in such ideas operates by once again
privileging music above other expressive domains: musical means were
considered to be the most effective ones for bringing the godless to
God (Ferrete 1985). And alignment with mainstream musical ideology
continues. The Indians were captivated by the viola, we are told, be-

they were accustomed to accompanying singing voices with wind instruments, and the sound of the ten strings fascinated them utterly. They were "seduced" by this new sound. To prove their case that rural genres emerged in this contact situation, many today emphasize the union of language and music in the birth of the important rural song type known as the *cururú*. Ariovaldo Pires argues its inception occurred when the Jesuits took an indigenous musical form and set Christian texts to it, employing the indigenous language of Tupí. In this way we are told that what would become a foundational Central-Southern rural song type provided the necessary aural seduction for conversion of Indians—all by way of a wily Jesuit employment of a mingling of Indian words and melody with Portuguese religiosity and instrumentation (see, also, Ribeiro 2006, 16–17).[6] So, music's seductive capacities mean that conquest and assimilation take place by way of guile and flirtation rather than brute force. In an explanatory move echoed by countless formal and informal historians of rural genres, colonialism is thus characterized as ever so slightly sexualized persuasion involving mixture rather than an outright coercion.

We have seen that rural genres focus on a slightly modified prioritization of the three races idea conventionally associated with Brazilian musical ideology. It is not that Africa is out of the picture, here, but rather, that it is placed more in the background. Furthermore, racial mixture has a different outcome. While the miscegenation of blacks and whites created the exuberance of samba in the hillside slums of Rio de Janeiro, the Indian-Portuguese *caboclo* appears perennially crestfallen. Rural music scholar Sant'Anna, for instance, argues that the Indians weren't happy because they were imprisoned in their own land—a diminished people struck down by both whites and disease (Sant'Anna 2000, 73). But the whites were also far from happy because of the discomforts of the unfamiliar tropics. Together, these races fashioned a collective well of tears that found expression and release in rural music. Here, then, is a Brazilian musicality that maintains the privileged position of music in the coming together of races while imbuing that mixture with an entirely different affective result.

Rural music also takes on a different cast from the mainstream Brazilian musical ideology by overwhelmingly emphasizing historicity, in particular, a state of reflection on the past. In the cover notes to música caipira performer Pereira da Viola's recent record (1998), anthropologist and scholar of rural São Paulo Carlos Rodrigues Brandão describes

Pereira's method of singing as a repository for quotidian affairs. Rural music becomes, for him, a kind of social document. Brandão reveals his support for Pereira's music as part of a broader drama:

> [Pereira] doesn't sing this way to please our minds. He sings this way because, in actually taking pleasure in what we hear, we might not forget those things that were not done to be remembered. Any good song is the best memory of what happened. Any good singer is the best history teacher. Because he remembers, artfully, not the doings of the greats—those fools with swords, on horseback—but the simple gestures of love and longing of the simple people we're talking about here. (P. d. Viola 1998)

It is by way of enjoying what we hear, as listeners, that we gain access to the past as common happenings. And music is what pulls the past into the present, mixing historical periods in a way that a listener may experience on an immediate level. Jeca's hills are brought forth for our inhabitance. We find a similar emphasis on music as something that calls up the past in an obituary for Xavatinho (of dupla Pena Branca and Xavatinho, discussed in chapter 2). One of the few who had not fallen victim to Pena Branca's charge of "forgetting," journalist and critic Luíz Nassif mourned Xavatinho's death in print, stating that the dupla he composed with his brother, Pena Branca, had embodied the entire nation in its music. He suggested that their collective way of singing "had lost that modern character and taken on that timeless tone that emerges from the depths of time and from Brazil" (Nassif 1999). He continued that the duo used a tone that was "plangent," the same "trembling" tone that his aunt had used when she sang to his mother, a tone that "makes up that mixture of intangible values that characterizes the Brazilian race" (Nassif 1999). Once again, rural musicality occasions reflection upon the past.

We can thus see that rural musical practitioners ground their musical ideology in many of the features that characterize other musical ideologies throughout Brazil: music as a significant domain of cultural reproduction, music as a philosophical and bodily enterprise, and music as both entailing and presupposing mixture of races, social classes, and genders. By contrast, in opposition to mainstream Brazilian musical ideologies, rural music de-emphasizes Africa and focuses on Indians and the Portuguese as it turns the results of racial mixture from exuberance into grief. Rural music becomes a domain for memory and what is defined as true social (as opposed to political) history—a place where the past, not as grand events, but rather, as daily affairs, is inculcated through the mingled acts of singing, playing, dancing, listening, and remembering. Finally, within a rural musical ideology, as we have seen in connection with the importance of brotherhood, the desire for the past takes on a gendered component, where men long not only for bygone days, but for a bygone love.

The following song by Chico Lobo shows how rural music emphasizes the desire for the past in the present, layering together the various ways in which rurality partakes of the Brazilian musical ideology. In the song's opening, the playing of the viola provides a tracking shot through time, mingling local experience with the embeddedness of the singing, dancing, and playing subject—all set within local weather conditions. The viola itself absorbs the qualities of the human voice. Note that that voice is "crying."

> The edge of the forest is good
> But the best thing of all
> Is when a viola is crying
> A pretty song, without going out of tune.
> Thoughts fly—pretending to fly away—
> Crossing the boundaries of time,
> Kicking up dust, coming back in a gust of wind. (Lobo 1997)

Elements of the landscape and the experience of being out-of-doors, framed by the hardships of country life, lead directly to poetic inspiration, and listening to songs which touch the heart:

> The best thing of all
> Is when the full moon
> In the sky, lights up our hearts.
> And we feel the poetry that inspires the caboclo
> In his simple life—
> Always hoping to have enough bread.

Then, the singer, inspired by nature, turns to the importance of heterosexual love. The lyrics of rural songs, it seems, are born of the cowboy's longing for his girl, set in motion by a desire for things such as rivers and rosemary:

The best thing of all
Is a girl in love
Who is wanted so much
By her cowpoke.

All of this points to the musicality of the oft-overlooked backlands, and, contrary to discourses which have marginalized them in the face of the ostensibly more significant African-influenced coast, they are figured as an important zone of Brazilian cultural production:

The troop, and the cattle herd
Following the pathways
Of this Brazil
That believes in the power
Resting in these backlands.

Mixture as sadness and historicity has characterized the rural approach to a Brazilian musical ideology, identifying both its differences from, and considerable overlap with, it. But the status of rural genres within the field of musical production is not simply defined by establishing their relation to the field's overarching ideology. It emerges also in acts of comparing rural genres to other genres in the field. Such contrastive exercises continue to unfold the tropic power of mixture.

Mixtures and Intimacies

The Brazilian field of musical production operates according to the ideological principles by which practitioners within that field orient themselves. In order to exist within fields of cultural production, participants carry maps with them that take into account each genre's position-takings in terms of a central ideology. Genres may then be evaluated in relation to the affinities and differences they exhibit with respect to one another. As I have argued above, in the Brazilian musical field, position-takings inevitably concern mixture. The way in which mixture produces and/or limits the degree of "cultural intimacy" with which a genre is associated has direct implications for Brazilian musicality.

Perhaps nowhere is this more obvious than in the case of rural music, which poses a conundrum for talk about social class in Brazil. In insisting on the way in which musical appetites indexed social class, many Brazilians I spoke with sounded like Bourdieu arguing that aesthetic tastes police and create class boundaries (Bourdieu 1984). With respect to rural music, journalists, music critics, listeners, and performers frequently proposed that commercial country music was produced for the lower classes, while other genres, such as MPB, jazz, and classical music, were for the middle and upper classes. Proof of the lower-class status of rural music came in the form of the oft-repeated statement that, once upon a time, música sertaneja was only played on the radio in the early morning hours, when rural workers who were getting up to go to work could hear it. Moreover, rural musical practitioners often ratify the lower-class orientation of their music, arguing that being lower class manifests itself in frequently feeling "lost for words," much like practitioners of American country music (Fox 2004). Furthermore, the cowboys that compete at rodeos, the soundtrack of which is Central-Southern rural music, call themselves peons (*peões*), proudly harkening back to nineteenth-century times in which cowhands served cattle barons.

However, arguments that rural music is somehow lower class should be understood as having more to do with a generically oriented approach to mixture than with a simplistic mapping of musical taste by social status. Unfortunately, the situation is much more complex than Bourdieu could have it. In postauthoritarian Brazil, record buying, attendance at shows in various locations, and observation of the musical tastes of music listeners reveal that the production and reception of rural music is not, in fact, profoundly class based—at least not in the sense of social class as representing control over material and social means of production. In accord with the work of ethnomusicologist Martha de Ulhôa Carvalho (1991, 46), who analyzed music in the town of Montes Claros, Minas Gerais, analysis of sites in the state of São Paulo reveals that Brazilians of upper and lower classes sample from a variety of high- and low-status musics. Indeed, just as many middle- and upper-class people listen to Central-Southern rural genres as do poor migrant workers or cattlehands.

This begs the question of what, precisely, might have been *meant* by statements that rural musical genres were somehow "lower class." Since neither listeners nor performers can reliably be confined to the lower classes, what, then, is at stake in the contention that they *are*?

Answering this requires detailing the relationship between mixture and "cultural intimacy" in a generically organized field of cultural production.

Mixture I—Tradition or Mutation?

Brazilian traditionalism proposes that certain musical genres must remain intact. Behind this assertion is the notion that Brazil is one of the last bastions of folkloric genres that may still be heard as they were one hundred years ago. Meanwhile what is portrayed as the menace of globalization threatens homogenization. Consequently, folkloric genres must remain inviolable. This formalism, which is well elaborated within scholarly, critical, journalistic, and performance domains preoccupied with the "folkloric," seeks to nail down, once and for all, where a certain music originated and where it might currently be performed in such a way as to maintain its integrity. This involves a historical imagination whereby performers, critics, and listeners mobilize the past in order to argue for the correctness or error of some aspect of current practice. In pursuit of these arguments, traditionalists tell birthing tales and punish infractions of their rules of instrumentation, subject, and tempo, with public censure. One viola performer, for instance, reported that he received criticism when he used a "digital delay" pedal[7] on one track of a record that traditionalists otherwise felt was superb. He used the pedal to layer short segments of acoustic ten-string guitar on top of one another, but the resulting sound, played back in stuttering fragments reminiscent of the experimental rock 'n' roll of the 1960s, was interpreted by the folklorically minded as a deformation.

Proponents of traditionalism strictly police boundaries via adherence to musical codes. As an example of this mode of thought, consider scholar of rural music Sant'Anna, who contends that the electric and digital performances so favored by commercial country music are bringing about the slow death of country's traditional form. Sant'Anna, who champions música caipira over commercial música sertaneja in a way that will become clear in the next chapter, stresses the importance of a "live" performance to traditional Central-Southern rurality. He also asserts that anything *other* than acoustic instrumentation distorts the sound; music accompanied "by orchestra or by electric instruments comes off as if it was decorated with false makeup" (Sant'Anna 2000,

67). In the same vein, he claims that the voices of the two singers in the dupla "tune in to each other much better if accompanied by acoustic instruments, as they do in live shows" (Sant'Anna 2000, 67). Electric and electronic instruments are thus incapable of being "live." Thus, for Sant'Anna, the traditional *caipira* voicing and instrumentation represent a way of preserving a culture which he deems to be truer to his "real" Brazil.

In contrast to this concept of genre within the musical field is the notion that Brazil is a place where there is a distinct *disregard* for folk-loric boundedness, and where unanticipated minglings innovate. I term this perspective on genre mutationism; when it occurs, sounds blur, and something entirely unexpected pops out. Subscribers to this perspective fail to adhere to the boundary policing associated with the unitary and formalist concepts of genre exhibited by the traditionalists. Whereas, for the folklorically minded, the genius of Brazil is in still *having* musics that have not been modernized or updated, in a muta-tionist stance, the genius of Brazil's approach to musical genre lies in flouting slavish adherence to boundaries, just as it has always done. This point of view is expressed by rodeo producer Fabian Chacur, who argues that frequent mixture with almost total disregard for generic boundaries was what gave rise, not just to Brazilian music, but to the Brazilian race itself:

> Without this spirit of 'mixing it all up,' we would never have had samba, *tropicalismo*, bossa nova, and modern sertanejo [commercial country mu-sic], just to cite a few examples. So it's hard to reprimand artists that, in a civilized and healthy way, mingle popular genres like sertanejo and samba. Where does this nose-in-the-air attitude come from, this "what are these caipiras doing with my beloved samba," or "what are these *pagodeiros* thinking, playing sertanejo"? Really, it's all Brazil. Clearly, some mixtures work, and some don't. But to censure someone for want-ing to make something new, is, at the very least, narrow minded. The more Brazilians are open to music made in their own country, whatever region it's made in, and whatever race or creed produces it, the better. (Chacur 1999)

Thus, Chacur elaborates a theory of national development that relies upon promiscuity within an intergeneric field.

Mutationism receives support among scholars, musicians, and jour-nalists who work to trouble formalism, emphasizing places within the

Brazilian field of musical production where generic mixture seems to be taking place in the present. Noteworthy in this respect is the work of Hermano Vianna, whose book on samba had the temerity to ask how this once little-known Afro-Brazilian genre from the slums of Rio de Janeiro could possibly have become the national music. But Vianna's work has also moved into other less strictly scholarly domains. Most important for our purposes, he musically "mapped" Brazil for MTV in a miniseries in 2000, with performer and songwriter Gilberto Gil, now minister of culture, narrating. In this work, Vianna dismisses traditionalists, proposing that mixture is the Brazilian musical talent par excellence. The principles according to which he claims to have assembled the various acts and locations for a musical "map" of the nation are not simply folkloric, then: "Rescue is what you do for kidnapped people, or people who have accidents," not for musical genres, Vianna argues (Gasperin 2000). "This [television] show," Vianna continues in an interview, "did not set out on a hunt for purity and lost authenticity, nor did it search for the 'real' national music, 'uncontaminated' by the radio. Everything has potential. It just depends who uses it" (Gasperin 2000). Vianna's show refused to discriminate against genres like música sertaneja, which were commercially successful and employed electric or electronic instrumentation; this troubled traditionalists.

Let us sum up the opposition of the two perspectives and point out some consequences. Traditionalists often justify their formalist approach to genre by drawing upon the thesis of racial mixture we have identified as partaking of the Brazilian musical ideology—a theory of Brazil's mutations from the past, occasioned by the union of Indian, African, and European elements. According to this line of reasoning, Brazil's musical history created highly unusual minglings which resulted in what must, in the *present*, receive treatment as inviolable musical forms. Past mutation requires present codification. Mixture in the present threatens this. Mutationism, by contrast, inverts most of these traditionalist terms and requires the flouting of distinct genres. However, it is worth noting that revelatory mixture results from bringing distinct genres together. Mutationism thus requires the idea of genre as a fixed entity against which to cast its ostensibly revolutionary permissiveness.

These two indigenous approaches to the concept of genre—as inviolable or promiscuous—shape musical practice dialogically. Across this dialogic space, practitioners focus on the concept of mixture, on what it meant in the past, and on what it might mean in the future. Tradition, almost by definition, orbits in the officially sanctioned portion of the musical field. Mutationism, on the other hand, may occupy various positions with respect to "intimacy." Unless it conforms to delimited rules, it finds itself in decidedly "lower-class" circles. On the other hand, various forms of mutationism also take up officially sanctioned "high" positions. In the event, the degree of intimacy of a particular genre depends a great deal on how it handles quotation of, and reference to, other musical genres, a subject to which we now turn.

Mixture II—From Elsewhere

Within the context of discussions of mixture, borrowing from abroad receives special scrutiny. MPB, for example, which is categorically glossed as a higher-status music than música sertaneja, borrows self-consciously, calling attention to what it is taking precisely *as* borrowed. MPB songwriters and performers sample with an ironic "wink" à la Clifford Geertz (1973b), which lets the observer know that the performer quotes from this *now*, in this moment, but could just as easily be quoting from something *else* in the next. The MPB singer and writer propounds self-awareness about what she has musically appropriated, preserving distance between the genre involved in the act of borrowing and the musically constituted identity in play. In the course of a single record or live performance, the MPB performer maintains several simultaneous borrowings, giving equal time to each. For example, during Caetano Veloso's tour of 2000, he quoted from rock 'n' roll, rap, samba, jazz, classical music, and *nueva canción*.[8] He read from Brazilian and foreign literature onstage. Listeners knowledgeable about Veloso's corpus knew that these were just a few of the appropriations he had undertaken in his career—indeed, that his musical origins in his tropicália movement were predicated on the concept of eclecticism.

Practitioners of Brazilian Popular Music (MPB) such as Veloso ground their practice in the second of this chapter's epigrams. Most famously, a musical movement that called itself tropicália, spearheaded by Gilberto Gil, Caetano Veloso, and Tom Zé, shunned folkloric parameters that they felt forced them to compose within overly restrictive bounds. These performers proposed a cannibalistic technique along the lines of Oswald de Andrade's "anthropophagy," using electric guitars, Beatles harmonies, and Hendrix-style improvisation, while borrowing tempos and melodic lines from Brazilian musics. Despite their having been criticized for this initially, these days, MPB's "highbrow" system of borrowing allows it to share official sanction with traditional genres, despite the fact that MPB is largely mutationist in its orientation.

MPB's modes of quotation contrast sharply with commercial country's. Música sertaneja performances borrow heavily, but almost entirely from genres deemed rural. The borrowing that takes place does not "wink," at no point signaling its borrowing with ironic distance. While MPB artists describe themselves as "inspired" by other musical genres, música sertaneja artists offer little explanation for their "influences" and are subsequently described by music critics and traditionalists as simply "copying" (S. Martins 1999). Indeed, música sertaneja performers often abet such statements by offering note-for-note versions of Nashville country songs translated into Portuguese, such as Chitãozinho and Xororó's version of Billy Ray Cyrus's "Achy Breaky Heart" (see Dent 2005), Edson and Hudson's rendition of Keith Urban's "Raining on Sunday," or Leandro and Leonardo's cover of John Michael Montgomery's "I Swear" (Leandro and Leonardo 1998).[9] Música sertaneja also borrows substantially from international and Brazilian "pop" music, another genre that evidences a high degree of intimacy.[10] Música sertaneja signals its borrowing in a profoundly different way from MPB by drawing upon a delimited array of genres, where MPB samples widely.

For English Ears—Mixture's Intimate Generativity

This analysis of rurality within the field of musical production and the central ideology that structures the position-takings of the musical field's various genres reveals the way in which music provides a crucial site through which to manage and reflect upon a preoccupation with mixture. By signaling conscious control over mixture, genres position themselves with respect to one another and reveal their degree of cultural intimacy.

With respect to intimacy, British social anthropologist Peter Fry, who came to Brazil in 1970 in order to, in his terms, bring social anthropology to the State University of Campinas (UNICAMP), edited a series of his early papers in 1981 under the title "For English Eyes." The title toyed with his status as a Brit in Brazil. But more importantly, his title quoted a common Brazilian expression, that when something is done to the letter of the law in Brazil, a nation where things are more often jury-rigged, it is obviously being done not for Brazilian eyes, but "for British eyes." Fry notes that at least two explanations for this common expression circulate in Brazil—both historical. The first suggests that as Britain tightened its antislavery blockade of Brazil in the mid-nineteenth century, slave ships had to be disguised as different kinds of vessels so the British wouldn't detect them. Second, Brazilians working under British supervision during the days of the British-run railway of the late nineteenth and early twentieth centuries had to do things just so, instead of doing them briskly as they would have preferred. When they did them just so, they did them "for English eyes." Both explanations suggest that performing actions "properly" in Brazil is a response to colonial power. The second argues that a more truly Brazilian mode of operation, which was less concerned with following instructions and more with simply finding the quickest way to get something done, exerts so much power over Brazilians that they must make an effort to suppress it.

So, "for English eyes" suggests that there is a degree of embarrassment, bolstered by the threat of punishment inherent to *brasilidade*. As Fry notes, "English" conveys a sense of needing to suppress the wish to do things, in some sense, "incorrectly." And this is not simply ascribed to one class faction or the other. This polarity between English and Brazilian, Fry argues, encapsulates many of the apparent paradoxes of Brazilian society: "this opposition between 'the Englishman' and 'the Brazilian' tends to coexist in everyone. One position or the other is invoked situationally, in accord with the interests in play" (Fry 1982, 18).

This reveals, then, a broader preoccupation with questions of intimacy than might be captured by pat ascriptions of social class in relation to musical taste. One viola teacher once railed to me against the absurdities of middle- and upper-class people calling rural genres "lower class." He stated flatly that countless middle- and upper-class people throughout the Central-Southern region endlessly listened to música caipira and música sertaneja, though they often did so hidden, in the privacy of their houses. As we can see, certain aspects of identity may be considered "a source of external embarrassment," but these sources of identity "nevertheless provide insiders with their assurance of common sociality, the familiarity with the bases of power that may at one moment assure the disenfranchised a degree of creative irreverence and at the next moment may reinforce the effectiveness of intimidation" (Herzfeld 1996, 3).

The next chapter delves further into the nature of the polarizing discourse between those things which are embarrassing and those things which are not by building on the definition of genre begun here. The approach is an activity-oriented one that focuses on how genre creates an empirically observable agentive horizon of possibilities, or a body of resources from which individuals might select, in musically enacting processes such as role recruitment and inhabitance, the fashioning of national character, and the navigation of day-to-day activity.

~~ **4**

Hick Dialogics

From this point of view, novelty would take its
chances against tradition.
—GREG URBAN, *A Discourse Centered Approach to Culture*

Despite their different models of subjectivity, the shared meta-
linguistic apparatus creates a common terrain of exploration
that might be described as an intergeneric tension field out of
which new forms of subjectivity develop.
—BENJAMIN LEE, *Talking Heads*

In the northern portion of the state of São Paulo, close to the border with adjoining state Minas Gerais, lies the town of Barretos, which
has been a center of Latin American beef production since a large
slaughterhouse and refrigeration plant was constructed there back in
the early 1900s. In 1955, a group of local bachelors calling themselves
"The Independents" (*Os Independentes*) proposed an annual get-together
involving competitions in horsemanship, races of various types, and
soccer games. The following year they actually held their first "Peon
Party"—"peon" being the deliberately chosen archaic term for cowboy
now universally employed in the designation of Brazil's six-hundred-
odd rodeos as *Festas do Peão*. As years went by, the annual event grew,
and by 2004, this once modest gathering had developed international
links to Canada, the United States, Australia, and Mexico by way of a
transnational rodeo circuit.

Barretos, along with other large-scale Brazilian rodeos such as Americana and Jaguariuna, currently shares some features with its international counterparts, such as bull riding; the techniques used to ride
bulls in Brazil were brought back from the United States by a cowboy
who had been competing there in the early 1980s.[1] At the same time,

however, Brazilian rodeo displays distinct attributes, such as the kind of announcing that happens during each cowboy's ride; in Brazil, announcers speak quickly and excitedly, like radio sportscasters pumping fans up when the soccer ball gets close to the net, whereas in the United States, announcing is much slower and more laid-back. Barretos's almost 1.5 million annual visitors over ten days near the end of August make it the largest rodeo in Latin America and one of the largest in the world.[2] The physical plant of the festival, which was housed under a circus tent for its first season, took its current form in 1989, when The Independents built a reinforced concrete park and stadium planned by Brasília's architect Oscar Niemeyer. During the rodeo in 2004, the way that Barretos's organizers had scheduled *música caipira* and *música sertaneja* events within the physical space of the park had important consequences for the way in which fans and musicians could experience and fashion history, politics, and culture.

Barretos, São Paulo: Saturday, August 21, 2004

In the last chapter, we looked at rural genres broadly speaking by examining the way in which they inflect the Brazilian musical ideology with sadness. Toward the end of that chapter, we established some of the musical field's affinities and extremes, and we began to see ways in which música caipira and música sertaneja differ from one another. In this chapter, we concentrate on those "extremes" (Boon 1990). We begin this process with the differences between these two genres as exemplified during the Barretos rodeo of 2004. Our purpose is to deepen the analysis of the way in which genre not only provides a way of thinking about position-taking within fields of cultural production, but also orients its users to the world (Hanks 1996, 246). Our subject, then, is the way in which genre provides what we might think of as a horizon of possibilities within which participant "experiences" take shape. We will explore generic horizons by looking at the way in which language has been used to distinguish between *caipira* and sertanejo, drawing upon and defining notions such as race, social class, and geography.

To continue with our treatment of Barretos: the open-air stadium, in which thirty-five thousand people can be seated, or, according to several security guards, close to seventy thousand could stand, housed the main attractions. On the August 2004 Saturday in question, events in

Figure 1.
Spaces of
Caipira and
Sertanejo in
Barretos's
"Peon's"
Park.

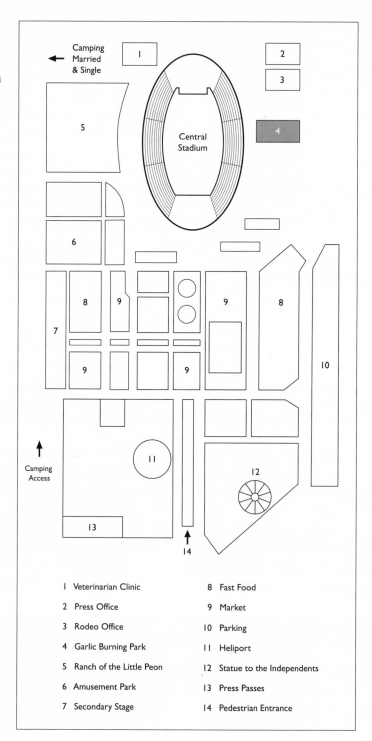

1	Veterinarian Clinic	8 Fast Food
2	Press Office	9 Market
3	Rodeo Office	10 Parking
4	Garlic Burning Park	11 Heliport
5	Ranch of the Little Peon	12 Statue to the Independents
6	Amusement Park	13 Press Passes
7	Secondary Stage	14 Pedestrian Entrance

the main stadium were due to begin with the usual rodeo roughstock events (bull and bronco riding) and timed events (penning, roping, and barrel racing) at around seven in the evening. These were to last till about midnight, when a musical show consisting of two commercial country duos would begin. The central stadium, then, provided the space in which commercially successful *duplas* sertanejas played into the early morning hours to sold-out crowds from the Central-Southern region and beyond.

Música caipira occupied a much more marginal space and time. Off to the side of the stadium, there is a fenced enclosure called "the Resting Spot" (*Ponto de Pouso*—intended to refer to the camp that cowboys would have pitched at the end of a long day's cattle drive). This resting spot contained trees, some lean-tos constructed just a few years ago to look a half-century old, and tiny paddocks. There, the rodeo's organizers held an annual cowboy cooking competition called "the Garlic Burning" (*A Queima do Alho*). During this competition, each team took up residence within a tiny paddock, using primitive implements and open cooking fires to prepare four dishes briskly. They aimed to recreate both the kind and speed of preparation of recipes "the cowboy way." In this fashion, they attempted to reenact what the cowboy cooks of the past must have done to feed hungry cattle herders of the late nineteenth and early twentieth centuries out on the trail, by producing simple fare over fires set right on the ground with almost no tools. The name of the event apparently derives from the ridiculousness of men cooking; "he's going to burn the garlic," the early twentieth-century cowboys are supposed to have said in anticipation of their compatriots' ignorance of garlic's properties and general culinary clumsiness. In 2004, the results were judged by local radio personalities, politicians, businessmen, and teachers.

In the afternoon hours, long before the evening's rodeo events were due to begin, the stadium itself lay empty. But the cooking competition off to the side of the stadium bustled. Judges circulated, writing thoughtfully on clipboards as they chewed. They were using three categories to evaluate the teams: "work" (*trabalho*), which included the implements and techniques; "performance" (the English word, *performance*, note),[3] which included deciding whether the competitors' movements represented the style in which the cooking would, once upon a time, have been completed; and "hygiene," which addressed the cleanliness of the process. Unsurprisingly, these categories enacted distinctly contemporary criteria for evaluating an ostensibly arcane practice; re-call from Jeca's theme that the historicity of Brazilian rurality is deliber-ately nonspecific.⁴ After the cooking was completed, locals and mem-bers of the news media sampled the cowboy rice, meat-and-bean stew, and grilled steaks that each team had prepared. The cooks were finally permitted a beer or two, strictly forbidden before that point.

Country music "in the roots style" added a sense of legitimacy to the garlic burning, providing an early twentieth-century soundtrack for what purported to be an early twentieth-century culinary practice. The musical accompaniment for this contest came in the form of another competition, this time a musical one where duplas performed folkloric Central-Southern songs: música caipira. Having a competition hark-ened back to the contests of the 1940s and 1950s, in which so many of the great rural music duplas had first won public recognition—duplas like Tonico and Tinoco. In Barretos, in 2006, pairs of men, often broth-ers, and always with one of the two members playing a viola (a require-ment), took to a tiny stage at the side of the cowboy cooking contest to sing and play. They were judged on the quality of the song they had chosen, their ability to present that song live, the twinning of their voices (afinação, or the brotherly in-tuneness emphasized in chapter 2), and their instrumental technique. The well-elaborated rules for this competition, equivalent in their complexity to those governing the gar-lic burning yards away, stipulated that no songs played on the stage could have been recorded professionally at any point. None of the musicians could be "professionals" in the sense that they could not have earned their living playing music full-time. And as noted, one member of the dupla had to play a viola while the other played a six-string guitar; two regular six-strings, common among nontraditional duplas, simply would not do. The afternoon's music was heard by a rotating audience of about twenty, composed mostly of passersby on their way into and out of the garlic burning, and for the most part accompanied the cooking and eating. The songs culminated in the prizewinning traditional dupla and song; this year it was the local Suleiman and Marcos Canela for "The Flower of Goiana," (flower from the Central-Southern state of Goiás).

As time passed and both the garlic burning and the música caipira competition came to a close, activity started to pick up in the other areas of the park. The sky darkened, and spectators began to arrive for the evening's rodeo events. On that particular Saturday, these events included the ever-popular bull riding, as well as family team penning. As a special treat, bull rider Ednei Caminhas would attempt to stay the required eight seconds on the bull advertised as the meanest in Brazil: Bandido.[5] (He failed.) Comic presentations, pyrotechnics, and a children's soccer game punctuated these events. As these attractions drew to a close toward midnight, many hours after the caipira musicians had sung their final chords, people started to arrive in droves for the evening's música sertaneja performance. Tonight would feature the famous dupla Rionegro and Solimões, which had actually won the old-fashioned viola competition here back in 1986, before going commercial. They would be followed by the up-and-coming brothers Edson and Hudson. Close to seventy thousand ticket buyers were expected, and while some of them had come to see the rodeo events themselves and the music, at least a third would not arrive until the first dupla was almost ready to step in front of the microphones; the head of security informed me that this was common. Many had come chiefly for the commercial country music.

As the rodeo events wound down and the organizers prepared for the two duplas sertanejas, the contrast between música caipira and música sertaneja could not have been clearer. Música caipira, with its explicitly traditionalist bent, attracted far smaller crowds and was relegated almost entirely to folkloric sidelines, while its commercial offshoot, música sertaneja, packed the central arena. Although música caipira's performers and fans could claim the kind of "roots" that would make a cowboy cooking competition using turn-of-the-century methods feel more authentic, música sertaneja seemed to be what most ticket buyers had paid to see. The divide between these two rural musical genres so clearly enacted at Barretos impacts broad domains of cultural production which we will now explore. But let us first inquire into the nature of "genre" itself.

Defining Genre

A genre certainly "goes without saying because it comes without saying" (Bourdieu 1977, 167). In other words, genre is frequently inculcated below the level of consciousness, forming an aspect of what Bourdieu calls "habitus": a durable body of dispositions that shapes and is shaped by participants without their having to think much about it. However, genre is also linked to conscious doings, as a form of ideologically oriented activity. Genre, thus, forms part of the "horizon" of shared practices (Hanks 1996, 259–65) that participants consciously and unconsciously use to direct their activities across various domains of social life.

Genre, on its simplest level, may be thought of as a kind of template for making and understanding a "text," musical or otherwise.[6] In this sense, a genre is "a constellation of systemically related, co-occurrent formal features and structures that serves as a conventionalized orienting framework for the production and reception of discourse" (Bauman 2001, 79). But following Bourdieu (1993a, 1993b), we must also understand genres as embedded within "fields of cultural production." This is another way of saying that we must address genre's "systematicity." To clarify systematicity using a famous example, that of sonic systematicity in languages: within a language, a given sound (or phoneme) represents not only the demarcation of a meaningful portion of the vast spectrum of humanly possible sounds for the establishment of meaningful difference—the kind of difference that marks, say, "beg" and "bug" as differently sounding words that *also* happen to *mean* something different. But as we note this difference of meaning that hinges upon a remarked difference of sound (/e/ instead of /u/), we must also understand that the differing sounds involved omit an even greater number of other possibilities. In Standard Average North-American English, "beg" spoken nasally by someone with a head cold does *not* result in a different word than "beg" spoken by someone breathing clearly, despite the fact that this nasal "beg" differs from the sound of the not-congested "beg."[7] "Bug," however, *does* result in a different word. Another way of saying this is that elements in a given system (a phonetic system, for instance) are defined as much by what they *are* as by what they are *not*.

And so it goes for genres, musical and otherwise. Practitioners of música caipira and música sertaneja view themselves, and are placed by listeners, producers, and critics, in relation to other musical genres which they at times resemble, and at times distance themselves from. This requires position-taking within a field of other possibilities, a rejection of, or affiliation with, those other positions. Thus, we can see that intergeneric practice forms one of the pillars of a coherent theory of performativity. Participants in a given communicative event require some sense of "what is going on here." In other words, participants need to be able to determine the extent to which a particular "set" to the message has been successful or not (Herzfeld 1996, 147). Genre is one of the primary ways in which they co-create this sense of success or failure in real time. Performativity therefore requires a metacritical faculty whereby participants continually monitor "what is going on here" for its suitability, or lack of suitability, for inclusion in a transforming set of co-occurrent features. And in this monitoring, genres change. They are therefore not fixed entities that participants bring out from some cognitive toolbox in order to apply them, returning them to the box once the work is done. As we shall see, through their interrelation, genres are continually being worked out, worked upon, and worked through.

Boundary Work as Metageneric Practice

Within the rural field, música caipira and música sertaneja are involved in a kind of dance with each other. For starters, música caipira's listeners sometimes criticize música sertaneja as "fake." This criticism helps música caipira to fashion an "unreal" against which to counterpose itself, a "reality" further abetted by its trumpeting of itself as pure in every sung note and plucked string.[8] On the other side of things, música sertaneja has its own ways of naturalizing itself, often by promulgating what is "realistic," what "people want to hear," or what "sells" (see chapter 6 for consideration of how these beliefs impact circulation).

One of the ways in which the continual emergence of genres becomes evident is through precisely this sort of boundary contestation. With the emergent quality of generic practice in mind, we can see that caipira and sertanejo oppositionally fashion distinct "ideologies" and "hegemonies" (J. Comaroff and J. L. Comaroff 1991, 23, 24). In more detail, proponents of música caipira may portray música sertaneja as a deformation of their own legitimate caipira practice via unwanted rationalization and urbanization. With irritation, *sertaneja* singers might respond that those who cleave to música caipira are being too old-fashioned to recognize "progress." Música caipira fans and performers sometimes take offense at the notion that their music has anything to do with música sertaneja; according to them, at such moments of offense, música sertaneja represents a profound forgetting, while caipiras remember. But música sertaneja practitioners worry that too much tightly circumscribed remembering is not a good thing; continuing to perform the same old material that the música caipira crowd so cleaves to means that rural music will get left behind, and that it will receive little radio play—a suspicion that appears well founded in light of música caipira's minuscule sales and radio statistics. I use "might" and "sometimes" here because where and how these positions are taken up depends on the context of interaction, as we shall see.

Distinguishing caipira from sertanejo involves looking at how their different position-takings police the interdiscursive "gap" between current performances and antecedent ones (Bauman and Briggs 1992, 149; Silverstein and Urban 1998, 2). Música caipira keeps the gap between antecedent and present-tense performances small, underscoring the importance of fidelity to what came before. Caipira duos perform classics from a tacitly agreed-upon repertoire, while fans use performers from a Golden Age (roughly 1930–60) to classify the vocal, instrumental, and storytelling styles of today. Commentators describe caipira dupla Zé Mulato and Cassiano, for instance, as "three-in-one" because they mingle characteristics from three duplas of yore: Zé Carreiro's and Carreirinho's romantic blending of a deep melodic bass voice (Zé) with a higher harmony voice (Cassiano); the superb viola work on par with that of Tião Carreiro (Zé); and the funny storytelling of Alvarenga and Ranchinho, most of it executed by Zé, with Cassiano providing short bursts of verbal support. Critical comments such as these are just one of many ways in which interdiscursive gaps are minimized in practicing música caipira.

Música sertaneja, by contrast, enlarges such gaps, striving for what its performers and fans describe as a rural "modernity." This is figured in terms of standard language use instead of a hick accent, electric or electronic instrumentation over the acoustic, and ornately produced live shows instead of simple two-microphone affairs. At the same time performers hold true to the notion that their music must speak both to and from the heart (*coração*). At other musical sites, such as Brazilian rock 'n' roll, to use just one example among many, a large gap between current and preexisting practice might point to something like the "originality" of the band. Here, however, música sertaneja's celebrated gap employs selected fragments of the ostentatiously modern, somewhat paradoxically in order to highlight the past (a process we will explore in detail in chapter 8).

Statements about generic coherence or lack thereof enact interdiscursivity, underscoring the textual play of the rural field and establishing distance from antecedent productions, or proximity to them. Some common polemics within the rural field appear, paraphrased, below. Note that the first numbered point (e.g., "1") contains the paraphrased opinion in italics, while the decimal that follows (e.g., "1.2"), contains the essential context of the utterance and identity of the speaker(s).

1) *Música sertaneja, that ultrapopular and debased musical genre that sells so well these days, has nothing whatsoever to do with its música caipira roots, or even with what we called música sertaneja back in the 1960s and 1970s. More than half of what currently gets called música sertaneja is really just pop with two voices.*

1.2) A radio DJ in his fifties in Itapira uttered this. It was an opinion matched in numerous contexts by those who currently practice música caipira or what they feel to be "real" música sertaneja.

2) *Referring to all rural musical genres as música sertaneja, a practice that began in the late 1950s, was a mistake from the start. In fact, música sertaneja was always specifically the music of the rural Northeast of Brazil, although the term began to be used, wrongly, to refer to all rural genres in the late 1950s. Today, we should call rural music of the Northeast música sertaneja, and music of the Central-South música caipira, and all other debased forms, simply pop.*

2.2) Cornélio Pires's nephew, Ariovaldo Pires, whose role in the practice of rural music on the radio between 1930 and 1970 can hardly be overstated, wished to correct what he perceived to be erroneous terminology in his 1985 biography by Ferrete.

3) *Calling us caipira is just fine. In fact, despite the past pejorative connotations of the term, nowadays it's flattering because calling us sertanejo could lead to us getting confused with those other guys.*

3.2) A prose translation of the lyrics that open current música caipira duo Zé Mulato and Cassiano's 1998 record *Sailor among the Generations* (or, *Sailor within the State of Minas Gerais*). We will encounter a version of this claim in chapter 7.

4) *Current ultrapopular música sertaneja is the only popular Brazilian music that really speaks from the heart. It makes you emotional. It grew out of música caipira.*

4.2) A São Paulo lawyer working for the city and driving me to a bar for a night out uttered this, while playing me Leandro and Leonardo. Leandro had just passed away. This opinion was echoed at música sertaneja shows, in fan club chat rooms on the Internet, in letters sent by fans to magazines, and in countless informal conversations and interviews.

5) *Música caipira is all well and good. We used to sing it. Our música sertaneja grew out of our wanting to make música caipira modern. And why should we be ruled by tradition? Most of the backcountry farmers use machines and have the Internet. Why can't we update too?*

5.2) Música sertaneja dupla Chitãozinho and Xororó (Nepomuceno 1999). We will revisit this claim below, including the linguistic ground of "modernity" that it, in part, rests upon.

These statements, culled from written and oral sources, forefront the importance of the boundary work that distinguishes caipira from sertanejo, constituting the rural musical field.

Within discussions at concerts, around the bar table over a beer, in newspapers, on television, in cover notes, or on the bus, differing positions on Brazilian music and the contrasting perspectives on society that such differences index often hinge on definitions. Indeed, statements about genre voiced in this fashion reveal a preoccupation with definitional practice. Commentators operate according to the logic that finding the correct label for past songs and singers has considerable import for the present. This suggests more than a simple fixation on reference. Polemics surrounding genre place the act of labeling squarely within the domain of musical production, as participants state their desire that correct labeling will *conjure* modes of participation as much as it presupposes existing ones. And for this reason, the rural field shows no sign of tiring of the quarrel over nomenclatures, fashioning new ones that future contributors may accept, reverse, or ignore altogether. Some claim that bona fide "música sertaneja" (which they sometimes also call *música sertaneja raíz*) applies solely to material recorded between 1930 and 1960. In those days, they report, traditional male duplas harmonized in parallel thirds and accompanied themselves on acoustic guitar and ten-string guitar, without so much sloppy romance and "Americanization" of instrumentation and melody. Others argue that the accordion was always a crucial component of this equation, such that duplas were always backed up by an accordion player.[9] Whatever the instrumental configuration, for those adhering to this position, what currently passes for música sertaneja is not only a pale imitation. It is more serious than that, in that it is considered to be an injunction to forget the real instantiations of a genre ostensibly about remembering.

The classificatory schemas of scholars both absorb and enact this back and forth. In 1988, for instance, Mário de Araujo (1988), using the term for kitschy, tacky, or tawdry (*brega*), suggested that commercially successful música sertaneja should be called *brega sertaneja*. Four years later, Suzel Reily, having read Araujo, but following instead the recommendations of musicians she worked with in the periphery of the city of São Paulo, proposed that commercial rural music ought to be called *música sertaneja jovem* (youth música sertaneja) (1992). And one year after this, Martha Ulhôa de Carvalho, having read both Araujo and Reily, proposed that the genre ought to be termed *música sertaneja romântica* (romantic) (1993). Note that the establishment of nomenclatures in each case selects an attribute of sertanejo, making it emblematic of the genre as a whole. In these three cases the attributes are quality of sound and inability to control emotions (brega), audience orientation (jovem), and subject matter of lyrics fused to melodic formula (romântica).

Thus do these scholars and other commentators hope to establish greater precision. The construction of a particular nomenclature sometimes forms part of an attempt to correct the occlusion of what is portrayed as a genre's true historical development (see Ferrete 1985; J. d. S. Martins 1975). Arguments that a particular set of terms errs sometimes climax with the notion that such reckless imprecision impedes the preservation of tradition, silencing music deemed legitimately Brazilian, which is to say, folkloric. At other times, arguments establish the notion that the need to apply so many qualifiers covers over the essential similarity of old-fashioned rural music to its current practice. Here, the argument is that current practice simply continues what went on before; it's *all* just música sertaneja, so what's the fuss? By this rationale, the application of so many qualifiers impedes the ability to simply listen to rural songs.

An ethnography of the elastic space between música sertaneja and música caipira, as revealed by the details of the matrices in which music circulates, together with such arguments over terminology, may be condensed into a list of distinctions and approximations (see table 3). Listeners and performers provided some of these categories in the act of discussing their approach to rural music. Other categories arose through analysis of conversations, shows, magazines, newspapers, radio stations, television programs, record stores, and illegal CD kiosks in bus stations and on street corners.

Table 3. Generic Features of Música Caipira and Música Sertaneja.

Generic Quality	Música Sertaneja	Música Caipira
Language (see below)	Monoglot Standard Portuguese[i]	Nasalized, hick with its hard /r/s, /r/s substituted for /l/s, and dropped /s/s at the end of plural words; Caipira vocabulary—i.e., Central-Southern hick
Instrumentation	Synthesizer, drum kit, electric bass and guitar	Viola and guitar, or, occasionally, viola with limited acoustic bass and simple acoustic percussion; orchestra of violas
Production	Digital; multitrack; heavy use of enhancement effects such as reverb, compression, and pitch-correction; various effects may be used on guitars	Digital and sometimes 2″ analogue tape; minimal tracks and layering; limited to no "reverb"
Licit Sales[ii]	10–13 percent	Less than 6 percent
Illicit Sales[iii]	Approximately 20 percent	Approximately 10 percent (música caipira); *música de viola* 0 percent
Dress	Hip urban or American country	Caipira (straw hats and checkered shirts); or in the case of música de viola, casual (jeans or khakis and a plain buttoned shirt)
Borrowings	North American country; all forms mentioned for música caipira	The Paraguaian *guarânia* and *rasqueado*; some Mexican *ranchero* and *mariachi*; Argentinean *tango*; *bolero*—all pre-1980
Theme and Topic	Heterosexual breakup; unrequited passion; the intensity, impossibility, and inevitability of love; occasionally, the enjoyment to be had at rodeos	Sadness due to isolation from nature or home; political humor; jilting and revenge; returning to the country after trying, unsuccessfully, to live in the city
Products Sold	Beer, furniture, electronics; pickup trucks; rodeo tickets and products	Frequently appears in concert halls, or "cultural spaces" built by banks such as Banco do Brasil in Rio de Janeiro and Itaú in São Paulo

(*Table 3. continued*)

Generic Quality	Música Sertaneja	Música Caipira
Performance Contexts	Rodeo; "country" dance clubs; radio stations; mainstream television variety shows; stadium shows	Rare spots allotted for folkloric content at rodeo; folkloric radio and TV; roots music clubs; the "cultural" performance spaces of banks like Banco do Brasil and Itaú; universities and other educational institutions such as SESC; the MST (Movimento dos Trabalhadores Rurais sem Terra, or Rural Landless Workers' Movement)
Song Forms	Classics from the música caipira and música sertaneja repertoire; Latin pop music's romantic ballad; American country; Mexican ranchero and mariachi	*Toada; moda de viola; cururú; pagode de viola; batuque;* these are often named in performance and almost always on record jackets (see chap. 7)
Configuration of Singing voices	Duo—usually of brothers	Duo—usually of brothers; also, solo viola with no voice
Harmony	Parallel thirds and sixths, with some limited soloing by the melody voice	Parallel thirds, and sometimes sixths, but the melody never solos
Radio Play	Romantic stations; música sertaneja/country stations; small-town mixed format stations	Cultural radio; limited play on MPB radio; small-town mixed format stations; "roots" segments of música sertaneja stations
Degree of Cultural Intimacy	Extremely high, such that many users conceal their affection for the music	Medium to high; users experiencing the music as "folkloric" are less likely to deny that they listen to it in certain contexts based on intimacy

i. Silverstein's treatment of Monoglot Standard English could easily be employed in a Brazilian context, where a Brazilian *Academia Brasileira de Letras* ostensibly directs acceptable rules for Portuguese from Rio. Though this centralizing institution modeled on that of France is frequently derided for its inefficacy, it pronouncements on language do have a concrete effect on practice, for instance, the removal of written accent-markings deemed gratuitous in the 1970s.

ii. Approximately 50 percent of all sales in Brazil are of legal copies, made by record companies themselves.

iii. Approximately 50 percent of all sales in Brazil are of illegal copies, most likely made by entrepreneurs using legitimate CD plants owned by the Big Five recording companies.

Table 3 presents a broad set of differences that spill over from music into economic and political spheres. In this way we can see that the interplay between these two rural genres creates a dialogic field in which participants are called upon by, and call upon, these genres in various social domains. Battles over naming and claiming are part of this. One of the best places to begin to explore the import of the boundaries of genre for elaborating the interrelationship of musical and social structures is in the domain of language. An archaeology of language use in rural genres illustrates the way in which this music laminates together race, social class, space, and time.

Minimal Effort and Central-Southern Hick Talk

Performers, listeners, and critics suggest that the qualities of the language in which lyrics are sung and in which performers speak onstage between songs, conceived phonologically and semantically, furnish one of the most significant means of distinguishing caipira from sertanejo. More precisely, the marked linguistic practice of caipira is interpreted as being highly localized to the antiquated interior of the Central-South, for better and for worse. Música sertaneja, on the other hand, despite the fact that it employed linguistic conventions currently deemed caipira as late as the 1960s, today aligns itself with Monoglot Standard Brazilian Portuguese—an alignment most often read as the *absence* of a hick usage. Here, "Monoglot Standard" refers to a set of practices surrounding the hegemonic reproduction of an ostensibly clearer mode of using Portuguese (see Silverstein 1996). This has a history; in seeking to modify their stance vis-à-vis caipira pronunciation and vocabulary, música sertaneja performers and producers of the 1960s attempted to delocalize their linguistic-musical practice. They sought to escape from caipira ways of talking because *caipirese* was believed to be a sort of "restricted code" that stipulated inferior cognitive abilities (Bernstein 1977). When this shift in language use took place, rural modes of identification had been associated with racial classificatory schemas applied in a Lamarckian way to the countryside. They had also been associated with a backward glance rather than the forward-looking, future orientation so important for the economic "miracles" desired by Brazilian governments between 1964 and 1985. Transforming the way in which music employed language thus represented an attempt to remove a degenerative and antiquated component from the rural side of the urban-rural divide.

In the present, the difference between caipira and sertanejo ways of talking and singing indicates that language use is thought to create a distinction between past and present, country and city, degenerate and progressive, working class and elite. As this analysis will show, much of this preoccupation with language fixates on how it *sounds*. Concomitantly, it also reinforces the idea that language, particularly sung language, participates in cultural production and reproduction in an unmediated way. In other words, the logic of language use in these rural musical contexts rests upon the idea that language makes culture happen directly and effectively, and the other way around. To capture a dialect is to capture a locality, or, less charitably, to employ a dialect is to be trapped in an inferior place and way of being.

Analysis of the dynamics of the Portuguese language in the rural field must begin with the concept of "caipira" itself as it came to be understood in the late nineteenth and early twentieth centuries. Roughly translatable as "hillbilly" or "hick," in the early twentieth century the urban middle classes sometimes used "caipira" as an epithet to describe the supposedly lazy and shiftless residents of the backcountry of the state of São Paulo. Newspapers around the turn of the century often contained cartoons featuring the unfortunate caipira as resigned, sad, and dull. Proponents of progress such as prominent writer Monteiro Lobato cited the caipira as evidence of social decay. In essays published in *The State of São Paulo* newspaper in 1914, Lobato created the stereotypical caipira character called Armadillo Joe, or *Jeca Tatú* (in name, if not in tone, the same Jeca of chapter 1), and described him as nothing short of an ailment. The final chapter of Lobato's book *Urupês* (1998), called "The Old Disease," was devoted to a description of the caipira, his habits and customs, and the ills he purportedly visited upon the nation.

According to Lobato, the caipira, accompanied by his vermin-filled dog, could be found sitting on the porch of his dilapidated shack smoking a corn-husk cigarette instead of working. Due to agricultural practices innocent of crop rotation, the caipira burned Brazil's virgin forests to prepare the ground for a planting schedule that would leave the soil exhausted in three years. When this exhaustion arrived, Lobato concluded, rather than replenishing the soil, Jeca simply moved on to repeat the process, gradually destroying the fertility of the interior. But despite the effectiveness of the caipira's perambulatory destruction of the backcountry, Lobato's Jeca was at root unspeakably lazy. Jeca was the enemy of a modernization that favored hard work; he was the "priest of the Grand Law of Least Effort" (Lobato 1998, 170). And this laziness was both evident in, and produced by, his language use, in which he neglected plurals and failed to pronounce words fully, cutting them off instead. Jeca also simplified certain vowel and consonant clusters and used archaic vocabulary. In short, for Lobato and his pro-modernization sympathizers, Jeca's tongue was as lazy as the arms and back he ought to have used in a more rigorous agriculture. Lobato wrote large portions of his essays and stories in caipira dialect to show that he knew of what he spoke.

In his incarnation as a public-health crusader during the First World War, Lobato moderated his tone with respect to Jeca, proposing that the ridiculous hick was the way he was because he was filled with parasites. In effect, Lobato now claimed that Jeca was "sick."[10] Directly addressing in print the Jeca he nonetheless still assumed was illiterate, Lobato wrote: "It has been proven that you [Jeca] have, in your blood and guts, a zoo of the worst kind. . . . It is this cruel bestiary that makes you pudgy, ugly, slothful, inert" (cited in Borges 1993). Though Lobato's second pronouncement might seem to have softened somewhat in obviating Jeca's direct responsibility for his destructive indolence, an essential attribute endured from Lobato's previous screed: the caipira was a health problem. Indeed, so powerful was the caipira's association with illness that a prominent pharmaceuticals firm used Jeca in leaflets circulated during the early twentieth century to educate the nation about concerns such as ringworm. Many of the people I interviewed in Campinas recalled these leaflets as a primary source of their stereotypes of the indolent and mentally impaired caipira.[11]

These treatments of the caipira used language as a way to address degeneration as a social disease. The concept of degeneration, fed by the popularity of Spencerian and Comtian approaches to society, contributed to the view that Brazilian society was an "organism" (Borges 1993, 235), and that the organism's problems might be viewed in terms of sickness: "from the 1880s through the 1920s, the national ailment that the medicalised social thought of Brazil most often diagnosed . . . was degeneration" (Borges 1993, 235). Such theories of degeneration did not simply revolve around skin color, though color was frequently at least a part of their argument. In this Brazilian context, race was a social category influenced by cumulative breeding within particular climatic zones and social classes. Language contributed to this cumulative process. Thus, interbreeding and lazy talking, in social circumstances deemed isolated, backward, and climatically challenging, led to the proliferation of this retrograde type.

As we have seen, such racial politics had famously found voice in da Cunha's *Os Sertões* (*Rebellion in the Backlands*), where da Cunha argued that the leader of the religious and antistatist rebels (named Antônio Conselheiro—or Anthony the Counselor) was simply the natural product of a stunted landscape known as the Northeastern *sertão*. Similar ideas applied in the contemporaneous Central-South. Around the turn of the century the term "caboclo" was explicitly racial in its focus and pointed to the mixture of Portuguese with Indian. But it was the term "caipira," with its emphasis on degeneration in primitive, peripheral, and poor circumstances, that underscored early twentieth-century hegemonic racial theories even more than "caboclo." According to mainstream characterizations of this ruralized human type, the caipira's chief degenerate attributes were his laziness, his backwardness, his poverty, and his stupidity, all evident in, and reproduced by, his inadequate use of Standard Portuguese. In an early twentieth-century caipira grammar and dictionary largely sympathetic to Central-Southern hicks, journalist and dictionary-writer Amadeu Amaral described just this sort of view when he wrote about a nineteenth-century Rio-based intellectual who apparently feared establishing law schools anywhere in the state of São Paulo. The intellectual's idea was that merely operating there would be linguistically impossible since the clarity of legal discourse was at odds with the linguistically instantiated locality (Amaral 1982).

Such understandings of the caipira's language use were not universal, however. Also in the early twentieth century, jack-of-all trades Cornélio Pires suggested a positive valence of caipira as an antidote to the characterizations of Lobato and those who agreed with him. Pires was a kind of working-class intellectual who had held down numerous jobs, among them folkloricist, rural music popularizer, physical education teacher, circus tent director, newspaper copy editor, brick factory owner, and troop entertainer for the rebellious São Paulo forces that had attempted to overthrow the newly centralizing national government in 1932. He copiously replied to Lobato in print (Pires 1927, 5) and onstage.[12] For Pires, the caipira was a wily and self-aware backcountry type. Pires's caipira, with his dry wit, sparseness of self-expression, and laid-back manner, was able to criticize the absurdities of modernity incisively. For instance, in one Pires song about a streetcar, "Bonde Camarão," literally "Shrimp" Trolley (a colloquial reference to its shape and color), the ostensibly hapless caipira's simplicity allows him to comment on the strangeness of cramming human beings into tiny spaces without regard for old-time proprieties of gender, hierarchy, and religion. Had urban life entirely dismantled important social categories, the caipira narrator in the song wondered, to great comic effect? Pires's caipira was furthermore able to voice the great sadness that many Brazilians felt about urbanization, a sadness found in, for instance, the song "As Tristezas do Jeca."

Pires's poetry, published initially in newspapers and later compiled into best-selling books, was voiced in caipira dialect. His work partook of a category of literary production dubbed "regional," which was, at the time, growing in popularity both in an expanding city of São Paulo and in the interior of the state. Pires mirrored his literary use of caipira language in live contexts. At a famous show at Protestant MacKenzie University in the city of São Paulo in 1910, Pires laid the groundwork for a kind of performance art in which he recreated caipira rituals and told caipira stories, transforming himself into a Central-Southern hick. In this first show, Pires and his caipira helpers put on a hillbilly funeral, complete with songs and amusing stories about the deceased, followed by a short lecture delivered by Pires on the subject of hick customs and speech. Pires's caipira proudly employed the hick diction that Lobato had used in a written form to conjure the height of ignorance. Pires also brought duplas from the countryside to sing. But most importantly, the linguistic features Lobato had marked as backward pointed, for Pires, to an incisiveness that allowed the caipira to shortcut urban bombast. In one of Pires's stories, a stuck-up urbanite on a walk in the back-country stops at a caipira's house for some water. While the caipira fetches the drink, the urbanite asks if various pictures of people in the humble home are family members, to which the caipira repeatedly replies "yes." "Is this your mother? . . . Yes. . . . Are these your children? . . . Yes." Finally, the urbanite settles on a photograph of a donkey and asks his host if this, too, is a family member. "Oh, that one's not a picture at all, sir," replies the hick, returning deferentially with the water. "It's a mirror."

Through a brief analysis of Lobato and Pires, we can see the way in which the caipira becomes a site of contestation beginning in the early twentieth century, with one group portraying hick backwardness as a social blight and another using it as a way to comment upon urbanity as overconfidence. Across both appropriations, features of *caboclo* talk, sometimes within songs and sometimes surrounding them, provide a way of understanding the contemporaneous linguistic grounds of rurality. Some differences exist, of course. Pires frequently inhabits the caipira as a social persona and clearly uses hick language with pride, which is not the case for Lobato. But at no point does Pires accuse Lobato of having gotten caipira diction wrong. Both essentially agree on features that linguistically represent Central-Southern hickdom. These may be viewed through one of Pires's poems—a sonnet (of form *abab abab cc deed*) called "The Ideal Caboclo" from his first book *Caipira Muse* (Pires 1985):

Ai, **seu** moço,	Ai, **senhor** moço,	Well, young sir,
eu só **quiria**	eu só **queria**	I would only want
P'ra minha **filicidade**	**Para** minha **felicidade**	For my happiness
Um **bão** fandango	Um **bom** fandango	A good dance
por dia,	por dia,	each day,
E um pala	E uma pala	And a good
de qualidade.	de qualidade.	poncho.
Pórva, espingarda	**Polva**, espingarda	Gunpowder, a gun,
e cutia	e cutia	and rodents to hunt
Um facão	Um facão	A big knife
fala-verdade,	fala-verdade,	that means business
E **ûa** viola	E **uma** viola	And a harmonious
de **harmunia**	de harmonia	*viola*
P'ra chorá	**Para chorar**	To cry away
minha **sódade**.	minha **saudade**.	my longings.
Um rancho	Um rancho	A little farm
na **bêra** d'água	na beira d'água	on the riverbank
Vára-de-anzó,	Vara de anzó,	A fishing pole, a watering hole,
pôca magua,	pôca magua,	and a whip
Pinga **bôa**	Pinga boa	Good *pinga*
e **bão** café . . .	e **bom** café	and good coffee
Fumo forte de sobejo,	Fumo forte de sobejo	Strong rope-tobacco
P'ra compretá	**Para completar**	To complete
meu desejo,	meu desejo	my desires
Cavallo **bão**—	Cavalo **bom**—	A good horse,
e **muié** . . .	e **mulher**.	and a good woman.

Pires's original poem, penned in caipira dialect in such a way that its readers might accurately *pronounce* what prescriptive grammarians of the time would have decried as "incorrect" Portuguese, appears above on the far left, as Pires published it. The middle column contains the poem as one might render it into Standard Portuguese. The far-right column translates the poem into English. The bold type in the first column draws attention to lexical items that Pires chose to render by transcribing caipirese pronunciation. Their corresponding standard forms are also in bold in the middle column for contrastive purposes, to make the following adumbration of caipirese easier to follow.

These types of dialect-laden texts, composed of songs, written and spoken poems, and stories between songs, oriented users to the link between certain features of language and Central-Southern locality. Thus, the items in bold above were the means by which Pires linguistically fashioned his caipira self as a token of the social type that hailed from the humble interior of São Paulo. Comparing these versions reveals the sort of phonological patterns Pires chose to mark. Similar patterns are easy to identify in present residents of the São Paulo interior, no doubt in part *because* of Pires's selection of them back in the early twentieth century. Among these are the substitution of /r/ for /l/ in evidence in the poem in what would be the Standard Portuguese term *completar* (to complete)—here, *compretá*. This word reveals a further tendency within Pires's version of the caipira dialect—the deletion of /r/ in word-end position, particularly in verbal infinitives, but also, for example, in *senhor* (sir or mister, *seu* in the poem) and *mulher* (woman, *muié* in the poem). This way of pronouncing the word for woman in Central-Southern Portuguese leads to vocalization of the palatal lateral /lh/ sound found in words like *milho* (corn) and *velho* (old); following the pattern of the caipira pronunciation of *mulher* as *muié*, the /lh/ sound simplifies, creating *mio* and *veio* respectively. The denasalization of a nasal vowel in word-end position, fairly typical of caipira talk, can be seen in *bão* (line three of the poem), a word that speakers and singers strategically emphasize to index caipira speech in 1910 as today. The caipira deletion of the semivowel of the falling diphthong in *saudade* (nostalgia, longing) is evidenced in Pires's *sodade*. Note from a distributionalist perspective that not all of these features are the exclusive province of Central-Southern speech; many of them appear with some frequency in other regional dialects throughout Brazil. For instance, the contraction of *para* (for, to) into *p'ra*, may currently be heard in locations urban and rural, northern and southern. However, the concatenation of these various phonological features marks this text as striving concertedly for caipira.

What is worth underlining here is the set of beliefs behind the notion that the caipira way of talking might be rendered by transcribing and speaking selected aspects of its phonology, together with some marked lexical items, and incorporating these into rurally themed poems, songs, and stories. Pires was not alone in his preoccupation with the way caipiras talked and the way the transcription or recitation of that talk might contribute to an understanding of Brazil in all its regional wonder. Though the valences were switched, as noted above, Lobato employed the same linguistic features in his writing in order to convey hickishness as a danger. But more important, the aforementioned Amadeu Amaral, Pires's uncle, produced the first detailed analysis of caboclo language of the Central-South, and in it, devoted considerable time to phonology. In this work, Amaral asserted that language was a direct and complete means of indexing culture. Channeling a version of the Herderian belief in language and folk as intertwined, he believed that a virtually unmediated correlation existed between a way of talking (accessed, as noted, mostly phonetically, though somewhat lexically) and a social type. Such ideas circulated broadly. São Paulo journalist Hélio Damante, a contemporary to Pires, summed up the folkloricist's efforts by suggesting that in focusing on the caipira's way of talking, Pires had grasped the most effective way of "capturing" the caboclo's very "spirit" (quoted in 1999). In effect, a focus on phonology was thought to be part of Pires's genius: "Transforming those phonemes via graphic representations, faithfully facilitating the capture of that [caboclo] reality—was something that had not been explored before Cornélio Pires" (1999).

Despite such celebrations of Pire's written caipira, not in evidence in this poem, but crucial to understand, is the hardened caipira /r/, undoubtedly the clearest index that the speaker hails from the Central-Southern interior. This /r/ sound was, in Pires's day, as it is today, a significant marker of caipira role-inhabitance. Standard Portuguese proposes an uvular mode in creating this sound, where the back of the tongue articulates with the uvula, as in the French *raton*. The caipira, by contrast, articulates this sound decidedly toward the front, as in the English *right*. In addition to this hardened /r/, other prosodic features in evidence both in recordings made by Pires and in current efforts to render the caipira live are not recoverable from Pires's purely written texts and would have required live delivery to be conveyed. Among the most important of these is the highly nasalized way of singing and talking, combined with a slow delivery; caipiras take their time. But whether Pires's innovativeness was to be found in his creation of a way to translate the sound of caboclo talk into writing so that others could *read* it the way it was supposed to sound, or whether his genius was in getting prosodic and suprasegmental features correct so that his live audiences could *hear* hillbilly speech the way it was supposed to be spoken, the emphasis that he and many of his contemporaries placed on the sonic aspects of language is nonetheless clear. What was important was to capture the *sound* of the caipira because, in so doing, one might capture his *spirit*.

This is not to say that an interest in vocabulary was absent from such linguistic analyses. Pires published a glossary at the end of his first book, *Musa Caipira* (1985 [1910]), which he later republished in other works prefaced by the cheeky label "Brazilianisms, archaic expressions, and corruptions" (Pires 1927, 173). Similarly, despite treating phonology in some detail and syntax much less, Amaral devotes the burden of his pages to listing words transcribed in the Pires mode, providing entries such as those found in a dictionary. Amaral argues that rather than corrupting Standard Portuguese, the caipira in fact *preserves* antiquated terms and pronunciations; this is a layover from the past, then. But note the importance of phonetics, with semantics in its service. A substantial portion of both Amaral's backcountry dictionary and Pires's glossary operated, once again, on the sonic plane in showing how caipira pronunciation was what was distinct, but at the same time, they were always at pains to show the Standard word "underneath" its backcountry gloss. Note, for example, from Pires's "vocabulary": "**livé**—nível" (1927, 195, Pires's boldface), "**Siá**—Senhora . . . **Siô**—Senhor" (Pires 1927, 204). Such usages were thought to index the caipira's stuck-in-time quality in that they represented a Portuguese leftover from colonial times. Furthermore, this attention to lexical items in a sonic register also pointed to the caipira's tendency to *remove* syllables—to make things shorter, in sum, to expend less effort in pronouncing words than might be required in Standard. The caipira talked through his nose, without bothering to open his mouth much. Note the way in which the chronotopic parameters of this ideology function: the spatial and temporal isolation of the hick are presuppose and entailed by what are read as the "slow" aspects of his language use. This allows for the likes of Amaral, Pires, and even Lobato to hone in on clearly segmentable aspects of language which were particularly transparent to userly consciousness: the "simplified" pronunciation of certain terms, the substitution of certain phonemes, the elision of plurals, and so forth. The transition that a speaker of Standard would need to make in order to arrive at caipirese here becomes a question of substituting certain phonological features and lexical items (many of them phonological "simplifications" of Standard terms) in a relatively straightforward fashion, but always measured as a *subtraction* from the Standard.

Significant is the way in which caipira slowness in other domains of social life reinforced, and was reinforced by, slowness in language: slow to speak, slow *when* speaking, slow to change *ways* of speaking, and so on. Further subtractions were apparently in evidence in terms of prosodic variety. In opening his book's section on phonology, Amaral notes that caipira prosody is simply not like that of Standard, where "Portuguese," in his phrase, designates "Standard": "the general tone of the phrasing [of caipira] is slow, even, and equal, without the variety of inflexions, of tempos and dispersions that enrich the expression of emotions in the pronunciation of Portuguese" (Amaral 1982, 3). Yet another example of laziness by omission appears in the notion that the caipira language is filled with "conservations" from what are deemed previous, colonial phonologies. Pauses are longer. The lexicon "is, naturally, fairly restricted, in accordance with the simplicity of life and spirit, and therefore, with the scanty necessities for expression of those who speak" (Amaral 1982, 9). Amaral continues that the rural São Paulo vocabulary contains "elements native to the Portuguese used by the primitive colonizer—many of which have become archaic in refined language," and it contains "terms in use in the indigenous languages" (Amaral 1982, 9) left over from times in which contacts with Indians were more frequent than in the early twentieth century. All in all, the caipira's status as stuck in time seamlessly evidenced itself in his language, while his language continued to reinforce it. Amaral writes in the early twentieth century:

> Today's genuine caipira lives, with few differences, the way he lived two hundred years ago, with the same habits, the same customs, the same well of ideas. From this we can understand the willful conservation of so

many archaic features [of language]—and also so many special terms
which, though they still exist in European Portuguese, are at times entirely unknown, here in Brazil, among city people. (Amaral 1982, 17)

In this way, Amaral blurred the distinction between language and culture. The hick's language iconically indexed his having been sealed off
from urban change in a backward context of intermixture, nature, and
repose.

In part due to the overwhelming emphasis on the sonic components
of language use, music, a sonically focused communicative practice
(see chapter 7), provided a particularly salutary vehicle for promulgating things caipira. Ever the entrepreneur, Pires soon set out in just such
a musical direction. When Pires approached Columbia Records in 1929
with a request to record singing caipiras—a story famous among current rural musical practitioners, and one to which we turn in chapter
5—rural music in Brazil was not unheard of. For example, Catulo da
Paixão Cearense (awkwardly rendered in English as "Catulu of the Passion to be found in the Northeastern state of Ceará," referencing, in
highfalutin' fashion, Catullus) had launched a successful career in early
twentieth-century Rio de Janeiro as a sertanejo (backland) poet and
troubadour. He had written a series of oft-circulated rurally themed
songs, among them the still famous "Backland Moonlight" (Luar
do Sertão). In the Central-Southern region, recording star Paraguaçu
(whose artistic name was culled from the tremendous waterfall on
Brazil's border with Argentina) had sung various rurally themed sertanejo hits, among them murder-ballad "Cabocla Tereza" (or, Tereza,
Woman of the Backlands). But in all cases, performers of rural music
and poetry had made no attempt to recreate the language and special
sound of rural people. Catulo's and Paraguaçu's pronunciations were
largely Standard despite their laudatory approach to the countryside.
Moreover, they sang in the full-throated tenor of the salon, not the
pinched nasal whine of the backcountry. Therefore, Pires's intervention
in the musical domain in the early twentieth century opposed itself to
this standard sertão with his caipira records and shows.

A Broader Backcountry

To return to our archaeology of the term *caipira* itself and the implications of this term for its dialogic relation to *sertaneja*, despite the tre-

mendous popularity in terms of record sales and radio time that música caipira enjoyed, particularly in São Paulo in the 1930s and 1940s, the term *música caipira* fell into disuse in the 1960s. One aspect of its diminished importance as a marker of musical rurality lay in the commercial domain. Musicians describe a particular baptismal moment in which the term sertanejo returned to common usage. It is attributed to Palmeira (Diogo Mulero), a producer of rural records on two record labels (first RCA, and later, Chantecler) and a busy dupla performer himself. Palmeira was responsible for several innovations in the late 1950s. He was, for instance, the first to integrate electric guitars, basses, and drum kits into rural genres. The sertanejo coinage was yet another memorable contribution. During a recording session he was trying to categorize one of the country records he was producing, which Chantecler[13] was about to release: "Forget música caipira," his assistant reports that he exclaimed. "Now, it's all música sertaneja. These duos are recording *ranchero* songs [a Mexican rural genre], they're recording boleros [Spanish], tangos [Argentinian]. It's not caipira anymore. Now it's all sertanejo!" (quoted in Freire 1996, 84). In this way Palmeira suggested that while *caipira* referred specifically to the countryside of the Central-South, the term *música sertaneja* could index borrowings from the rural genres of other places in Brazil—the Northeast, for example—as well as various genres from Mexico, Spain, and Argentina.

The term sertanejo was, in a sense, available for just such employment as an indicator of rurality broadly speaking. The term sertão had taken on broad significance with da Cunha (1944), even though da Cunha referred specifically to the Northeast. Another sense of *sertão* arose in connection with novelist Guimarães Rosa's characterization of it in his first work of fiction, his 1946 collection of short stories, *Sagarana* (2001).[14] Rosa defined the sertão not simply as Northeastern, but rather as the interior of Brazil's Central-South as well. So it is not as though Palmeira executed this transformation without precedent, taking a term used to refer to Brazil's Northeastern rurality and applying it to the Central-South at one stroke.

Along with this transformation of the musical label, producers like Palmeira began an equally important and connected shift. They began to encourage songwriters and performers to produce rural musical song texts in Standard Portuguese. An emphasis on caipira pronunciation began to make way for Monoglot pronunciation and word choice. The reasons for this emerge from our analysis of caipira speech, above, reinforced by the relationship between Brazil's racial topology and its approach to social class. Those inhabiting rurality, across class lines, wished to transform the figuration of rural space in terms of racial degeneration that caipira speech iconically brought forth, while maintaining an emphasis on the dupla form, retrospection, and Jeca's all-encompassing desperation. The clearest way to enact this distancing was by standardizing hick language while maintaining an affect where males pined about lost loves and countrysides. Across the newly named música sertaneja's rather broader audience this represented a desire to transform the associations of the rural so as to excise its backward slide. It also sought to *modernize* rural genres by signaling the desire to participate in a broader speech community. No longer would the music limit itself entirely to a Central-Southern locality in its talk.

In song texts from this period, there is evidence as to why caipira practitioners of the time might agree with these changes, as Jeca's absorption in his grief becomes an absorption in "the city's" determination to misconstrue "the country." We see caipira narrators who had moved to the city from the countryside growing tired of the prejudice of city-dwellers. And the wily caipira of the Pires variety no longer provided a comic response, retorting, this time, with bitter words. Consider the song "The Hoe and the Pen," made famous by dupla Zico and Zeca in 1954. In the opening, an urbanite, referred to as the "pen," goes for a walk in the countryside and comes upon a rural worker, the "hoe." The "humble" hoe moves to greet the pen, who recoils in horror at the latter's filthiness and reminds the hoe that he should remember his station. The pen brushes shoulders with important people, such as the wealthy and the politicians, and he writes down their ideas and laws. A rural worker should not, the pen suggests, forget this. Note that both characters are workers, which makes the rural laborer's response all that much more appropriate, though it takes the arrogant pen off guard. The hoe informs his writerly acquaintance that his haughtiness is ill placed since he, the hoe, is the one responsible for the fundamental material production that allows the pen and his cronies to survive:

> The hoe responded: who hits the earth
> To clothe and feed your patrons?
> I came first in this world—back to the time of Adam.
> If I didn't sustain it, there would be no learning.
> Get away, you proud pen, shame of your generation

Your high nobility is nothing but pretentiousness
You say that you write everything?
I'll bet there's one thing you don't write.
It's a pretty word called education. (Zico and Zeca 1954)[15]

The rural musicians who cited this song as evidence of the continued prejudice against caipiras in the course of my fieldwork in 2004 did so with anger, stating that what marks the caipira nowadays is not so much that he's dirty. What marks the caipira after all this time is still the way he talks. The minute a caipira opens his mouth, that *sound* gives him away. With this song in mind, largely cleansed of hick diction, we can more accurately discern one of the crucial axes of the transition from caipira to sertanejo, as well as the current practice of distinguishing between them. Indeed, far from the corporate, top-down imposition that the move from caipira to sertanejo is often portrayed as being by current traditionalists (see, for example, a diatribe voiced during a show by Zé Mulato and Cassiano in chapter 7), practitioners of what had once been termed música caipira seemed content to adopt the new música sertaneja label and more Standard pronunciation.

This attempt to move musical practice into a more modern space by way of language had important consequences for the way in which rural genres developed in the course of the twentieth century. And it continues to have implications for the way in which the two rural genres approach and retreat from each other. Furthermore, this analysis reveals the way in which generic boundary work plays a crucial role in rural performativity, recruiting domains of social life such as race, social class, space, and time into musical practice.

~ 5

Teleologies of Rural Disappearance

INTERPRETING RURAL MUSIC

> The point here is that students who wish to critically assess
> the position of *the* peasants in rural society must first come
> to terms with *the images* of them. Failure to do so runs the
> risk of pursuing a reified type, a will-o'-the-wisp that has been
> projected onto the countryside by urban intellectuals.
> —MICHAEL KEARNEY, *Reconceptualizing the Peasantry*

The dialogic tension between rural musical genres is in part made
possible by interpretive practices that are used both to make sense
of and to fashion musical texts. This chapter concerns modes of understanding rural music in Brazil through the twentieth and into the
twenty-first century. Rural music relies upon ideas about "the country"
that, in turn, require calculated elisions. The countryside must be a
place of simplicity in social relations, economic production, and political action. Signs of social complexity, economic diversity, layered identity, and multiplicity of communicative practice must be temporarily
erased in order for rural performativity to function. This necessitates
the selection of particular details in telling about the country. We will
examine the elisions that notions of country rely upon by comparing
the story of Brazilian rural music's "first recording" with journalistic
and academic accounts of disappearing "peasant life" by way of "urban
migration." Across these domains, we will consider the way in which
tropes of rurality rely upon fully inhabiting social, emotional, and economic disempowerment.

With respect to the way that modes of understanding function, I take
it for granted that rather than providing some kind of supplement to an
ostensibly underlying activity, interpretation constitutes an important
aspect of any practice *as* that practice takes place. As Geertz (1973a,
452) has shown and the linguistic-anthropological literature on meta-

pragmatics confirms in considerably more detail (see, in particular, the papers in Lucy 1993), interpretation does not exist at some comfortable distance from communicative practice. Rather, metadiscourse (Bauman 2005) always emerges as a centrally constitutive feature of any action. As we have discussed throughout, the capacity for categorizing "what is currently happening here" is an essential aspect of social life. Rurality takes shape as a cluster of features, available to actors at certain times and in certain places, within a field of cultural production. These features include: a set of possibilities and impossibilities for the way rural genres take shape, which Hanks (1987, 672) has referred to as forms of generic "finalization"; modes of role inhabitance that participants may call upon in emergent interaction (A. Fox 2004, 42); and structures of voicing whereby interactants may align themselves consciously and/or unconsciously across communicative space (Silverstein 1999).

The interpretive practices brought to bear on "country" under consideration in this chapter most often rely on formalisms that sample materialist (country is economic relations), literalist (country is spatial relations), and temporalist (country is the past) approaches to social life. These readings key "country" almost exclusively to some durable concatenation of listeners and musicians "out there"—most often, a poorly delineated social category referred to as "rural migrants," though also "the working class." "Country's" signification is limited to an essentializable social attribute, or, in more recent scholarship, a badge of something called "identity" for some strictly demarcated group, fixable in terms of race, social class, occupation, and educational level. The kinds of stereotyping in play across these essentialisms are central not only to musical practice itself, in part defining what the "country" may be. Such essentialisms also undergird the maintenance of rurality's "intimacy."

The point I wish to make here is not that formalized interpretive practices are, in some sense, "wrong." It is not as though no one identifiable by means of conventional social indicators listens to Brazilian rural music, or that nothing might be learned through an analysis of who those people might, in a demographer's sense, *be*. Nor do I wish to indict scholars and journalists for failing to account for some "full" social context of musical circulation by oversimplifying. Rather, I am suggesting that analysis of Brazilian rural music must take full account of interpretive practices within the ambit of the field of musical production. This analysis thus argues that interpretive practices brought to bear on Brazilian rural musical genres not only partake of the same historical moment in which participants fashion their rural music. More emphatically, rurality cannot even be conceived of without its rural metadiscourse, here defined as its reflexive mode of monitoring and commenting upon interaction as it takes place.

Several historical examples elucidate the emergence of interpretive patterns in the present. Into the early twenty-first century, journalists, critics, and scholars comment upon "country," endorsing musical shows and criticizing, as well as blessing, given performers. Current commentary on rural genres in the news media, in the academy, and in numerous informal contexts overwhelmingly fashions some hypothetical "rural" subject, suspended between a bygone cooperative and inherently social lifestyle and a citified regime of individuated consumption where he may only behave as a consumer and producer. In most cases this rural subject is referred to as a "migrant" and the activities of this ideal type are then brought to bear to explain transformations of musical and vocal structure, stagecraft, dress, and record sales. Changes in musical genre must simply be the result of poor farmers coming to the city and performing an ostensibly transparent procedure known as "urbanizing" their music. Hapless country-born wanderers are "pushed" from the backlands and "pulled" toward the city by the usual cast of "forces." This focusing in on a stereotyped individual as representative of some musical demographic—a sort of Jeca—relies upon essentialist modes of explication. Such interpretive practices provide the grounds of possibility for rurality itself, not just for scholars and critics, but for practitioners of rural genres themselves.

Consistently, these lines of argument emphasize the perpetually disappearing pure rural that occurred to Raymond Williams one morning sitting at the breakfast table reading yet another newspaper article about the fact that the British countryside was gone for good, really and truly this time: for *good* (Williams 1973). He'd been reading such reports since he was a boy, he suddenly thought to himself. The newly "forever lost" suddenly seemed passé. And in this Brazilian case, too, "country" must continually recede at the very moment we might reach out and touch it. This, in turn, means that Jeca is always sad, not only because he has lost his home, his love, and his self (a mingled loss, as we have seen) but because, to add insult to injury, he is forever about to cross over into extinction. In an ineluctably world-historical mode, human affairs are doomed to become urbanized, and then, as part of an incumbent process, they will be "globalized." Naturally, as this takes place, "true" rurality must vanish. Enter the great rationalization and demystification of the world. And it is not only elites who have been enchanted by such notions (Saler 2006, 693). In Brazil, across class lines, the countryside gets pulled along behind, or left in the dust altogether, and is always the disempowered actor. The elisions and inclusions of such an approach and the role they play in rural musical understanding and practice, appear clearly in the story of how Central-Southern rural music's father figure is thought, by current performers and fans, to have delivered the genre's first 78 RPM record.

The Rebirth of a Birthing Tale—To Music

I met José Manuel dos Santos at a performance by Almir Sater.[1] Sater is one of the *viola* players credited with revitalizing the instrument through his songwriting collaborations with Renato Teixeira in the late 1980s and early 1990s, and through his appearance on several Brazilian soap operas (*novelas*) both as a character and on the soundtrack.[2] José listened impatiently to the music that night. He had come in order to confirm what he already knew. Sater was an imposter—a middle-class kid who had first learned to play guitar and had then taken up the viola much later in life on a whim. For José, Sater had not been *born* to Central-Southern rural music; instead, he had simply stepped into it like a new suit of clothes. Sater was evidence of the fact that, these days, everyone seemed to have an opinion about the "right" way to play the viola, one that lacked serious backing by way of life experience in the countryside.

José provided little information about his own country background, though details accrued over time. He had been born into humble circumstances, one of several brothers and sisters, in the interior of São Paulo. A picture of the tiny rustic house that had been his childhood home adorned his breakfast table. Though he had never been able to attend university, José had always been an autodidact, particularly in the sciences, as well as in expository writing and foreign languages. He had gone to work as a tire technician for a Goodyear affiliate in his twenties and had traveled throughout the Central-Southern region to train salesmen and those who installed the company's tires on cars, trucks, and tractors. He had done this for over thirty years before retiring early, in his fifties. He had never married and had no children. He had, throughout his life, practiced the *viola* intensely, writing music and lyrics, establishing friendships with many of the industry's important instrumentalists, singers, writers, and producers, and performing with his brother in his own *dupla*. He had become close with famous rural musician and viola player Tião Carreiro, and though José would never corroborate this, several of his friends independently informed me that he had even doubled Tião's viola parts in the wings offstage toward the end of Tião's life, when Tião had become too sick to play but nonetheless needed to appear competent onstage.

On the night we met at the Sater show, José explained that he had retired early from his job because his spiritual counselor, a spiritist medium, had informed him that it was time for him to devote himself full-time to his music. He considered my appearance shortly thereafter to be propitious; my foreigner's interest in Central-Southern rural music was a good sign, and he would teach me the true history and practice of rural music. From the start, José was impressed that I had taken the time to read some of the accounts of Central-Southern rural music because this had provided me with some basic knowledge about its most important figure: Cornélio Pires. José informed me that the histories I had read were by and large quite incorrect, according too much importance to certain performers and not enough to others; he was able to cite the specific errors, chapter and verse. But at least these writers had explained that Pires was the one who had first recorded Central-Southern rural music. In addition to helping me pick out a student-model viola from the music shops of downtown Campinas, José agreed that night that he would assist me with my research, taking me to meet the important characters and teaching me to play.

Part of what José saw as my apprenticeship involved taking me to Pires's birthplace, the São Paulo town of Tietê. As we drove there, José reinforced to me that one of Pires's most important accomplishments was presenting the first rural music show in the city of São Paulo in 1910 at Mackenzie University. But most important, Pires had been the first to record the music to record in 1929. On the outskirts of Tietê, these claims were reinforced when we visited the house in which Pires had been born, which was currently being rebuilt by the town government as a park with a historical theme. This revitalization suggested to José that all was not entirely wrong with the world, as the town had finally granted some space and money to this unbelievably important man.

Back in town, a bust of Pires perched on a red granite pillar in the central square. The back listed sixteen of his books, though none of his records. The Pires "museum," two large rooms in a mansion in the center of Tietê, contained pictures from Pires's career and copies of the many 78 RPM records he had recorded, including the first ones, from 1929. From the walls, and by way of José and the self-taught historian who took care of Pires's artifacts, a story of how Pires had recorded the first Central-Southern rural genres took shape. And despite José's dismissal of the history books I had read, the tale that emerged matched written versions, in turn, most likely, derived from the tale woven by Pires's nephew, Ariovaldo Pires.[3] Both my guides that day, as well as critics and scholars of Brazilian rural music, cited Pires's first recordings as the moment rural music was born.

That birth goes like this. In 1929, Cornélio Pires visited the newly installed headquarters of the Brazilian outpost of Columbia Records in the city of São Paulo and proposed that *música caipira* ought to be recorded on 78 RPM discs. At the Columbia office, Pires was sent to the American manager of Columbia in Brazil—Wallace Downey. Through Ariovaldo, the only person in Pires's party who spoke even marginal English, Pires managed to make his case. Downey rebuffed the idea, countering that there was no market for hillbilly music. In all these tellings, Downey's response proves the urbanite bias against rural popular culture. This hubris is always carefully built up for the fall it must take by the end of the story. The fact that Downey was American goes unaddressed; Downey's North American ignorance of Brazilian musical "markets" joins seamlessly with the ignorance of Brazilian city-dwellers of the rural interior.

The gregarious and forceful Pires pressed his point until Downey insisted that a record of backcountry music could only be recorded if Pires were able to raise, not only the funds for the recording session, but also what would be required for the one thousand pressings customarily made of a first release. Columbia could not be asked to take such frivolous risks. Tellings pause again here, this time to reinforce Downey's ignorance of Pires's influence and power, in assuming that a hayseed would be unable to collect the necessary funds. Downey was therefore said to be horrified when Pires returned later that day with the money. Narrators puff their chests with pride here to report that Pires's reappearance turned the tables and allowed the hick to dictate to the record company executive for a change. Pires was so utterly certain of his correctness in this endeavor that he asked to record not one record but five. Further, he would produce not the customary one thousand copies of a first release but five thousand of each. Downey's citified doubts apparently remained, but since he was now in no position to take on much risk himself, he apparently acquiesced. As Pires handed over the cash, he delivered what is portrayed as his final stroke, stating his intention to sell these records himself rather than through Columbia's existing distribution networks. And last, these records were to have their own bright red label and numeration that would set them apart from other Columbia recordings in Brazil at the time, which were labeled with burgundy and uniformly numbered. We might speculate that this might well have been Downey's attempt at damage control, disassociating Columbia somewhat from the hick records, but listeners to this version of the story of the birth of rural music are asked to assume that Pires *demanded* his own labeling; he wanted his *own* series, not one associated with Columbia's other music.

Pires's miraculous efficacy continues. When the five records (twenty-five thousand actual discs) were ready several months later, he set out with two trucks for the interior town of Bauru to sell them. According to most tellings, Pires paused for two days just east of his destination, in Jaú. But instead of making it to his planned stopping point, Pires sold every single record in Jaú and wired Columbia that before he could go on to Bauru, five thousand more pressings of each record would be required. In the course of each rendition of this narrative, this phone call brings Downey's ignorance fully home, and Pires's expert knowledge of the rural interior bursts forth in a knowing wink. The rural trumps the urban for a change.

Thus, tellers continue, began the boom in the sale of rural music that continued into the 1950s. Months later, competing companies Victor and Odeon, not to be left out of what was clearly a trend, started their own rural recordings in the Pires style. Some of them even employed Pires and the group of performers he had assembled for Columbia under pseudonyms.[4] Pires enthusiasts end the story here with "thus was Central-Southern rural music born." Instead of international companies using "us," I was reminded, in case I had missed the point, "*Pires used them.*" One triumphalist history went so far as to portray Pires as "the first independent record producer in Brazil" (Júnior 1986) despite Pires's clear reliance on one of three giant contemporaneous multinational record companies. All of which might seem to fly in the face of rurality's reveling in its lack of power, as indeed rurality must, except that the triumphalist tone of these tellings so profoundly under-scores the tellers' sense of rurality's continual losing. In other words, the triumph of the story arises from the way in which rurality's victory, here, is to be understood as a wonderful anomaly.

Toward tracing this narration of a victory in the midst of so many defeats, it is worth noting that the details that are left out of this birthing tale are as important as what finds its way into it. What is omitted suggests that Brazilian rurality must negotiate several tensions. To be-gin with, renditions of the story reveal the necessity of obviating the fact that Pires's sale of rural music required mediation.[5] The Central-Southern rural music Pires was recording could no longer resemble the music which accompanied lengthy parties, and popular Catholic and secular festivities. The music Pires had first brought to Mackenzie in 1910 existed in the backcountry in the form of pieces that stretched sometimes for hours, stressed highly repetitive lyrics rather than fo-cused narratives alternating between verse and chorus, and was often played on poorly tuned instruments, sung by nasal untrained voices. For Pires's new recordings, the songs had to fit on one side of a 78 R P M disc, thus requiring substantial shortening. They also needed to be played on well-tuned instruments because anything else would simply reinforce mainstream ideas about hicks as musically challenged. Fi-nally, their lyrics would have to change substantially, such that relatively open-ended and improvised pieces became specific songs, with au-thors, which followed narratives with a clear beginning, refrain, mid-dle, and end. Mediation had these concrete requirements.

Second, in tellings of Pires's dramatic victory, we see little trace of the economic complexity of the state of São Paulo. In more detail, there is hardly a trace of the way an economy of coffee cultivation in the interior of São Paulo in the mid-nineteenth century had given rise to a series of supportive crops and industries such as rice, beans, corn, cotton, steel, farming implements, and textiles. The tremendous success of the cof-fee industry also relied upon a supporting infrastructure of railways and roads like the ones Pires used to drive his two trucks to Jaú. All this construction and local manufacturing led to the development of what is often referred to as São Paulo's "coffee bourgeoisie" (Fausto 1994, 203). It would have been this bourgeoisie and those affiliated with it that could afford records and already owned turntables, which were pieces of equipment that represented a substantial outlay of funds.[6]

Third, the state of São Paulo exhibited strong regionalist tendencies in the early twentieth century. At this moment, São Paulo was the economic powerhouse of Brazil through its production of coffee for foreign export. This hegemony did not go uncontested, however, and São Paulo continually engaged in power struggles with Minas Gerais, which mainly produced milk and hides for local, rather than international, consumption. This rivalry of "coffee with milk" politics often translated into the São Paulo resident's inherent sense of his state's superiority over the rest of Brazil—a regional loyalty in part maintained by the state's frequent leadership in Gross Domestic Product, but also grounded in its assumption of the superiority of its local culture (Skidmore 1967, 17, 37). Paulistas were therefore attracted to Pires's records not just because they were humble "country" people, but because of the way the music inimitably presented pro–São Paulo sentiments. Merely recording *caipira* music was a regionalist affirmation in and of itself, which occurred at a time in which regionalist sentiment was high. In fact, that sentiment had exploded in rebellion in 1928 and would do so once more in 1932 when Pires himself, unable to serve in combat on São Paulo's side due to his age and obesity, entertained the state's troops by making them laugh, and ardently supported independence (Dantas 1976, 147).

Fourth, far from spurning Pires's sort of fare, recording companies around the world frequently pursued regional musics during this period. Pires's Columbia story must therefore also be read within the context of developments in the global phonographic industry. Record companies had pursued local markets in the United States via race records such as African-American jazz, or records for immigrant populations, among them Ukrainians and the Irish (Peterson 1997, 195), as well as hillbilly records. There were three large record companies functioning in Brazil at this time, Victor, Odeon, and Columbia, the first two based in Rio de Janeiro and the third in São Paulo. All three hoped for precisely the kind of local market that Pires delivered. Despite Columbia's initial resistance to Pires's idea, therefore, in the end he provided a wonderful gift to the international phonographic industry. The speed with which the three companies began their own series of rural recordings in Brazil several months later was thus consistent with their corporate strategies throughout the world. But in this story celebrating rural music, an urban record company, its urban manager, its urban recording studios, and its urban record-manufacturing facilities simply must not appear.

Fifth, Pires was not, himself, a peasant, at least not in any meaningful sense of the albeit problematic term we are about to explore. Indeed, his family had considerable means, owning a brick and tile factory. Pires owned his own circus at one point. Despite the fact that he held a number of jobs throughout his life, he was avidly entrepreneurial, at one point taking on one of the first beverage sponsorships to be awarded to a traveling circus in Brazil from the Antarctica Company. Pires's employees, and the singers and instrumentalists with whom he worked, were well aware of the divide between them and their employer. To illustrate, one story appears in biographies of Pires in which someone came looking for Cornélio at his family's brick factory and farm and asked some of the peasant workers where their boss had gone. They wryly informed the visitor that Pires was off traveling somewhere, getting rich "by imitating us."

In this sense, we can see that this interpretation of Pires's story as the victory of a peasant over international corporations, the music he recorded as the spontaneous outpouring of a pristine backcountry culture, the triumph of "independent" production, and the steadfast opposition of the city to the country, requires calculated blindness. My point is emphatically not that some obscuring of "what really happened" has taken place. All historicities have their blindnesses. Rather, the point is that this blindness says a great deal about the current importance of rural music's discursive fashioning of an urban-rural divide. Furthermore, many of the occlusions this story relies upon in turn flow from a concept of the stereotypical rural subject: the peasant. It is thus to the historical imagination that supports a Brazilian rural subject that we now turn.

Crisis at Pretty River: Materiality and Separation

Rural public culture, not just in Brazil, but across time and space, relies upon the impending sudden disappearance of a once timeless "country" and its subjects. But what counts as country in various locations shifts along with transformations in space, economic relations, and social class, among other things. Wordsworth's pastoral farms green to their very doors ("Tintern Abbey") are not precisely the same as the tears in Hank Williams Sr.'s beers ("There's a Tear in My Beer"). Said differently, the cluster of institutions, actors, and practices gathered under the umbrella of "modernity" in its varied guises and locations over the last five hundred years has generated a country-city dialectic wherever it has alighted (R. Williams 1973, 302). But due to cultural differences that distinguish these locations, this alighting has created a plethora of "countries."

Music is only one of many mutually reinforcing modalities in which a country-city dialectic may play itself out. This dialectic also grounds social-scientific approaches to society and culture. In a critical engagement with twentieth-century anthropology, Michael Kearney (1996) discusses the way in which the discipline "invented" the peasant at a moment in which anthropology's traditional "others" became less viable as objects of study, partly in response to the increasing importance of postcolonial nationalisms. Yet, the peasant was not "other" in a way that anthropology's previous others had been. Whereas the tried and true subjects of anthropological inquiry had been easier to conceive of *outside* of modern structures, peasants resided very much *within* nation states, which meant that their use in the fashioning of nationalist discourses, at the very least, problematized any straightforwardly peripheral status that might have been ascribed to them. The peasantry was "a Third World poised historically and politically *between* the First and Second Worlds" (Kearney 1996, 39, my italics). This betweenness called for new categorical fixity, which rurality could supply; everyone needed to be able to point to a countryside that was being buffeted by the grand modernization of the world. "The Great Transformation" (Polanyi 2001) had surely touched down all over, though there were small pockets which it seemed to have temporarily overlooked. It would get there soon enough, of course, but, it was to be hoped, not before these nearly forgotten corners could be photographed, sound-recorded, and otherwise documented.

Ruralist discourse in the twentieth century in Brazil has given rise to an analytics of country space and time in relation to the urban, figured in terms of the disappearance of the former due to the latter. Take the set of Brazilian actors, institutions, and practices participating in the production and reception of journalism, scholarship, and criticism of rural musical genres, and the way in which they partake of precisely the same kinds of assumptions that undergird the music itself. Essentially, scholars seeking to explicate rural music and the culture from which it derivatively "springs" rely upon and encode a plangent regret for a bygone time of idyllic wholeness, a time in which Brazilians lived in the interior, free of urban influence. These attempts to analyze rural public culture from a discursively fashioned scientific remove rely upon inter-pretations of history that ratify materialist, literalist, and temporalist understandings of social reality. These, in turn, perpetuate the country-city dialectic on which the music depends.

Perhaps no single work illustrates the importance of formalism to arguments about rurality better than Antônio Cândido's *Os parceiros do Rio Bonito*, or *Sharecroppers of Pretty River* (Cândido 1979). Cândido is one of the most respected literary theoreticians and scholars in Brazil, best known for his tireless effort to place literature into its social con-texts. His analyses of the emergence of Brazilian poetry and prose over-whelmingly underscore the way in which literary production is always, simultaneously, social production. Cândido's first academic work was inconsistent with his stated career goals in two ways, however. First, and more significantly, it did not ascribe meaningful social productivity to the public-cultural form it analyzed, favoring a materialist mode of explication, as we shall see. Second, and more simply, his thesis was not about literature per se, but began with music. As he tells it in the preface to *Sharecroppers*, his interest in the rural began with a "sung dance" called the *cururû* from the interior of the Central-South. Appar-ently, Cândido began to notice, back in the 1940s, that this rural song-and-dance varied widely within the state of São Paulo (Cândido 1956). In some areas, it was entirely rustic, such that uninterrupted bouts of song lasted for hours, and musicians were unpolished, somewhat out of tune, and sang through their noses. In other locations, the dance was much tighter, the songs shorter, the singing smoother and more full throated. In Cândido's eyes and ears, the archaic forms of the song and dance evidenced in this first cluster of features seemed to coexist with the modern ones evidenced by the latter. What might explain the simul-taneity of seemingly distinct historical periods indexed by this dance, he wondered? To answer the question, he suggested that the multiple temporalities of the contemporaneous *cururû* pointed to a broader state of affairs in Brazil's Central-South, where older ways of life were dying out as newer ways were coming in, largely in response to the growth of cities and the linked demise of the countryside. A desire to look care-fully at the cultural material that was, according to his way of hear-ing Brazil, on its way out, led him to a detailed study, not of the *cururû* itself, but of the particular region in the interior of the state of São Paulo in which an antiquated *form* of the *cururû* still existed: Bofete, also known as Pretty River, a zone in transition. For Cândido, the old-fashioned *caipira* was at a crossroads here, as a new system of values based on capital, savings, and profit butted up against an older system based on reciprocity, sharing, and production at the level of a social unit no larger than the small village:

> And here, we can see that the process of urbanization—a civilizing process, if we encapsulate it from the perspective of the city—presents itself to the rustic man by *proposing* and *imposing* certain traces of material and non-material culture. It *imposes*, for example, a new rhythm of work, new ecological relations, certain manufactured goods; it *proposes* the rationalization of work, the abandonment of traditional beliefs, the passage to an urban life. (Cândido 1956, 218, his italics)

Note the discursive way in which this model apparently functions. Cândido's city almost seems to speak to its hick subject: you *might* want to do these things (proposition), but you *will* do these (imposition). Cândido's caipira is not entirely without choice in the short term, it would seem. While he is forced to accept some of what Cândido describes as imposed, he may choose to accept some or none of the *proposed* possibilities. But over time, that which is proposed will become obligatory. Cândido's rustic man is definitely a dying breed, caught between a rock and a hard place, stuck in the ways of the past, but being forced, by degrees, to move to the future.

Cândido sets all this down with more than a few tears of his own, rendered in careful prose. We get the sense that he ardently hopes that his hicks will fight hard as they go down. The critical bite of Cândido's analysis here takes on a Marxist bent. He ends his seminal work in the words of the great philosopher himself, here rendered in English, from Cândido's Portuguese translation from the original German. As for Marx, according to Cândido, the city is truly the result of

> the concentration of population, of the instruments of production, of capital, of goods, of necessities, while the country shows just the opposite, isolation and separation. The opposition between the country and the city can only exist within the context of private property. It is the most gross expression of the subordination of the individual to the division of labor and a determined activity that is imposed upon him. A subordination which makes of one, a limited beast of the city; of the other, a limited beast of the countryside, reproducing each day the conflict of his interests. (Cândido 1956, 226)

Thus Cândido invites a reading of the opposition between country and city in the broadest terms. For him, the opposition between them under capitalism speaks volumes about exploitation and alienation and must be perceived as embodying the contradictions of the overarching economic system. The subservience of the country to the city is also, simultaneously, the subservience of the individual to the division of labor in society, which relegates actors to highly specialized roles and places only the capitalists in possession of the means of social and economic production. Capitalism apparently creates its "country" through exploitation.

Despite Cândido's avowed interest in reading literature as a social practice, his argument orients rustic sociality by means of the material, in this case, the production and consumption of food. In a sense Cândido's book almost becomes a meditation on sustenance in Bofete and on its absolute centrality to social life. Drawing on readings of contemporaneous peasant studies by those such as anthropologist Robert Redfield, Cândido considers what crops the backcountry resident is able to grow, in what quantities, and with what frequency. This analysis of a means of production forms the basis of his definition of what, precisely, rural society is. Cândido suggests that this disappearing "rustic" operates according to a delicate balance between what is produced and what is consumed. Caipira society is a minimal means of existence; a life in which what is *required* is produced, and no more. The notion of a surplus lies entirely outside of this state of affairs as an urban encroachment. For Cândido, material necessity *defines* rusticity. This involves being forever tied to the bare bones, embedded in a particular landscape, and reliant upon specific crops and cooperative methods for growing and harvesting them. These define the terribly fragile rural subject. Rurality in its purest form here orbits around perpetual necessity, precluding ease, profit, or surplus. This also means that the rustic community must be self-contained (Cândido 1979, 57). Recall the necessity of Jeca's isolation. The caipira is wedded to the landscape, laboring from sunup to sundown, harnessed to the "cycle" of growth (Cândido 1979, 123), tied by requirement to his neighbors, to his family, and to the land. And this humble embeddedness of rural man in his bucolic locale is on its way out. Already, in 1947, when Cândido embarked upon his ethnographic work in the small municipality of Pretty River in the state of São Paulo, Jeca was to be found only in small, isolated, pockets. He would soon be gone.

Significant for this contrast between idealized caipira sociability and the capitalist forms that threatened it is the fact that the hick does not compete. He cooperates. But the expansion of the market economy into a larger and larger area has made cooperation more difficult and has begun to turn the rustic into one who frames his work as a solitary endeavor, something able to be done only for his own "interests." The caipira is starting to become an "individual" in the modern and urban sense, Cândido informs us. This requires alienation. His past reliance on his neighbors for help (Cândido 1976, 216) is becoming impossible. This, in turn, has made backcountry work less effective than it once was at actually *producing* what is required to sustain rustic life:

> Today, the economic dimension has reached the point of destabilizing the caipira situation. The expansion of the capitalist market has not only forced the caipira to multiply his physical efforts, but it has also tended to atrophy the collective forms of organizing work (mutual aid), cutting the possibilities of a more active sociability and a harmonious culture. (Cândido 1976, 169)

The capitalist system thus strikes at the heart of possibilities for collective organization, which in turn, it would seem, precludes "active" sociability and "harmony." By way of its inveterate individualism, then, the city brings passivity and disunity to a once self-sustaining system. These problems are brought about by the increasing importance of a market, rising population density, and the lack of available arable land (Cândido 1976, 216). These factors hem the backcountry resident in, turning him more and more into someone who works alone, is passive, lacks a sense of cultural integration, and has no land to call his own. Farewell to an older, closed, society and enter a newer, ostensibly more open one in which the *caboclo's* walls are nonetheless closing in. The seminomadic requirements of caipira agriculture are now circled by factory farms and cities.

Cândido's *Sharecroppers* ends with a plea for agrarian reform in Brazil. According to his analysis, the caipira is simply fleeing to the city to escape a bad situation; the destruction of his culture and the material possibilities of his self-support are all but complete, and no new coherent economic system has taken shape. And for this reason, rustic man's move to the city stands a good chance of making his life worse, Cândido fears. He suggests that the antidote to this dire situation is to be found in a more sensible governmental policy: "without rational planning, the urbanization of the countryside will proceed more and more as a vast cultural and social trauma, in which hunger and anomie will continue to prowl around their old familiars" (Cândido 1976, 225).

Despite its scholarly execution, the ideas behind this book, which Cândido defended as his doctorate in 1955 and eventually published in 1964, nonetheless animate much of the Brazilian conception of the relations between the country and the city in literature, song, and picture. The book is continually called upon in rural musical practice. I was repeatedly referred to it by those seeking to help me with my work. Many of my interlocutors saw it as a social-scientific treatise on rural music despite the fact that its author had quite candidly confessed to spending much of his time discussing food. The ethnography of Brazilian rural musical genres that occupied me had already been done, many informed me: had I read *Sharecroppers of Pretty River*? The book had also inspired several musicians in their musical practice. The Paulo Freire of chapter 1, for instance, cited it as instrumental in his decision to stop playing the guitar, deepen his study of the viola, and move to a small farm in the interior of Minas Gerais for several years to engage in manual labor by day and music by night (he also cited Guimarães Rosa). *Violeiro* Ivan Vilela told me fondly of the party at which Cândido's book had been reissued in April of 2001. Cândido and the book's publishers felt that it was essential to accompany the reissue with a performance of viola music by Ivan. In the words of one press release announcing the event, "nothing could be more appropriate than a concert of the caipira viola by Ivan Vilela for rounding out the evening's programming."

Oppressing the Humble:
Commodification as Embarrassment

An analysis of Cândido's work goes some distance toward clarifying the shape that the rural subject takes within discourses of rurality and the precise ways in which urban-rural relations must be portrayed in order to fashion the rural as disempowered and materially distinct from something called the city. However, a further development of these details, which deepens the relationship between rurality and cultural intimacy, finds voice in prominent Brazilian sociologist José de Souza Martins's *Capitalism and Traditionalism* (1975). Martins, a complex scholar whose laudable political achievements include being an early supporter of the Rural Landless Worker's Movement (the MST), engages more extensively with music than Cândido, devoting the final chapter of his book entirely to its consideration. The chapter begins by historicizing rural genres, and in so doing, Martins unites Pires's birthing tale with Cândido's dirge for backcountry simplicity. He opens with the necessity of distinguishing música caipira from música sertaneja according to his understanding of the commodity form. This clarifying of terminology anchors his concept of rurality. For Martins, recording backcountry music in 1929 put an end to música caipira once and for all. What Pires put on disc at that time was not, therefore, música caipira at all. Instead, it was an industrialized product: música sertaneja, a rurally themed mode that no longer expressed the social life of the simple caipira, but instead conveyed the conservative backlash of those hurt by the Great Depression's decimation of coffee prices. Música sertaneja was a commodity, unlike the simple and "real" rural music that had circulated in caipira communities before recording technology made its destructive entrance. The preindustrial makers of caipira music did not separate music out into some demarcated domain *as* music, but rather simply considered it to be an integral part of social life. Only under capitalism, Martins thunders, do we find something called "music" being split off from daily routines and circulated "for profit." Nowadays, music contributes to alienation. Martins argues that in the 1950s and 1960s the music industry used rurally inflected musical products to "adjust" newly migrated rural workers to city life. This took place in the rationalization of Brazil where local traditions were bulldozed by modernity and urbanity, producing, we are told, an increasingly homogeneous society. And note that the rural and its subjects must be acted *upon* in such a formulation—that the country must be passive in the face of the city's brutishness. The industrial product known as música sertaneja, he noted, appealed first and foremost to the poor working-class migrants seeking to adjust to city life.

For Martins, música sertaneja encapsulated the "humiliations" that were so deeply constitutive of migrant identity. Lyrics seemed to rail against the injustices of a system that treated rural people as second-class citizens. But at the very same moment those lyrics ended up *endorsing* this unjust system. Workers thus clearly found in música sertaneja both a means of framing their discontent at being treated as inferiors under capitalism, and, at the very same time, paradoxically, a

justification for their remaining in that oppressed situation. The music seemed to empower, and then, at the last moment, it utterly disempowered. For Martins, this duality finds itself clearly expressed in the lyrics of one of the classics of música sertaneja in the early 1960s, *The King of Cattle (O Rei do Gado)*, by Teddy Vieira. Here, the song opens in a bar in the interior town of Ribeirão Preto, where a dusty man enters and asks for a shot of the local sugarcane rum, called *pinga*. The bartender serves him, at which point a well-dressed and wealthy patron kicks up a fuss. The stuffed·shirt demands that the bartender explain: how can you serve such filthy and insignificant people here? Can't you see that this is an affront to the people of importance here present? I am the King of Coffee, and I do not wish to drink in proximity to such rabble. Martins is careful to point out that the cowboy's disheveled appearance indicates that he has been *working*, whereas the King of Coffee is squeaky clean and has had others doing the work *for* him. Martins's idea here is that the song's listeners should sympathize with the feelings of a person walking into a bar, dirty from work, and hence looked down upon by some pompous patron who has never gotten grit under his nails. But then, according to Martins, the song twists in a different direction:
In a courteous fashion

> That cowboy responded to the guy
> "Your riches don't scare me,
> I bet I can top them, by any measure.
> For each of your coffee trees
> I can grab a bull from my pasture
> And to close this subject, I guarantee
> That I'd still have some left over."[7] (Tonico and Tinoco 1968)

The cowboy's words shock those present because they suggest that this dusty worker is, in fact, every bit as wealthy as his blustering critic: dirty and rich, to boot. The cowboy cements his words and worth in the final verses:

> There was a deep silence.
> But that peon left people even more shocked
> By paying for his pinga with a thousand cruzeiros
> And telling the waiter to keep the change.
> "Whoever wants my address

> *Don't hesitate, because it's no big deal.*
> *You just go to Anradinha*
> *And ask for the King of Cattle."*

According to Martins, its once rural, now urban, listeners will feel sympathy for the King of Cattle. They, too, have been disrespected because they look like they've been working. Furthermore, listeners will identify with the cowboy in experiencing pride in that hard work; labor therefore becomes a noble pursuit. But this work does not keep the dirty cowboy poor. Martins suggests that listeners will believe that just as hard work has brought the King of Cattle his wealth, manual labor may provide the path to amassing great wealth for them as well.

Yet, Martins notes that though this first experience might be realistic, the second one is not. The dusty laborer does not get rich, we are told. Thus, far from sending some liberating message, "The King of Cattle" is in fact a finely tuned instrument for keeping rustic, newly urban, listeners in their status-quo position. Mainstream society will continue to view hard manual labor as something that is less than desirable, and hard manual labor is extremely unlikely to create the kind of wealth the song's jousting kings display. And there is a further paradox. Wealth has corrupted the King of Coffee and made him into a prig. Yet, wealth is also what enables the King of Cattle to reply to the King of Coffee in the first place, enabling him to answer the coffee baron on his own terms. Wealth simultaneously corrupts and liberates. Thus for Martins, música sertaneja (all rural music after 1929, recall) was both the result of, and the engine for, classic alienation. It hemmed in its working-class listeners on all sides.

The neutralization of migrant discontent and naturalization of migrant inferiority, rendering abhorrent the very goals migrants were apparently being taught to pursue, played somewhat differently for the middle and upper classes. Martins informs us that these groups, who were much less important to a consideration of this musical genre anyway, but who nonetheless bore some brief consideration, simply loved hearing the well-greased gears of their capitalist machine. The upper classes who, for Martins, control the production and circulation of this music, celebrate it for the way in which it maintains the class-structure that supports them. So the limited number of upper-class fans enjoy the music because, in its harkening back to days of yore, it enacts a regret for the disappearance of a time in which social hierarchies were clearer than they are "today." At its first moment of "industrialization" with Pires, the upper classes could listen to and enjoy the stuff because it seemed to mourn the passing of the hegemony of the agriculturally driven system of coffee export in which the deference of rural laborers to their bosses was assured. With the entrance of import substitution industrialization after 1930,[8] the once strictly regimented systems of country-driven economic production gave way to the beginnings of an organized urban proletariat and the destruction of once crystalline social roles: capitalism over traditionalism. Even three quarters of the way through the twentieth century, long after coffee's hegemony had passed away, Martins believed that the upper classes could still experience the music as a forlorn statement on the good old days in which the workers knew their place.

Returning to formalist explanations of rural music, Martins essentially takes up where Cândido left off. Cândido's once isolated hicks have now fled to the city in Martins's account, and they must be *adjusted* to their new mode of subservience by the powerful. To this end, music becomes a classic instrument of alienation for the working classes. Only the upper classes may listen to it free of contradiction, though they do so very little, we are told. For its largely working-class constituency, here is the paradigmatic "castration moment" à la Adorno (1938) in which the subversive possibilities tantalizingly dangled by "mass culture" are brutally crushed by that same text moments later. In this way, Martins's analysis vociferously reproduces the poetics of shame on which rurality balances and upon which its intimacy relies. Música sertaneja is to be reviled because it is an industrial product that destroys the pure countryside, castrating the working classes in the bargain.

A series of scholars writing since Martins and Cândido have reinforced the theoretical and methodological templates these scholars established. Important to this discussion is the work of Waldenyr Caldas (1977, 1987), whose two works transposed Adorno's notions about the social control exerted by a "culture industry" into a Brazilian context through the analysis of Brazilian rural musical examples from the 1970s and 1980s. Caldas argued that commercial rural music created subjects obedient to a rapacious Brazilian capitalism in league with an authoritarian military government, often in cahoots with international development. Once again, for Caldas, the original caipira is long gone, aped in grotesque fashion by commercially successful música sertaneja. And once again, the rural subject has no power to choose the public culture he consumes.

One of the most quoted historians of Brazilian music, Luiz Ramos

Tinhorão, transposed the critique of rural genres into a slightly different register by framing their circulation in terms, not only of "urbanization," but of an incumbent "Americanization."[9] For Tinhorão (1986), rural genres provided a powerful record industry with the opportunity to homogenize the Brazilian public by presenting expressive forms in an American mold. Note that in the case of both Caldas and Tinhorão, following Martins, an original and pristine rurality has been distorted and put to use in the name of class warfare and imperialism. The true rural is essentially gone, and current rural music is nothing but an instrument for the replication of obedience. How embarrassing.

For the most part, these scholars read lyrics as their method, treating them purely as the reflex of industrial conditions of production and the transformation of the countryside enacted by the city, or of Brazil by the United States. It is thus worth pointing out that the country-city dynamic as it is presented here, relies not only upon a certain poetics of place, time, and self, but also on a set of methods for establishing the ways in which public culture is permitted to signify. The reading of lyrics out of the context of their direct engagement with a musical structure, and by a lone analyst, suffices. The *words* in songs become the preeminent means to determine a song's argument, while the more strictly "musical" elements fall by the wayside. We will explore how this ideology of the relation of music to language itself replicates a certain rurality in chapter 7. In the meantime, suffice it to say that these materialist, formalist, and literalist approaches to country-city relations relied upon specific interpretive practices which sealed the past off from the present and argued for an ineluctable destruction of the world via capitalism. This went hand in hand with an emphasis on textuality-as-lyrics which, in turn, involved an insistence that the places in which music is most meaningful can be found in the excerpting of words from musical structures of participation.

Such notions and methods reinforce the rural-urban dichotomies in other portions of the field of musical production. The growth of the popularity of música sertaneja and what is often described as a linked phenomenon, the expansion of rodeo, partake of the tendencies we have established in our analysis of Pires's birthing story, as well as the critical work of Cândido, Martins, Caldas, and Tinhorão. The countryside must be perceived as profoundly different from the city, its difference cemented by material relations of production. And the cultural intimacy with which rurality must be treated is the result of shame over the *way* in which the countryside has changed.

These "changes" appear in the news media in yet other variations. Within the most superficial analyses, rural public culture in Brazil is nothing more or less than "fashion," part of the vogue for things rural, of which the increasing circulation of American country music via música sertaneja, cowboy boots, Wrangler jeans, chewing tobacco, tasseled shirts, and ten-gallon hats are but other indicators. Such accounts suggest that a weakened "country" public longs for things that appear new, as magpies covet shiny objects. In these explanations, the rural becomes merely the latest fad. By this rationale, an "industry" seeks to sell "products" to "consumers," and it accomplishes this by promulgating what seems "novel." And here, because this hapless country public has no knowledge of its own history (which, apparently, ought to dictate "tastes"), "new" can simply be something quite old that the current generation fails to recall. The idea is that sooner or later, this country fad, too, shall pass. The consumers of such products are, themselves, thought to be of rural origin—although what this might mean is rarely specified—and rurally derived listeners are particularly prone to whoring after the latest trend since their cultural moorings are so poorly fastened. Consumers of the rural are therefore highly vulnerable to what become the predations of an urban culture industry.

In an only slightly different vein, the popularity of rural public culture may be traced, as in Cândido, though on a much larger scale, to agricultural production. In the fall of 1999 (May is autumn in Brazil), the editors of the newsmagazine *veja* devoted an entire edition to the Central-South, focusing on its economic power and its fixation on things "country." Entitled "The Strength of the Interior," and featuring a cover with a rodeo cowboy poised to pounce from his horse onto a sprinting calf (an actual event called "bulldogging," at rodeos in Brazil and abroad), the authors of five short connected pieces treated the phenomenon of the increasing popularity of things "country" as the reflex of material production.[10] This series of articles needs to be viewed in the context of the summer of 1998, when economic crisis struck "emerging" markets in Latin America and East Asia. At this time, São Paulo state's agricultural production, particularly soybeans, oranges, beef, wheat, and rice, generated sufficient profits to allay fears that Brazil might be the next economic domino following Malaysia, Russia, and Argentina. Therefore, those wealthy farmers and their families from "the interior" had every reason to be proud, the magazine's editor stated in the issue's introduction. Brazilian manufacturing had performed abysmally as compared with agribusiness during this period, so perhaps the nation was really turning "country" at its very core after all. The irreverent joy in things country—irreverent precisely because of rural public culture's intimacy—was thus to be explained as the economically grounded chest thumping of Central-Southerners. Long live "the *agro-boys*," *veja*'s reporters seemed to be shouting, somewhat mockingly. The popularity of música sertaneja, American country music and boots, rodeo, and chewing tobacco *just made sense* to *veja*'s editor and reporters because everybody knows that someone who's "on top" does as he pleases, even if some people believe that "what he pleases" is embarrassing.

Channeling Tinhorão's arguments, other explanations offered in varied contexts link the turn to the rural to a desire on the part of many Brazilians to be like the United States, and in this sense, describe this "turn" as a kind of cosmopolitanism gone awry. Many fans of regional musics, for example, suggest that the agricultural nouveaux riches responsible for managing Brazilian agribusiness, together with the poor migrant workers who toil on their farms, are yearning to be American, and thus striving for a sort of progress-by-cultural-emulation that seems to echo Sir James Frazer's ideas about sympathetic magic; perhaps contact with things American might *make* them American. Thus, cultural nationalists, among them many scholars, describe this country "fad" as the efforts of an intellectually low-status group to attempt to prosper by *being* as much like Texans as possible, as though Texas somehow represented the zenith of American popular culture in the United States itself. This group brands música sertaneja as a "sellout" and therefore a lower form of cultural production compared to those deemed indigenously Brazilian, such as MPB, *samba*, and explicitly folkloric music. Furthermore, for cultural nationalists, this aping of America causes even more nausea than the aping of another Latin American country such as Mexico might. Note that one of several epithets applied to música sertaneja is *serta-nojo*, or *serta*-nausea. The reasons for this are that to copy the culture of America, the apex of an oppressive world system, facilitates utter capitulation and sickness.

Other attempts to explain in the news media the rising popularity of música sertaneja and rodeo suggest, in concert with Martins, that the music is a corporate tool for manufacturing conservative ideology. Evidence for this contention is not difficult to find, as the practice of música sertaneja and the growth of rodeo have some links with right-wing politics. Note that corporate champion and Brazilian president between 1990 and 1992 Fernando Collor de Mello (referred to simply as Collor), together with his wife, vocally supported the genre and entertained several prominent duos at the presidential palace before his fall from grace in 1992. Live música sertaneja animated the then-president's birthday parties, and many of his most ardent supporters were, and continue to be, admirers of the music. Liberals and media critics read this as proof that the neoliberal and, ironically, anticorruption President Collor had no "taste" when it came to music: taste, here, employed in its Bourdieuian sense (Bourdieu 1984). Despite the fact that other politicians across the political spectrum had used música sertaneja in state elections since the 1940s, and that Getúlio Vargas had enjoyed the *dupla* Alvarenga and Ranchinho in the 1930s, the intellectual establishment deemed it scandalous that someone as high up as the president should enjoy the music publicly in the 1990s. A president with "good taste," critics proposed, would have listened to Brazilian Popular Music (MPB), samba, or, at the very least, something folkloric (*regional*). In an interview I conducted, one musician and filmmaker launched an invective on the way in which all of this "pride" in things rural sounded very much, to him, like the platform of an ultra-right-wing political party and advocacy group called UDR (The Democratic Ruralist Union).[11] Just as commodification has knocked the bloom from the caipira rose, so, too, does conservative ideology strip good taste from the public sphere, in a rural mode.

Establishing Rural Disempowerment

Much of the journalism and scholarship considered here would seem to criticize rural music, particularly current commercially successful instantiations of it. However, these interpretive practices actually endorse the underlying categories of rurality on which commercially successful rural music currently relies. All of this engagement with rural musical genres evidences a hunger for a pristine rurality that has little power to influence its own unfolding; it is defenseless. In one set of formulations, the city becomes that which has moved forward and simply forgotten about the countryside. In another, the city has moved forward and hauled the countryside along *behind* it as a kind of unwanted appendage. The rural has either disappeared for good, or is in danger of disappearing for good quite soon. It has no power in the face of the city's onslaught. The rural subject has no will and falls victim to unseemly desires in the face of corporate pressure, or sometimes pressure from abroad.

Within these formulations, the sadness of those who decry the commercialization of rural genres as the product of urbanization and late twentieth-century American imperialism is as shrill as the sadness of commercial country music itself. Indeed, such critiques are phrased using the same idiom. Arguments frequently begin and end with materiality. Economic demand creates the need for rural people, and, with them, for rural music, to move to cities. Then, once the move has taken place, the music "urbanizes," and, according to some, "Americanizes." Or, as we have seen, their music may be used against its own fans to naturalize subservience. Such notions frequently receive statistical support. In 1940 Brazil's urbanization rate was 26.35 percent, which means that just over a quarter of its people lived in cities. In 1980, this level had reached 68.86 percent, and by 1991 it was 77.13 percent (Carvalho 1993; Nepomuceno 1999; Reily 1992, 2002; M. Santos 1993).[12] The thrust of such presentation is to try to show that between 1940 and 1990, in the space of fifty short years, Brazil went from being a largely "rural" nation to being an "urban" one. The music also changed, the story goes.

Scholars and journalists view the transformation of música caipira into música sertaneja and the popularity of rodeo largely as the results of this movement from the countryside to cities. But the current variety of performance contexts of ultrapopular música sertaneja, the breadth of sales across class lines, and the diversity of locations from which performers and fans derive show that rural migrants are not now, nor were they ever, the sole pillar of rural music's circulation and popularity. The notion that they are must not only be conceived of as a shortcoming in the scholarly and journalistic study of music. More importantly, the insistence that rural migrants are the music's sole fans, the notion that the music hails from an entirely separate economic segment traceable through material means, and the theory that the music involves an unwanted commercialization of a once pure space, are all crucial to the reproduction of the music itself. Indeed, without these supportive discourses, Brazilian rural musical genres would be impossible.

In this analysis of attempts to explain the current and past popularity of música sertaneja via urbanization, these culturally intimate portrayals of the turn to the rural propose that the history of the music itself is about loss of innocence. But perhaps most importantly, we see that these interpretive practices establish the rural as a zone of disempowerment. The rural must be acted *upon*. Any sense of empowerment that emerges from rurality must always address this fact, as we shall see in our analysis of modes of circulation.

∿☉∿ 6

Digital Droplets and Analogue Flames

THE CIRCULATORY MATRICES OF BRAZILIAN COUNTRY

> Piracicaba River
> Will throw up water—
> When the water arrives
> From the eyes of someone crying.
> In the neighborhood where I live
> There's only one spring:
> It's the spring that's my eyes
> Which have already made a stream.
> So close to my house,
> There's already a lake
> Full of my tears
> Because of someone.
> —DINO FRANCO AND TIÃO CARREIRO, as performed
> by Lourival dos Santos, Tião Carreiro, and Piraci, *River of Tears*

As we saw in chapter 1 by way of all the flowing in "Jeca's Sadness," Central-Southern Brazilian rural music attends to its own motion by necessity. For Jeca, singing brings forth tears that flow to the sea. Hearing the song makes you cry. Strumming the *viola* does too. The process of music making thus embeds the singer, the listener, and the instrumentalist in a hydraulic loop by way of sentiment, which becomes physically instantiated through its emergence in watery form as it runs off to a liquid infinite. The mingled circulation of music and memory thus becomes constitutive of rural subjectivity itself.

These days, to hear "Jeca's Sadness," and perhaps shed some tears of your own, you can pick up a copy of the song on any one of a number of digitally reproduced recordings, or go to hear it, amplified onstage, at the local cultural center when a *violeiro* comes to town. As we shall see, within the field of rural public-cultural production, the space between these types of mediation—the space between water and compact disc as conveyances for, and elicitations to, a certain interiority that may then become manifest on someone's "outside"—is sometimes not so great in this rural field. At other times, the space is very large indeed.

Producing and Consuming, Singing and Listening

It is to these interconnected processes of hearing, making, exchanging, and experiencing rural music that we now turn. We inquire into when "natural" ways of moving, involving water and fire, overlap with arithmetic and financial modes, and when they are perceived to run in different channels. My point here is that performativity frequently reifies its circulation, though we are concerned here with the particular choices made within Brazilian country music. This chapter thus seeks to contribute to an understanding of the distinct patterns of "interdiscursivity" (Agha 2005; Silverstein 2005) associated with Brazilian rural music. Our subject in this chapter is therefore the way in which participants in the field of rural musical production conceive of the dynamics of musical practice. Music moves through radios and televisions sets, through singing voices in live performance, and through digital recordings copied illegally in large CD pressing plants in the Free Trade Zone of Manaus, then sold at the central bus station in downtown Campinas. Across these various domains, we are concerned with the way in which musical participants, from those absentmindedly overhearing a song on television while cleaning the floor, to those performing that song in front of a live audience, trace out the "circulatory matrix" (Gaonkar and Povinelli 2003, 386) that facilitates their public-cultural participation *at that very moment*. Circulation is often made manifest by way of materialities that recruit subjects to broader projects of local, national, and international import. These projects will become clearer as we consider the neoliberal significance of locality and cosmopolitanism in chapters 7 and 8, respectively.

One noteworthy characteristic of the rural field is the relationship between channels of musical circulation deemed natural, and broader arithmetic and technological ones. The buildup of emotion behind a "dam" of rational restraint, as one classic tune tells it, may well facilitate the arithmetic accrual of the "week's most popular" charts that appear in top-twenty countdowns and on the front page of the entertainment section of newspapers such as the *Folha de São Paulo*. A song, released like a messenger bird to bring back a long-lost love, may be inseparable from the sending of that song out "to all our friends and family on the Street of Fishes" on the "Big Sunday" live radio show I attended weekly at the Rádio Clube de Itapira. Over the course of this chapter, we will develop an understanding of the relationship between the natural and the arithmetic. In anticipation of this understanding, within the domain of the natural, music flows, gaining force as a river gets larger moving toward the sea, whereas in the domain of the arithmetic, iterations of a particular piece of music accrue numerically into a larger and larger number.

In the case of rural musical genres in Brazil, participants believe that the natural processes of circulation encapsulated by the music are paramount. Nature comes first in the composition and playing of a songtext. But then, these processes must be put to work within a system of exchange in which those natural flows are temporarily transmuted into something quantitative for the purposes of financial exchange. In alignment with rural music's celebration of the past in relation to a debased present, a well-aligned state of affairs in which the power of the natural circulation within a song aligns perfectly with sales very rarely exists "now." Indeed, one of the things wrong with the present is the frequency of the disjuncture between a broader system of exchange and the natural flows portrayed in rural music. If congruency does occur, it cannot last. Drawing attention to this disjuncture, while ardently hoping to erase it, forms one of the major components of rural musical practice. However, the rural-musical indictment of broad networks of arithmetically accruing, financially remunerative, and technologically advanced systems of circulation is not necessarily the same as indictments of financially reductive "markets" heard in the playing and hearing of other musical genres. This rural-musical indictment specifically indexes the past, the countryside, and the inevitability of the singing and listening subject's fragmentation, set within the frame of the dripping of water, the swirling of wind, the crackling of fire, the growing of plants, the pace of cattle, and the loss of love.

We will consider the actors and institutions of which the market is composed in more detail below. In the meantime, singers, songwriters, studio heads, and listeners characterize the system of financially motivated and arithmetic musical exchange in two major ways. The first is a consumption-centered version of the field, which holds that the field's existing structure is dictated by the appetites of those referred to as "Brazilian listeners"; the field works the way it does because people want to hear certain songs. This idea is grounded in the argument that "the public," understood in a conventional sense as a static concatenation of "listeners," gets what it wants, or sometimes, more critically, what it *deserves*. Musicians attain success because there is "demand" for what is thought of, in this paradigm, as their "product."

The second is a production-centered version of the field, which, still oriented toward the financially motivated and arithmetic, suggests the opposite: that some institution or social body, most often the large record companies that operate in Brazil, dictates taste and exerts substantial, or even complete, control over the field.[1] Listeners buy the records they buy and request the songs they request because the record companies *put* those songs, in a certain sense, *into* their ears. The purported force of these global institutions is thus credited with the fashioning of, once again, a "public's" appetites. Note that the act of production is empowered here with the ability to dictate the shape of consumption.

Both approaches may be used to support a policy of creating commercially successful music. The consumption-centered perspective may be employed, for instance, to argue for the unproblematic nature of the structure of the field of musical production. Practitioners of successful *música sertaneja* propose that there is no harm in supplying people with the music that they want. It's just the law of markets, they say. Trust that "consumers" will buy what's good for them. Or, on the production side, the powerful record companies have a profound influence on taste, but this is not necessarily problematic. This perspective thus proposes, quite literally, that it should be business as usual.

Both production- and consumption-sided approaches may also be brought to bear in a traditionalist mode, critical of the existing state of the musical market. Here, commercial music is public enemy number one. The consumption-sided approach to this opposite orientation begins with a reprimand to slothful listening, suggesting that the reason that musical options available to listeners are populated by so much commercial material is because people don't bother to learn their traditions. People are just lazy, and youth, in particular, are impressionable. It's "the audience's" fault for failing to want something better. Once again, the industry is supplying people with what they want, but what they want is lacking. This deprecation of listeners leads seamlessly into a production-centered scaffold for a critique of an unbridled free market, which suggests that rapacious corporations will erase Brazilian traditions and further the subjugation of the nation to foreign capital in an urban and North American mold. The harm in this form of musical inculcation will be great; these companies are making us forget who we *are*. This critical approach suggests that the way to fix this problem is by reforming the existing system of musical production, making it more "responsible," to use the critics' term. In the case under analysis here, the public should be taught to listen to music that is "truly rural." This perspective thus advocates a didactic approach to the market over a "free" one, as we will see in more detail in the next chapter on locality.

Despite the political differences between these two notions, rural music fans often listen to both commercial and folkloric rural genres. For instance, many rodeo parties place commercial and folkloric CDs side by side in the CD changer, and switches across genres go completely unmarked as an evening's socializing proceeds. The reasons why these sorts of combinations occur will become clear in chapters 7 and 8. In the meantime, suffice it to say that approaches to production and consumption designated as critical or mainstream both fashion notions of a "public" (Warner 2002) by relying upon technologies of accrual in the form of sales figures, radio requests, television airtime, and popularity charts. Free marketeers and revivalist champions of the folkloric alike use these tools to get a sense of what's "going on," whether they see the results as good or bad. In both cases, circulation becomes quantifiable in a numerical way, wherein certain songs may be portrayed as the most or least played of the day, week, month, or year, and record sales translate into thousands, or, in the case of the most successful records, into a hierarchy whose labels are taken from components used in the manufacture of jewelry (gold, platinum, and diamond, in that order). In this process, song texts, the actors that produce them, and the genres to which both are seen to belong are flattened into totals that might be used to make a point: that commercial country music is selling extremely well in Brazil these days, for instance, or that folkloric country music is *not*. This "sales" approach to musical circulation requires further attention if we are to understand Brazilian country "publics," the way in which participants orient their music making to listeners, and the kinds of periodicity involved in that orientation. Changes in the relationship between institutional practices of dissemination have influenced the shape of long-standing circulatory matrices. It is therefore useful to consider some broad transformations in the musical field in the late twentieth and early twenty-first centuries.

An Archaeology of the Neoliberal Musical Field

When Getúlio Vargas came to power as president of Brazil in 1930, he developed a template for collaboration between the state, private companies (makers of radios, investors in radio stations, and print media), and intellectuals, in order to promulgate a national musical culture, championing the *samba* of Rio de Janeiro as emblematically Brazilian (Vianna 1999).[2] Vargas's regime emphasized a coherent national culture as part of its continuing efforts to eradicate what it saw as the destabilizing effects of regionalism in the turbulent years leading up to 1930. Toward this end, as we saw in chapter 3, Vargas recruited a group of scholars to develop an ideology of music as a supremely important form of Brazilian popular culture, linking musical practice intimately to national character. What amounted to a new cultural cartography placed regional genres, among them rural genres, into a peripheral position with respect to more central Rio-based expressive practices. On a national scale, developing media conglomerates, often in partnership with the national government, promulgated notions of *brasilidade* as derived chiefly from carnival and samba and helped to maintain rural music's peripheral status.[3] This distinctive Brazilian mingling of private enterprise with state actors in the maintenance of a center-periphery arrangement is sometimes referred to as a "national-popular" way of organizing the field of cultural production (see, in particular, Hale 1997), and it relied, for control, on a delicate mixture of censorship, seduction, and incorporation. For instance, when rural *dupla* Alvarenga and Ranchinho's musical criticism of President Vargas could not be silenced by repeatedly arresting them, the two were invited to the presidential palace for a semiprivate show in which Vargas guffawed at their mockery of him and bestowed upon them the status of honored entertainers of the nation. They were never arrested again.

Subsequent authoritarian governments between 1964 and 1985 continued to promulgate the coherence of public culture as a way to cement political stability, drawing upon this national-popular approach. The mid-1980s brought a political "opening-up" (*abertura*), an end to dictatorship, at least from a strictly governmental point of view if not from the standpoint of policing and economic disparities. It also brought changes within the field of musical production. During this period, the role of regional music shifted into locality-producing and cosmopolitan molds, as we shall see. Groups of practitioners of some genres began increasingly to incorporate electric and electronic instrumentation and production, and several of these new fusions exploded in popularity. Included among these were *forró* (a Northeastern accordion-driven dance music), *axé* (a heavily percussive Northeastern dance music with roots in Brazilian black-power movements of the 1980s that have now largely been erased), *pagode* (a sped-up and technologically enhanced form of samba, rather than the rural form of pagode), and música sertaneja. Música sertaneja grew to be the most popular of these (ABPD 2001; IFPI 2001). The expansion of these genres heralded an increase in the quantity of domestically produced music (Chacur 1999). Before the opening up, music produced in Europe and North America had represented a larger percentage of the material sold at record stores and played on the radio. However, after democratization, practitioners of these newly expanded genres became the largest selling acts in the land. As a result, more of the music that Brazilians purchased in record stores and on street corners, listened to on the radio, and watched on television was composed by Brazilians, who wrote lyrics in Portuguese and put that material to tape somewhere in Brazil. This material, which was mainly oriented toward Brazilian listeners (Dunn and Perrone 2001, 30), is often glossed as "domestic production" (IFPI 2001). Its growth may be reflected quantitatively: domestic music accounted for 58 percent of all music consumed in Brazil in 1992. That figure rose to 75 percent in 2000 (ABPD 2001; IFPI 2001).

There were those who criticized the increased sales of these expanded genres on culturally nationalist grounds. Some musicians began simultaneously to augment composition of, and encourage listening to, music in folkloric molds deemed regional. These were often ensembles and composers claiming to practice the "true roots" of now best-selling genres such as música sertaneja, despite the fact that their fans often listened to both ultrapopular and folkloric modalities. These groups began to produce their own CDs and to advocate detailed research of the folklore that they felt grounded their musical practice. For example, "methods" for studying the *viola* (Corrêa 1989; B. d. Viola 1992) called urgently for a "rescue" of viola technique that had been threatened by a present-day lack of attention to traditions. Where use of regional genres had occasioned critique of authoritarian politics in the 1960s and 1970s, this developing group of local practitioners now shifted its criticism to the propensity for globalization to produce what they thought of as debased Brazilian music. What was characterized as the crass "anything-to-sell-records" attitude embodied by newly popular axé, pagode, forró, and most of all, música sertaneja, became a prime target.

An increasing focus on commercialism in genres such as música sertaneja oriented toward a certain cosmopolitanism (see chapter 8), plus the focus on the production of locality as in folkloric genres (see chapter 7), thus characterizes the musical component of the economic and political liberalization that followed close upon redemocratization. This liberalization was in large part impelled by a cluster of nationally instituted economic laws that intensified with the inception of Mercosul (Mercosur in Spanish) in 1991. These laws led to a series of changes within the field of musical production that gave shape to the transformations we have just discussed. The large international record companies also played a vital role.

Among these transformations, transmission of recorded music, which had initially taken place on LP and cassette in the 1980s, moved entirely to compact disc, an alteration so comprehensive that vinyl and prerecorded cassettes were essentially no longer commercially manufactured for legal sale in Brazil by the late 1990s. This happened quickly, so that cassettes, which were still quite popular when the change began to take place, were almost entirely wiped out. Collections of old records and cassettes had to be thrown out or placed into long-term storage, leaving participants with the sensation that a shift in the technology of reproduction had led to a change in what they could listen to and how they could listen to it. The transfer to compact disc has also played a role in the growth in the size of the informal economy of music sales, sometimes referred to as a "black" market in "pirated" music, which continues to increase despite, and perhaps because of, concomitantly growing corporate attempts to stamp it out.[4] This growth in the informal economy took place mainly in the latter half of the 1990s, particularly with respect to CDs, such that, whereas in 1997, contraband CDs accounted for only 3 percent of national sales, by 1998, this figure had jumped to 30 percent. It is now closer to 50 percent. Participants are therefore aware that licit CDs, which are quite expensive at official stores (currently R$15–30), can be had for a third of the price on the street (R$3–4), while the "sound" is precisely the same. They can therefore buy more music, more often, than if they purchased it at official stores.

The number of companies whose discs were being illegally copied and sold at *camelô* (informal markets) decreased dramatically in the neoliberal period, beginning in the early 1990s. During the late 1990s, there were five labels: Universal Music, Sony Music, BMG, EMI, and Warner Music Group. Since then this number has reduced to four. In order of licit sales, the "big four" now are: Universal Music, Sony Music/BMG, EMI, and the Warner Music Group. Congruent with neoliberal mantras of "efficiency," these international companies divested themselves of duties they once held, such as the support and "development" of songwriters and performers and the maintenance of recording studios. Consequently, artists began to produce records themselves at independently run studios. They then promoted themselves on a small scale, usually by way of some local group of fans and clubs, often making use of the Internet. At times, small independent labels took on some of the costs of recording and distribution. Only after artists had achieved substantial success through these means, including selling thousands of their own records, might the larger labels take notice. At one time then, a major label might have shepherded an artist through a process of growth, but this is no longer the case. Those wishing to produce music therefore feel that they must "take responsibility" for the process. The dream of being "discovered" has been supplanted by market-driven notions of hard work, localized entrepreneurship, and individual creativity. As critical as independent artists may be of what they characterize as the monopolistic tendencies of the big four, they nevertheless espouse highly individuated, entrepreneurial, and neoliberal beliefs about how to "launch" their own careers. In conformity with neoliberalism, where competition is perhaps the most important principle, they even see themselves to be in competition with each other for market share. We will see how this plays out in the rural field below.

The distribution of these former major-label duties to a more diffuse set of actors was facilitated by the strength of the new currency, launched in 1994: the *real*. This facilitated the purchase of previously unattainable foreign-manufactured digital recording and reproduction equipment,[5] which, in turn, made recording, reproduction, and circulation more affordable for small labels and private individuals. The tools for making a "radio-ready" record, free of tape-hiss and other kinds of degradation, were thereby spread to a larger group. Previously, the only way to attain pristine sound quality was through extremely large and expensive two-inch analogue tape machines. Now, specially equipped personal computers could perform the task. Also at this time, as mentioned, several foreign companies invested heavily in CD plant-reproduction capacity in the Free Trade Zone of Manaus with the hope that this region would eventually produce CDs for other Latin American markets.[6] And finally, radio and TV networks, forced to collaborate with military politicians during the years of dictatorship, had to re-negotiate with emerging civilian politicians and strike new bargains with international corporations (Costa and Brener 1997; Galperin 2000; Waisbord 1998). Often these local politicians were businessmen of some kind, who, having thoroughly bought into the importance of entrepreneurship, frequently used media to shepherd themselves or their allies to political power. This has given those working in news media a sense that there is a broader pool of interests and actors with which they must coordinate activities. We shall see the significance of these transformations for the rural field below.

Technologies of Arithmetic Accrual

Within the context of these broad transformations, industry analysts and chart compilers focus on strictly demarcated channels of circulation, drawing out a bottom line by way of sales and radio or TV itera-tions of a song. Pragmatic institutional goals establish links between what is called "popularity" and notions of participation. This guides record companies in orienting research and development money and structuring radio and television programming. As we shall see, the pedagogically focused champions of locality aspire to popularity as much as the commercial cosmopolitans of mainstream country.

Such notions of sales entrench reified understandings of genre within the field of musical production, creating a largely static picture of musi-cal practice. Chart compilers parse the field into genres of greatest statistical importance, leaving the details of precisely what co-occurrent features constitute each genre to readerly common sense. Everyone is just supposed to *know*. By these sorts of analyses, in 2000, for in-stance, "Domestic Pop" accounted for 18 percent of sales, "MPB" for 15 percent, "International Pop" for 14 percent, and música sertaneja for 13 percent.

Genre here becomes a stable and fixable entity, and listening to genres becomes imaginable from a mathematical perspective. Some "public," discursively enacted by sales figures according to genre as represented in the figures above, creates what Susan Gal (1995, 418) refers to as "decontextualization and depersonalization." Such percentages deliberately elide the periodicities of the publics they claim to represent, the ways in which listening calls publics into being, and the way in which music balances the simultaneity of an experience of interpellation with the understanding that everyone within earshot might be so addressed. To spell this out further, fashioning publics by percentage simultaneously reinforces two notions: The first is that all genres are equally oriented to the everyone hypothetically addressable as part of an overall 100 percent; the second is that a reader might view her own participation as in some sense *carving out a portion* of that whole—as in, I listen to these genres, and *not* to *those*. My remarks aim at description rather than critique. The important thing to understand is not that these practices are somehow wrong, but that this deliberately flattened notion of musicality becomes one of the technologies of musical circulation.

Such approaches to circulation focus on the channels in which music flows, here thought of in terms of locations in which songs play so that people may hear them. In so focusing, arithmetically grounded discussions of the field focus on mass-mediated contexts that may be surveyed by means of counting. This locates musical participation in highly specific circulatory matrices. Numerical approaches cite percentages of play-time, amounts of revenue generated, and numbers of requests made. Contexts in which this sort of data might be gathered in Brazil begin with television and range from advertisements playing certain music as background to MTV playing music videos which people sit and avidly watch. Most Brazilian families own television sets or have access to one.[7] Many Brazilians also own radios, and there is a large web of both legal and illegal radio stations in both AM and FM covering the nation.[8] Many also own CD players.[9] Of Brazil's twenty-six states, São Paulo buys by far the most records, with 23 percent of national sales.[10] The Escritório Central de Arrecadação e Distribuição (the Central Office of Collection and Distribution, or ECAD) is a performing-rights organization much like the American Society of Composers, Authors, and Publishers (ASCAP) and Broadcast Music, Inc. (BMI) in North America, and it parses channels of mass circulation in the following way: television accounts for most of the revenue that is not generated from the direct sale of records, at 25 percent. Radio accounts for 13 percent, shows and events such as rodeos and soccer games for 13 percent, live music for 7 percent, carnival for 5 percent. Other users, which include bars, restaurants, and miscellaneous public spaces, account for 32 percent of royalties.

The ECAD maps circulatory matrices into percentages in several ways. It administers the payment of artists and musicians when their songs are played in various public fora. It licenses television and radio stations, restaurants, clubs, and numerous other sorts of venues to play the songs of its affiliated artists, and then claims to do its level best to pay the artists according to how many times their song is played in those locations. It collects cue sheets from television programs, analyzes playlists from the radio, and sometimes even sends ECAD employees to listen to live shows. Clearly, public performance cannot be monitored constantly, however. So ECAD uses mathematics to simulate what it thinks of as actual musical circulation. Essentially, it determines how much a song is actually being played through statistical techniques of sampling airtime and then subjecting that sample to a somewhat involved set of equations based on, minimally, the time of day the song is played, whether it was background music or front-and-center, and the number of people thought to be listening to it at that moment. They then pay the artist according to the number thus derived. In this way, what is thought of as "listening" becomes mathematically, and consequentially, representable statistically. Once again, this involves a necessary *flattening* of reception whereby it becomes solely the fact of the song having *played* in someone's presence. It is impossible to conceive of the ECAD, and other performing-rights organizations, differentiating *attentive* listening from *distracted* listening and rewarding the artist whose music is attentively listened to more richly. The listener is stripped from the process except as a kind of hearing neuron. Listening therefore becomes playing a song where others may hear it. This building up of the song into something experienceable numerically integrates with long-standing traditions of accrual by way of counting (Hacking 2006; Poovey 1998).

A particular body of institutions reinforces and draws most heavily upon these mathematical means of conceiving of musical circulation (see figure 2). First and foremost among these are the internationally owned but locally managed recording companies, with offices in Rio and São Paulo: EMI, BMG, Sony, Warner Music, and Universal. Together, these accounted for 80 percent of licit global music sales in 2000 (Vicente 2002). As noted above, these big five have become the big

Figure 2. An Institutional Map of the Brazilian Field of Musical Production.

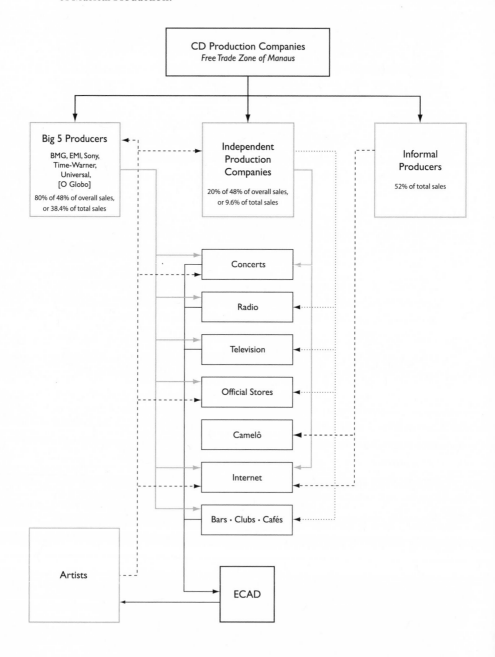

four, because Sony purchased BMG. In Brazil, media giant O Globo also owns two large labels, Som Livre and Editora Abril. Most música sertaneja is circulated by these six labels. In the 1990s and into the twenty-first century, much traditional rural music circulates on labels described as independent, such as Kuarup, Revivendo Músicas, Pau Brasil, Paradoxx, Velas, Lapa-Discos, Discos Corrêa, Vai Ouvindo, Estúdio Eldorado, Viola Shows Produções Ltd., and the state sponsored FUNARTE. Despite the smaller size of these labels, the belief structures that orient their productions are largely consistent with those of the majors in terms of a basic orientation toward sales, though in many cases, some other mission may play a role; Revivendo Músicas, for instance, reissues out-of-print material it deems to be classic. It nonetheless would love to sell as many copies of its material as it can.

This discussion of these means of coming to grips with musical circulation has shown 1) that participation can be figured through a mechanized approach to playing-and-overhearing, reducing subjectivity to accumulation and anonymity, 2) that participants view their ability to participate in the field as shaped by technologies of circulation that may shift precipitously in the Brazilian case, and 3) that the mathematically represented accrual of public taste yields, not only a specific periodicity, but 4) a sense of participation that aligns with some broader state of mind of a listening "public," as in 5) the release of a particular song's coinciding with its "catching on."

In a way that somewhat resembles the power of public opinion polls in other postdictatorial Latin American contexts (Paley 2001, 137; Paley 2004, 498), the Brazilian Institute of Public Opinion (IBOPE), founded in 1942, wields considerable force. It is cited in the news media on subjects ranging from political candidates to the sales of records. In fact, IBOPE has become a descriptor, such that "I don't think that will have much IBOPE" conveys "I don't think that will be very popular." Nevertheless, as powerful as these modes of musical engagement are, they exist in dialogue with other ways of coming to consciousness of musical practice.

Rural Circulation

A rural approach to musical circulation calls upon the kinds of natural processes in which participants cast rurality itself, revolving around an idyllic past in which interaction with plants and animals and embed-dedness in the elements such as wind, rain, and sometimes fire could be taken for granted. Conceptions of rural circulation also address the way in which rural song texts are able to interpellate listeners directly to emotional subject-positions that mingle sadness, longing, and desper-ation. In effect, rural musicians and fans believe that the circulatory matrices of rural music are operating in a "natural" fashion when those song texts are able to directly address and bring into being the grief of their listeners, not unlike the *gisalo* songs of the Kaluli, in Papua, New Guinea (Feld 1989, in particular chapter 5).

I illustrate the above points about circulation in the rural field by analysis of an interview with Marinho,[11] a prominent performer in a *dupla* that was widely recognized in the 1960s and 1970s, producer, songwriter, and musician's-rights advocate. I tack back and forth be-tween the interview and texts drawn from other times and places which support the points Marinho and his interlocutors make. We will try to understand Marinho's consciousness of the field through a song which addresses the way fire recycles the past. Music and memory, mingled, move in these natural kinds of ways. However, Marinho and his in-terlocutors also come to grips with the field of musical production through statistics. These perspectives thus intertwine.

Marinho's multiply determined position-taking thus telescopes a paradox of rural circulation, that is, how a sense of loss imbues its si-multaneous backward glance and its hunger for market share. Marinho inhabits both traditionalist and commercial quadrants of the field. Across this inhabitance, two things are worth noting. First, that com-modification itself is much to be wished for; the transformation of music into a CD for sale and circulation on the radio is the only way to be heard, he argues. Rurality and commodification are not only not opposed to each other, they are tightly connected. Second, the under-lying assumptions about how the markets work remain essentially un-changed across both traditionalist and commercial perspectives. Rural-ists do not criticize the market in and of itself. Rather, it is deemed to be problematic when the natural processes of musical and emotional cir-culation evidenced in rural lyrics and styles of playing fail to map onto the arithmetic and technologically mediated forms of circulation that mainstream music production relies upon.

These points are clarified in a meeting with Marinho, which had been arranged by my teacher, José, who informed me that Marinho had been playing rural music since the 1940s. I realized, upon arrival at Marinho's São Paulo office off the Praça da Republica that morning of March 14, 2000, that José's reason for scheduling this encounter had been twofold. Yes, he had wanted me to meet Marinho so that I could ask him questions. But José also wanted to consult with Marinho on a song which Marinho had written; José hoped to place the song on his next record. The meeting took place within the physical space that Marinho used to conduct his work for the ECAD, which, he informed me, he had helped to found. Indeed, during the meeting, Marinho's work for the ECAD provided a constant but nevertheless unmarked reminder of the importance of arithmetic modes of circulation to rural music. The meeting was punctuated by phone calls, faxes, and Marinho's brief absences as he proofread letters, checked song lyrics, and looked up publishers to help artists get paid for the playing of their songs in public space.

Moments after we arrived, I found myself in a side office with Marinho and José, evaluating circulation from the standpoints of song authorship and the rendition of a song text for later playback. Marinho, the song's author, would be teaching José what song form to employ— what mixture of rhythm, inflection, and key. The two were thus busily preparing to cassette-record the song. Using the cassette, José could then practice the new rhythm with his absent brother. José requested that I make a backup of the proceedings with my digital minidisc, in part for his own reference, and in part to show the device off to Marinho. For José, at that moment, the technological advancement of the equipment I was capable of bringing to bear on the project was a token of the quality of the work I could do on rural music. The two began to warm up and quickly fell into step. Marinho instructed José to sing the lead part as a way of practicing for the eventual official recording session where José would be singing lead to his brother's higher harmonic "second." Marinho pressed the record button on the cassette player, and I did the same on my minidisc recorder. Marinho then played the opening chords on his *viola* and seemed about to launch into the song, but instead surprised both me and José by making a declamation; José had actually leaned in toward the cassette recorder on the table to start singing and was forced to tip back suddenly. Far from the recorders hampering the proceedings, as ethnographers often fear that they might, in this case the devices had positively enhanced the occasion because Marinho took a new "footing" (Goffman 1979) with respect to the meeting: that of the seasoned warrior helping a neo-phyte (me) in pursuit of a worthy goal (academic research on Brazilian rural music). He addressed me by way of the cassette and minidisc, and the circulatability of his message, its future playability, channeled his speech.

> Um . . . Brother José, is visiting me today, and brought Alex—this guy I've had the great pleasure of meeting. He's Canadian—but he is . . . an APPRECIATOR of the viola, of the rural musical genre. And he's doing a wonderful study. It is necessary that many people in Brazil should wake up and grab this flag, to tell the story of our rural music, to show to our youth—the children—our *culture*, our roots music. So I congratulate Alex, for his marvelous work. Thank you, Alex. Thank you very much. And proceed with this fight. And whatever you should need from this old *caboclo*, whatever I can offer you, I'm at your complete disposal. . . . And now I'm going to sing a song with brother José—"Burnt Hitching Post"—a song he's going to put on the record he's doing. I'm going to do the first, and he's going to do the second.

In concert with rural musical song texts, Marinho presented himself as a *caboclo*, and then expressed concern that the ways of the past were under threat. I was directed to take up a "flag" and save dangerously exposed "roots" from death. The enterprise was pedagogical in that my work was to be used to educate children.

With that, they played through the song, which portrayed circulation not in terms of water, but fire. As in Jeca's case, in this song, memory becomes both the music's problem and its opportunity. And consistent with Brandão's notion that Brazilian rural music forms the repository for the quotidian (chapter 3), the narrator laments that life's small and seemingly unimportant moments are burned up by the passage of time. This is problematic because if memories all burn away, then nothing will remain of the self. The song furnishes hope, though, because memories may be recoverable in the ashes. Singing thus becomes the occasion for sifting through those ashes, calling forth the poignant memory of a boy's discussion with his father. Music both circulates and recovers memory, which, in this case, is a piece of the narrator's youth, off in those hills. Writ large, music restores a natural process of recovering trivial fragments of the past, thereby allowing you to remember who you *are*. Musical circulation thus constitutes rural subjectivity itself.

Consider the song in detail: "Burnt Hitching Post" begins with the narrator remembering a fire off in the distance, seen from his window when he was a boy:

> When I was still a child
> One night, long ago,
> I saw a flash of fire
> In the forest far away.[12] (Luiz Faria and Silva Neto)

The boy's father explains that he should not be afraid; the fire is not destructive, but portends new growth. The fire evidences man's interaction with the land because farmers burn weeds and undergrowth to prepare the earth for planting. But the hitching post is a kind of unanticipated casualty in this process. It catches and burns because of its closeness to the weeds, not because the farmer wants to get rid of it. It is this minor accident which provides the bright reminder of what took place long ago. The song thus celebrates serendipity:

> My father said: don't be afraid
> It's some hitching post still burning
> That's left over from the fire
> To prepare the ground for planting.

The narrator then uses this incident as a way to reflect on memory itself. He explains that the harsh realities of life burn up just this sort of seemingly unimportant happening, leaving us only ashes. And as we know, such memories are far from trivial. They are the means by which our entire life is recalled and retained, and the song, like the ashes, is the repository of the past which, in circulation, evokes the memories of listeners' very own "burning hitching posts":

> You might tell me that it's silly
> To remember things this way
> Things so little, but important
> I keep inside me to this day.
> In the smoke left by my passing
> Summers gone in tens and twenties
> I left that fire far away
> In the distance of the plains.

Chorus
Burnt hitching post
Together with my childhood dreams
On the plains of destiny
It became ashes, as did I—
Ashes of time
In the fire of memory
I am the ashes of that child
That the past has kept around.

After José and Marinho finished, we returned to the main office and sat down. The conversation moved much more freely now that the recording had facilitated the expression of half of the day's purpose, which was allowing these performers and songwriters to teach me, the outsider, about rural music in the Central-South. José, Marinho, and Edilson (a songwriting friend of Marinho's who had come to ask for advice—also a pseudonym) discussed their hopes. Edilson expressed his expectations for his upcoming participation in a song competition sponsored by a large São Paulo newspaper, the *Folha de São Paulo*. Winning the competition garnered radio airtime and sometimes major record contracts, or at least the possibility that a mainstream artist might record your winning song. Marinho explicitly "passed on" pieces of information to José, Edilson, and myself, particularly about song forms, and charged all of us with remembering them, attending to the fact that I was digitally recording the conversation. They all referred to the compact disc that José was in the process of completing; they agreed that the production of CDs provided the most important countermeasure to the recording industry's bankrupt politics. The recording of a disc would, it was thought, help to establish social networks that might be used to forward the cause of tradition.

Commodification

> Marinho: Cornélio Pires was the first to bring the *caipira* to disk. I had the great fortune of being carried on the shoulders of Cornélio Pires when I was four, and I'm proud of that.

As noted in the previous chapter, many rural musicians take note of the importance of Cornélio Pires's first recordings of rural music. Their triumphal stories about Pires might have begun with his first show of rural music at Mackenzie University in the city of São Paulo, in 1910. And yet, they do not. They begin, instead, with Pires's first *recordings* of rural music. The celebration of Pires's act of commodification in the present emphasizes current preoccupations with mediation. For Pires, the latest technology was the 78 RPM record. Today, it is the compact disc. Rural musicians attempting to launch a career continually called my attention to their new CDs. At the Americana Rodeo of 2006, for instance, Alysson and Alessandro, twin brothers just getting their start, immediately offered me a copy of their new CD. It was their calling card and proved their credibility. Their proud father, who had funded the project through his local business, stood by and beamed. And the record seemed to have worked in a way, in that the two got to open the night's performance of megastar Daniel (once of dupla João Paulo and Daniel). The CD was also important to those who circulated rural music in small towns in the countryside. In one small radio station, the host of one of the station's rural musical programs sat me down one day to lecture me on the importance of the CD. "I only work with duplas that have a recorded CD," he told me flatly. He went on to explain that the recorded CD indicated a level of professionalism, preparation, and the desire to be taken seriously. Thus, in concert with those who celebrated Cornélio Pires's first recordings, and in agreement with the likes of José and Marinho, this host believed that the recording itself, correctly employed, could and should be used as the means of conveying rurality.

José's approach to his career demonstrated what he and others referred to as the "conviction, dedication, and hard work" required for someone to establish his career in music. I noted, in the last chapter, that José had quit his job in order to pursue music full-time. He knew that if he was going to get anywhere, perhaps having his songs heard on the radio and played on television, he needed a professionally recorded disc. His first task, therefore, was the act of commodification itself; all other opportunities would flow from this.

He had thought long and hard about how he ought to create the CD. His planning process had revolved around evaluating other rural musical CDs, establishing which ones were good, and coming to an understanding of the mistakes in others. In order to demonstrate the criteria by which he thought a rural record ought to be judged, in this way revealing the "natural" constraints within which he felt he must operate, he played excerpts from many recent records for me. He pointed out problems and noted how he would do better. For instance, he told me that no *real* rural musician would play such an ornate viola fill in that spot; it was too "flowery" and indicated that the violeiro had studied academically. In another place, a particular player was described as not "playing from the heart." He was failing to acknowledge the simple fact that the viola as an instrument was "sentimental by nature." José attended carefully, not only to the musical features of the discs, but also to their visual attributes. Along these lines, he showed me a picture of a dupla whose record he found musically sound but visually unacceptable because the pair stood beside a painted concrete wall. A rail wooden fence was the correct thing to stand beside, or perhaps something natural, such as a forest, river, or tree. He would not make the same mistake and worked hard to find a photographer who would make the long drive into the state of Mato Grosso do Sul to photograph him and his brother beside the specific river that would adorn the cover of their record *Splendid River* (Rio Formoso)—one of several "sweet" water rivers near the town of Bonito.

He recorded the album over a period of a year, making trips to the interior every few weeks with his brother, the other half of his dupla. In 2002 the record was finally ready. He pressed one thousand copies and held a CD release party where he lived, in Campinas, at a local venue called the Via Roça (see chapter 7). He began to market the disc to local record shops. Some television and radio appearances on local stations followed. He sold the thousand copies in a year and made another thousand in 2003. He cautiously declared that things were going according to plan. The carefully produced record had opened some doors. He continued to hope that it might fling many other doors *wide* open, so that he could get a spot in the mainstream somewhere. As of this writing, this has yet to occur.

José's discourse about his record made it clear that he held great hopes. In our meeting with Marinho, he pulled out a recent disc he had done to show that he had not stopped recording rural music with the death of his longtime partner. What is important to note here is that for both José and Marinho, neither the process of commodification, nor the actual CD itself, was deemed destructive of rurality in any way. Quite the opposite was true. The CD simply became the conduit for rural ideas and hopes. Far from the "medium" in some sense being perceived *as* the message (McLuhan 2005), these users of the compact disc believed that it could transmit quite specific cultural messages (Turner

2002). Even more important, where we might have imagined that technology would be perceived as destructive of "real" Brazilian rurality, hailing, as it does, from nonrural locations, we see that in fact technology's products may well circulate in such a way that they harmonize with "country."

Natural Listening

As Marinho worked hard in the background of our conversation to see that artists were paid for their work, it nevertheless became clear that all three musicians worried about the circulatory process of rural music. As we have seen, they all believed in the possibility that rural music circulated on CDs could transmit each song's distinct emotional message. Thus, when the mainstream musical system was functioning properly, albeit a rare occurrence, the songs that were emotionally the most powerful were the ones that were selling, simply because people were moved by them.

However, the possibility that individuals might listen to a song for the wrong reasons emerged as a prominent anxiety. Here, an unwanted instrumentality entered the circulatory process in the form of money for bribes to play certain songs instead of others: a production-sided fear. "This makes it even harder for the rural musician to get himself heard," José informed me. Because the rural musician is, the story goes, of humble origins, he has no money to pay this *jabá* (in the United States, "payola").[13] Marinho gives the example of an acquaintance:

> I get really upset when I have the misfortune of watching Oswaldo Cunha's [a pseudonym] program on television. Because I have known Oswaldo Cunha since he was eight years old. Oswaldo grew up singing and recording rural music with his brother, a great viola player. Did you know his program was pulled off TV because of *corruption*?!

Such diatribes over payola can be heard all over the world. But the point in this Brazilian context is that the success or failure of a rural song ought to be based on that song's emotional power and the congruence of that emotional power with natural processes of flowing, burning, and blowing.

This sort of congruence may take place when songs are addressed to listeners through a personalized historical process. In these situations, the song simply calls out directly through its clarity of sentiment. In Marinho's words, a good song should simply "stop the audience dead in its tracks," taking it almost by force. Or, songs may be "sent" by one person to another. Many radio programs encourage call-ins, where those figured for the purposes of the sending as "listeners" can send songs to other listeners. With respect to Central-Southern rural genres, commercial radio maintains this practice, augmenting it at peak hours. Often listeners call in to offer a song to a member of the opposite sex to whom they wish to send a message of affection. In effect, rural genres fulfill this messenger-bird function a great deal in Brazil.

Similarly, hosts may choose to send out portions of the radio program to specific people. During my fieldwork I made weekly visits to the town of Itapira, where a Sunday rural music radio show was hosted by Marcão (a pseudonym), a warm-hearted and friendly character in his late fifties who supported himself as a barber and simply hosted the show on the weekends out of love for rural music. His show was intended to recreate an older style of radio program in which music acted as a kind of glue for the community. The show was about music as a practice embedded in family sociality and, by extension, family friends. He told stories about the duplas that had performed on the show, sent pieces of the program out to listeners who were having birthdays, who were sick, or who he simply knew were listening, and generally focused intently on the environs of Itapira, Mogi Mirim, and Mogi Guaçu, which were all within the Itapira Rádio Clube's reach. His show therefore created a kind of community of listening akin to those described by Spitulnik (Spitulnik 1997, 163). As an example, on one occasion he began the day's broadcast with the following:

> Our oration goes out today above all to all our Rádio Clube listeners, those who dig our program—to you, Donilda—to those here in the city who are affiliated with the Rádio Clube—this oration goes out entirely to you. I want to offer it to Chico, of Black Point, Dona Thereza, to Dona Luz, Chico's girlfriend, to Chico at the Itaú Bank, to Santa, my son Roberto, who's having a birthday today, to all our fans, to my wife, to all my kids as well, to Edson, Ronaldo, and all our fans—to Marcio Dinortes. I also want to offer today's program—today's oration—to Sergio Fonereiro, our friend, to Thereza Amira. To the directors of the Radio Clube, Ronaldo and Flávio, we ask Nossa Senhora, the patron of Brazil, to cover all the directors and workers of the Rádio Clube with her sacred mantle. I also want to offer it especially to the infirm of our hospitals, to

the elderly in the homes of our city, to all those who are listening to the Rádio Clube, to our violeiros, all our friends, our companions, I offer this oration to the patron of Brazil, Our Lady of the Appearance.

This was the way he almost always began his broadcasts, before launching into a prayer entreating Our Lady for her protection and care. Every once in a while he would demand that I, the Canadian, come up to the microphone and say a few words to "our listeners." In this way, the circulatory matrix of the show explicitly traced itself onto the physical and social space of the radio station's environs, reaching out beyond what was taking place in front of the microphone into what was emerging from radios out in the town. This represented not so much an attempt to blur the boundaries between something we might think of as a mediated text and that text's public, folding the roles of audience and musician into each other. Rather, by rendering a mass-mediated musical performance in terms of a much smaller, familial and face-to-face one, Marcão strove to map the natural circulatory patterns of rural music onto its technological ones.

A series of assumptions remains constant across both traditional and commercial approaches to rural music. Not the least of these is that commodities may carry rural sentimentality. When something called the market functions according to rural proclivities, music addresses listeners through emotional forces that flow, burn, and sometimes stampede. Rural music is therefore deemed to be most successful when the qualities of its circulation, mass, or otherwise, are in concert with the "naturally" occurring emotional attributes in evidence in rural song texts. In the next chapter, we will explore in detail the way in which traditionalists tie Central-Southern rurality to emotional states that emerge specifically from song forms. In the final chapter, we will explore the way in which commercially successful musical acts orient Central-Southern rurality toward a country cosmopolitan.

Producing Rural Locality

> With the fight for redemocratization and with the process of
> political "opening" that marks the end of the military cycle,
> old questions are beginning to become relevant once again.
> In this way, despite—or perhaps because of—a growing cen-
> tralization, we may now observe tendencies that run against
> this centralization, which manifest themselves through an
> emphasis on the necessity of a real federalism, the proclama-
> tion of the advantages of administrative decentralization, the
> clamor for tax reform that would give more resources to states
> and municipalities, and the affirmation of regional and state
> identities that emphasize their differences in relation to the
> rest of Brazil.—RUBEN OLIVEN, The Part and the Whole: Cultural
> Diversity in the Brazilian Nation

Producing Locality

In the last chapter we saw how, in the neoliberal period, a series of
genres once deemed regional began to appropriate electric and electronic instrumentation. At the same time, practitioners of these genres
oriented themselves toward larger publics than they had previously
aspired to; after 1985, sales of axé, pagode, forró, and, most of all, música
sertaneja blossomed. Within the field of rural musical production, a
quadrant of the field that opposed aspects of música sertaneja emphasized music's traditional possibilities instead. This portion of the field
claimed to dislike what it characterized as an alarming increase in the
commercial bent of the rural mainstream. Note that the arguments
involved a state of affairs in brisk motion. A "rapid increase in sales,"
together with the impending "crisis" such sales might bring, thus
bifurcated musical rurality. On one hand, commercial música sertaneja
grounded itself in an ethos of cosmopolitanism, which we shall visit in
chapter 8, the next chapter. On the other hand, música caipira relied upon
"locality," our subject here.

as a modern nation, diverse identity are being consumed? Locality prevents this?

Producing Rural Locality 187

Locality involves a group's sense of itself in relation to a larger whole, where generically acceptable texts are made first to agglutinate, and then to articulate with broader co(n)texts framed as national, and sometimes, international. Central-Southern rural locality manufactures consciousness through the stipulation of group characteristics from which participants may select as they fashion themselves as "country" people, tied corporeally to a "country" space. In order to produce traditional rurality, actors semiotically shape identity and agency (see Silverstein 1998a, 403). This requires mediation by way of such things as language, economic exchange, political participation, writing, or music in order to knit culture together with location. It is important to note that emphasis on the local derives from an epistemological crisis concerning the very possibility of its existence. Anxieties over an expanding commercialism emerge from the way in which commercialism is thought to index a reaching outward, *away* from "here," wherever here happens to be. This distal motion poses a threat. All in all, it is not so much that our current moment has severed locality from geopolitical space (Appadurai 1996, 1998), but that a building *sense* of delocalization has intensified the importance of focusing *upon* locality as something that counters cosmopolitanism. *too national?*

To elaborate, I focus on a concert that took place in Campinas on February 12, 2000, put on by the folkloric *dupla* of brothers Zé Mulato and Cassiano. The show was staged at a restaurant known as the Via Roça, which can be translated as country road(s), country path, country way of life, or country way of "doing things." I also step outside the concert to explain significant concepts using other performances, interviews, and readings. In the course of this show, rural locality accrues by way of emphasis on the *viola*, stress on traditional song-forms, valuation of the past, elaboration of *caboclo* ways of storytelling, a distinct mediation between music and language as modalities of communicative practice, and attention to plants and animals of the Central-South. Other important features include harmonization, audience participation, storytelling, and song selection. Finally, locality is framed here by food and the deliberately constructed "rural" space in which both food and music are to be enjoyed. These interlocking media are mobilized to tell a story about the too-quick urbanization of Brazil, and together they form the cornerstone of a discourse about the cultural distinctness of the Central-South within the ambit of an expanding postdictatorial Brazilian multiculturalism.

It is central to my argument that audience and performers collaborate in voicing their critical consciousness *through* music. As noted in chapter 3, though performers of folkloric regional musical genres reject the notion that samba holds the key to Brazilian musicality, they nonetheless adhere to the idea that music plays a crucial role in Brazilian life. According to them, música caipira provides a potent way for artists to transform their present by engaging with their past. It also provides a means to reflect and act upon the position of the Central-South within Brazil and its place in the world system. Música caipira targets local manifestations of globalization, particularly those in which Brazilians unreflectively appropriate generic features thought of as urban and/or foreign to transform música sertaneja into a commercial success.

The didactic nature of the show under scrutiny here is a concomitant of all of this. Zé Mulato and Cassiano believe that, in the act of playing music for others, they are, in fact, not just entertaining, they are *teaching*. Terms that make such pedagogy explicit emerge both onstage and in discussions of why what happens onstage matters. How did everyone present, including the audience, *learn*? They learned through a musically structured dialogue between mind and body. In acts of listening, clapping, singing along, laughing, and crying, I was told that audience members trained themselves to value Central-Southern principles that related sound production to emotional governance. Audience members thereby became more historically sensitive in a way deemed specifically Central-Southern. The musically instantiated body thus becomes the site through which philosophical arguments play out. For all involved, one of the ways this takes place is through the mediation between language and music as modes of communicative practice. But for the truly devoted student, this bodily and emotional learning may take place in that most transformative of practices: learning to play the *viola*.

My treatment of this chapter's material draws upon Paul Connerton's insights about practical activity, embedded structures, and the body for theorizing about social memory (1989, 71). Connerton distinguishes between two kinds of cultural practice important to memory: inscribing ones, in which participants pay explicit attention to the inculcation of memory, and incorporating ones, where memory slips in without much being said. Claiming that the social sciences have been preoccupied with the former, Connerton (1989, 100) wishes to focus instead on the latter. He argues that societies don't just remember through the edifying consumption of text artifacts composed and read as "histories."

Rather, they remember through performances that inculcate history through the physical experience of certain kinds of texts. As important as incorporating practices are, however, we must also consider the *relationship* between explicit and implicit components of memory. In other words, the always dynamic space between the ideological and the hegemonic provides the key to memory. Public rituals such as the one that I witnessed on February 12, 2000 operate simultaneously on an incorporating level, through listening, singing, clapping, laughing, and playing, and on an inscribing level, through lyrics, intersong banter, audience conversations, and discussions about the show after the fact. In considering "tradition," here defined as adherence to antecedent productions of a genre, we must be able to analyze the way that bodily participation (incorporation) and philosophical argument (inscription) fashion historical consciousness simultaneously.

The Show: Zé Mulato and Cassiano

Zé Mulato and Cassiano present themselves during their show on February 12, 2000 within the context of the overarching narrative of the popularization and commercialization of rural music that they hope their music counteracts. They recorded their first record in 1978 and struck listeners at once with their combination of three strands from música caipira history: sentimental power, comic political savvy, and superb viola playing. They recorded four more records between 1979 and 1982, at which point, as they tell it during the show, their record company tried to "modernize" them by dressing them in stylish clothes, arranging their songs with drum kits and electric guitars, and requesting more songs about love. They refused to comply. They claim to have been so nauseated by the commercialization of rural music which took place in the 1980s that they simply stopped recording altogether. They continued to play, but they did so mostly for friends and family, and when they faced an audience of strangers, it was only at small venues. Zé still wrote some songs, but the brothers supplemented their income with jobs outside of music. Zé, for example, worked as a security guard. These details and others like them come out in bits and pieces over the course of the evening and together add up to the dupla's version of a transformation of the musical field whereby once-folkloric rural music became commercially successful while Brazil went from a rural nation to a nation of rural people forced to live in cities. Though they, too, were forced to take part in the latter transition, they refused to participate in the former, and hence remained on the sidelines, watching as other brothers successfully adopted the formulas their producers had encouraged them to use.

Several developments treated in the last chapter on circulation returned them to recording. These included an increasing potential for independent production brought by low-cost digital technology, the proliferation of independent labels seeking to record traditional musics, and the presence of traditionalists with the wherewithal to push them back into recording. The traditionalists included dupla Pena Branca and Xavatinho, and later, viola player and folkloric composer Roberto Corrêa. He helped Zé Mulato and his brother assemble, produce, and record an LP entitled *My Sky*. Corrêa then arranged to release it on a small label called Velas in 1997. In addition to critical acclaim, this record won them the most prestigious musical award in Brazil, the *Prêmio Sharp*,[1] in the best "roots" category, in 1998. The press coverage this garnered relaunched their career, stepping up their schedule of shows. The dupla followed this success with another record in 1999—*Navegante das Gerais* (Sailor of Minas, or, someone who navigates the Central-Southern state of Minas Gerais), which was also a critical success. Their latest two projects, *New Blood* (2003) and *Best Days* (2007) were released on their own independent label, Brazilian Viola Shows Productions. Since the dupla Pena Branca and Xavatinho was halved by the death of Xavatinho in 1999, Zé Mulato and Cassiano are, arguably, at present, the most-esteemed música caipira duo.

Zé Mulato and Cassiano framed the music I heard that night in terms of a dark period of the commercialization of rurality—essentially, its transformation into current ultrapopular música sertaneja—followed by a hard-fought present-day reemergence into the light of the folkloric. The idea behind this was that despite the continued popularity of música sertaneja, there had been some small "space" opened up for their folkloric efforts, as evidenced by the slow but reliable sale of their recordings, but chiefly in their success booking shows such as this one at the Via Roça. The importance of promoting tradition at a time in which they perceived it to be under siege emerges, not just from the statements they make in interviews and before audiences, but from the urgency of their delivery. Both on- and offstage, they orient themselves toward preservation. Despite injury in a serious car accident in 2004, Zé and his brother have continued a busy schedule, and Zé has begun to write songs for up-and-coming folkloric duplas, which his manager and friend then release on the dupla's Viola Shows label. Composing songs for other duplas in the folkloric category is one way Zé feels that he significantly contributes to an overall effort to revitalize the traditions of the Central-South. He "offers" his songs as gifts to younger players so that they may, in a sense, ride them upward toward success.

A discussion of Zé Mulato and Cassiano's past in the music industry formed part of the February 2000 show. Two important additional details were in evidence on this particular evening. First, the show reinforced the simultaneous emphasis upon, and neutralization of, the social hierarchy discussed in chapter 2. Zé unquestionably led the pair with his viola playing, and his "second" lower voice carried the melody. His tone was deep and contrasted with Cassiano's higher one. Cassiano played a supporting role onstage, rarely interjecting spoken comments, and most often only doing so after Zé had initiated something that called for a quick response. In the pair's history, Zé also does most of the songwriting, only occasionally composing with Cassiano or other partners. Second, and more important for this chapter's argument about the mingling of incorporating and inscribing practices in the performance of locality, Zé's compositions run the gamut of música caipira song-forms. He creates pieces that range from melancholy to upbeat and amusing, and his lyrics match the tempo, tonality, and vocal delivery of the song form in which they are cast. His ability to command all of these modes of mediating between linguistic and musical communicative practice will be discussed in more detail below. But to establish this mediation and the various components that compose it, we turn to some of the other ways in which locality was produced in the course of the evening of February 12, 2000.

Country Roads

A series of actors needed to collaborate in order for the show to take place. The music was staged at the Via Roça, which opened in 1998 as a restaurant selling food from the interior of São Paulo and Minas Gerais. Owner Fifa speaks of her restaurant and musical space as emerging from her experience running a kindergarten in a rural town in Minas Gerais in the 1970s. During these years, she was appalled to learn that many of her young charges knew nothing whatsoever of their local folktales, dances, and songs, and she set about attempting to teach them the traditions of the Central-South. In the early 1980s she moved to Campinas and explains that she maintained her emphasis on the traditional, though no longer explicitly in the field of education. Instead of teaching school in Campinas, she opened a store that sold products such as furniture, fabric, paintings, carvings, and embroidery produced by artisans from the Central-South, especially Minas Gerais. However, after doing this for several years she wanted a change and felt that the combination of music with food would provide a more powerful means to preserve tradition. Her customers agree. Fifa notes that despite the overwhelming importance of the music, the food seems to be what keeps people coming back. It provides a kind of nourishing foundation, she ventures. And it is certainly true that on less crowded evenings, most audience members eat dinner either before or during the musical performance.[2] Diners note that the ability to do so is part of the place's appeal. Essentially, they feel themselves to be experiencing *caipira* music in its natural environs—on the porch, during or after dinner. But what is important here is that Fifa feels that she has arrived at the consummate method for preserving tradition. It is one that relies heavily upon folk theories of incorporation, not just of music, but of sustenance that diners literally take into their bodies (Mintz 1996; Wilk 1999, 244). Food, here, plays a vital role in the propagation of memory (Holtzman 2006).

Fifa is not alone in suggesting that caipira food and drink support rural music and a rural way of life. Celebrations of caipira food within the context of discussions of music often revolve around the flavor given to meats, bean stews, and vegetables by cooking them over a wood-fired stove. Nothing else tastes the same, we are told. In no other cuisine does one get the same mixture of aromas, often described as descending from mingling indigenous and Portuguese cooking, and at other times described as partaking of the conditions associated with cattle herding, as in the "Garlic Burning" of chapter 4. One web site called "Caipira World," run by a literature professor and a computer scientist from Goiânia in the state of Goiás, is devoted to the preservation of rural culture and offers recipes for what it refers to as caipira cooking. The site also sells caipira food, grills, and stills for making sugarcane rum called *cachaça*. Also, the personal site of the grande dame of música caipira, Inezita Barroso, host of the folkloric television show

Viola, Minha Viola, contains a section devoted to recipes. As a final example, José's record, the subject of so much conversation in the last chapter, contains songs about food, such as one in which he stresses that his favorite dish is manioc.

When Fifa opened her restaurant, she thought that she would host one performance a month of what she often calls "roots music." However, after an extremely well-attended show in October of 1999, which I attended and will address below, Fifa increased the number of concerts from one a month to one a week. The October show had convinced her that there was an audience for this kind of music. Not only had a large number of people turned out, but they had paid a great deal for their tickets. Since then numerous significant figures within the ambit of a música caipira revival have played at the Via Roça.[3] Moreover, as the restaurant grows in popularity, it has begun to host more than just concerts. Fifa offers a location for viola-playing competitions, June Festivals, stage performances of Three Kings' processions called *Folia de Reis*, traditional dances called *catira*, courses in viola playing, and CD release parties for local viola orchestras and musicians such as José.

The Via Roça is located in a rural suburb of Campinas, about ten miles from downtown. Though ten miles might seem like a small distance, the conditions traversed in order to get there make that distance seem large and provide an important aspect of the experience of listening to music there. The route resembles a series of deep scars of red dust and concealed ruts that fill with water when it rains. Often, by the time I arrived, I considered myself to be in the middle of nowhere, or perhaps to have traveled back to the past. Other audience members frequently commented on the isolation of the place, particularly in wet conditions. On nights when it rained, shows had to be held back, sometimes for hours, in order to allow advance ticket-buyers the time to show up. To make matters worse, the actual acts themselves sometimes found the way there impassable.[4]

Perhaps in part *because* of the tribulations involved in arriving there, shows at the Via Roça are often well attended, that is, they draw between fifty and one hundred people. Fifa advertises on posterboards outside the general store in nearby Guará, at UNICAMP (the State University of Campinas, and one of the most prominent universities in Brazil), and for more famous performers, she pays for spots on Rádio Morena, which plays MPB, folkloric material, and some jazz. The restaurant draws a literate crowd from nearby Barão Geraldo, the part of

Campinas where UNICAMP is located, and from the city of Campinas itself. At shows, I encountered university professors, schoolteachers, small businessmen and women, web designers, translators, journalists, musicians, and university and business administrators. The prices for tickets and food made the Via Roça slightly more expensive than other roadside places, but a good deal cheaper than expensive restaurants in Campinas itself. The Via Roça caters to a middle-class audience of people who have graduated from basic schooling and, most frequently, have continued with some form of postsecondary education. These people work in professional and educational fields. Some of them eschew commercial rural music. Most do not. But all of them enjoy traditional rural music.

The Via Roça itself consists of a small raised house with a porch that extends out to form a covered space holding up to two hundred chairs (see figure 3). It is constructed of heavy logs. The floor is cement. The ceilings are approximately fifteen feet high at the center of the structure. There is a small slightly raised stage at the front of this space, backed by a screen of saplings bound together. Mobiles of horses and armadillo shells, both from the state of Minas Gerais, hang from the ceiling—the kinds of items Fifa once sold at her store. Listeners are surrounded on all sides by forest. The car park is a grassy paddock.

The space itself is designed so that when you sit in it, you feel as though you're sitting on the enormous porch of a small house. The tiny house itself mimics a country shack like the ones appearing in the lyrics of so many of the songs performed at the restaurant.[5] The idea is that music should be experienced in a mode as close as possible to the way it would have been experienced in caipira society: on the porch, in the evening, over, or perhaps just after a meal, with a glass of sugarcane rum (pinga, or cachaça). You can sometimes hear the crickets chirping between songs. Thus the setup of the Via Roça argues for presenting music as an aspect of daily life, rather than in a concert hall. It enacts its highly formalized informality, and its in-the-woods quality often gets incorporated explicitly into the music.

A different show from the one under consideration in this chapter illustrates this fact especially well. Almir Sater played the sold-out concert that caused Fifa to augment her musical schedule in October of 1999. Midway through his first set, Sater concurred that this was indeed like playing at a house somewhere "well into the countryside." And Almir, normally known for shows with little dialogue between songs,

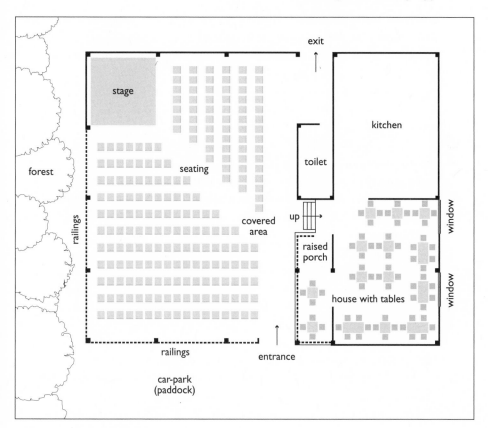

Figure 3. Plan of the Via Roça.

opened up in a way that none present had ever seen. He shared stories from his childhood, talked about his experiences as a soap-opera star, and gave detailed accounts of the writing of several of his most famous songs. A show that would normally have lasted only two hours stretched to over four because he spent so much time chatting. The audience listened to every word and note with rapt attention. And no one left the Via Roça until Sater had played two encores and it was quite clear that no amount of applause would produce a third. Those who had seen him play before were thunderstruck at his loquacity. Into the third hour of the show he paused, suddenly looking surprised. "Wow, I'm talking a lot," he said. "It must be this *place*." He finished his story and played the song. Thus are the special attributes of the performance location contextualized onstage. This particular performance was tied to a distinct set of circumstances, which indexed the countryside itself. Here, Sater is telling us, in this bucolic setting, rural music is at home, and I, a rural person, am at home. What more could a music that strives for at-homeness aspire to?

Setting the Frame

Let us return now to the show at the Via Roça on February 12, 2000. It took place on an evening in which the rain had turned the roads into mud slides, and Zé Mulato and Cassiano took the stage at eleven, three hours behind schedule.[6] They immediately set the frame for the evening's entertainment with an old-fashioned declaration harmonized in parallel thirds and unfolding according to a song structure called *moda de viola*, or simply, viola song:

> I'm here.
> My people—I'm here.
> To sing for missus and mister.
> To sing for missus and mister.[7] (Zé Mulato and Cassiano 1999)

Cassiano's nylon-string guitar only entered after the opening words, when the tune departed from the moda de viola song-form and entered a more lively beat called a *batuque*, in which the musical line is no longer tied to the rhythm of the singers' words. The brothers continued: "I'm here to show you a *real moda* (song), something *purely* from the countryside." Here, they cast aspersions on música sertaneja by implying that it is made up of *unreal* modas, things *impurely* from the countryside. Zé Mulato and Cassiano thus set a contrastive dynamic structure of expectations in place for the evening's performance. This dig has the audience chuckling and clapping from the first moments of the show. Of course, that this would *not* be an evening of commercial música sertaneja needn't have been pointed out. The traditional dress, hick accents, traditional harmony, song form, and the location itself spoke for themselves.

"Thank you, thank you," Zé responds to the applause for the opening number, "but none of you should really be clapping, because you're all *violeiros*." This remark frames the evening's proceedings once again and gets a burst of laughter. His false modesty amuses the audience, which

[handwritten margin notes: "Popular conceptions of music", "vs. rural"] is still cheering for the opening number. Zé's joke is oriented toward the presence of two *violeiros* whose CDs have received national attention and who regularly perform on stages throughout the country: Paulo Freire, and João Ormonde. Zé points them out next, though even those who don't know them personally already know they are present since Fifa has named them in her introduction. But Zé's opening remark is not only aimed at clarifying the presence of these particular audience members. It is also oriented toward the Central-South more broadly; the idea is that we are on Central-Southern music's home turf, and therefore, we might all be said to be viola players.

After Zé's establishment of the group of listeners that so importantly constitutes the space in which he will play and sing, he continues by placing the evening's events into a musical line that extends into the early twentieth century. He runs through a list of duplas stretching back to the 1920s. "There are so many great duplas you just have to listen to. You have to listen to Zé Carreiro and Carreirinho, Tonico and Tinoco, Raul Torres and Florêncio, [Pedro Bento and] Zé da Estrada, Pena Branca and Xavatinho, Tião Carreiro and Pardinho." You "have" to listen to them in the same way that students "have" to do their homework; the self-improvement that will result becomes a civic duty. The placement of Zé Mulato's and Cassiano's performance within the context of other greats from the history of música caipira continues throughout the night. Later, Zé will mention Roberto Corrêa, whom he declares to be perhaps the greatest living violeiro. Zé and his brother also play, late in the evening, a version of a song made famous by Tião Carreiro and Pardinho, noting as they do so that playing the song is a way of acknowledging those who came before them, their musical ancestors, so to speak. Through these citations, Zé provides a musical genealogy for himself and the audience, establishing the standards by which he expects to be judged. All of them played rural music and were either famous before what he will later call the "modernization" of rural genres that created música sertaneja, or they strongly resisted such trends and insisted on playing folkloric rural music.

Zé places himself and his brother firmly in the company of those resisting. Early in the evening, he criticizes the record company that recorded their early albums, a company he tells us he will not name.[8] He tells of the company's offensive attempt to "modernize" them by having them do away with their caipira accent, wear more urban clothes, arrange their songs with electric guitars and drums, and write about love.

Cassiano adds that the two of them, both short and stout, were even pressured to practice moving their hips seductively onstage, a notion the audience finds riotously funny. Throughout, part of what they present as their inalienable essence as hicks emerges in their rigorous use of the hick accent Pires both studied and employed. For these traditionalists, the accent is not only *not* something to be ashamed of. It becomes a badge of honor and proof that they are, at their very core, rural people. In contrast to those other romantic crooners who speak Standard Portuguese, we, Zé continues, speak *this* way, unapologetically.

Rattlesnakes, Graveyards, and Cantankerous Musical Machines

The viola plays an important role in the performance of traditional rural music and is spoken of as the musical embodiment of "country."[9] This is apparent in the opening declaration in which the viola doubles the singing voice. Zé's *viola caipira* executes different parts from Cassiano's guitar, which mainly provides the chord structure and rhythm. It is the violeiro who is prominent as the instrumental soloist, his instrument sometimes accompanying the singing voices. The viola is featured because it embodies sentimentality. As José once informed me in an irritated quip in the middle of one of our lessons: "The viola is sentimental by nature." Part of this sentimentality is thought to arise from its sound, produced by its hourglass shape, small body, and metal strings. These attributes combine to give it a more piercing tone than the nylon-string guitar. Well played, it is often described as sobbing in both song and speech.

In performance, violeiros frequently call attention to the instrument, most often by pointing out that it is notably difficult to tune. This is because it has ten strings, patterned in five pairs that are tuned "open"— which is to say that the instrument strummed with nothing fretted in the left hand produces a major chord (see figure 4).[10]

The bottom pair of strings, closest to the chin of the violeiro when he is playing, is tuned in an octave, as are the next two pairs moving down the instrument. The highest two pairs are tuned in unison.[11] Two ways of explaining the degree of difficulty involved in tuning the viola involve scientifically grounded acoustics. First, the frequency of doubled notes in the viola makes errors in tuning easier to perceive. Second, the differ-

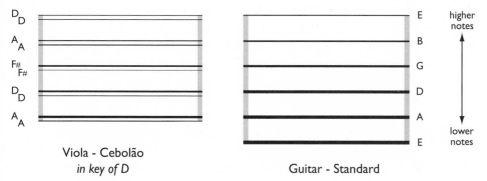

Figure 4. Viola (*Cebolão*) vs. Guitar (Standard) Tuning.

ent thicknesses of the strings tuned in the octave pairs mean that they are always slightly out of tune because of the level of the instrument's bridge. But viola players prefer other interpretive paradigms for understanding the trouble with tuning. Onstage, the act of tuning the viola often becomes the subject of a joke. Violeiros spend half of their time tuning their instrument and the other half playing out of tune, we are told. Or, alternatively, the viola is always out of tune before midnight when not enough cachaça has been consumed, and it is always in tune after midnight, when alcohol levels are sufficiently high. Remarks about tuning sometimes lead to the personification of the instrument. In this case, the joke is that the viola is in tune only when it *wants* to be and that it must be cajoled into consonance. Here, like a woman, the viola is unpredictable, willful, and only cooperative when seduced. You can't force a viola into tune because it just ends up taking more time to get it where you want it.

Thus, even to those audience members who are unaware of the practical difficulties associated with its tuning, the viola is presented as cantankerous, and the violeiro is elevated to the status of one who can govern a willful instrument. Sater verifies these notions. For him, the viola is

> a very primitive instrument, limited, hard to play, imprisoned within tunings that make it incompatible with an instrument that's tuned in a different way. If you want to make chords and harmonies—you can't do it on a viola. It has to be able to resonate—you have to be able to take advantage of the lower strings—and if you try to play it like a guitar, it just won't work. (quoted in Nepomuceno 1999, 397)

Recall, in this respect, José's discomfort with viola players who learned to play guitar first and switched to the viola later. "You can't treat a viola like a guitar," he lectured me numerous times, knowing that I had learned to play guitar first. The point of all this commentary on tuning is that the viola is portrayed as resisting the attempt to force it to correspond to other instruments and voices onstage. Tuning imposes a common tonality so that instrumentalists and vocalists can predict what each other will sound like. The viola, apparently, resists this commonality. It wants to be its own entity, set apart, and special.

Remarks on tuning the viola also lead to stories about what is required to learn to play it. Many players tell tongue-in-cheek stories about the necessity of making a pact with the devil. These stories vary in plot, but are invariably complex.[12] One involves visiting a church during a full moon, where a great violeiro is known to have died, while another encourages drinking a considerable quantity of pinga at a violeiro's graveside and then calling forth the devil. The one seeking the pact in such stories is often unsuccessful, suggesting that the method used to call forth the devil was wrong. Such stories are always framed by the fact that the current violeiro, the one actually telling the story, knows what went wrong and knows the method that ought to have been used to make the pact work.[13] At other times, stories speak of practitioners becoming good players by courting death. For instance, one player recounts how one might learn to play by caressing poisonous snakes and not getting bitten.[14] Finally, in terms of ways of talking about viola skill, the patron saint of violeiros, Saint Gonzalo, is sometimes invoked, either before a piece as a supplication for good luck, or after a piece has been played to account for why it might have gone well.

In these ways, the violeiro calls attention to a specific body of lore, grounded in magic, religion, danger, death, and legend that goes along with playing his instrument. Note that the violeiro often presents these stories as partial, indicating that he is holding information back; he could say much more, but chooses not to. But what is significant here is that across these practices violeiros do not speak of improving their playing by means of practice. They do not address technique onstage. Rather, they, speak of improvement through the cultivation of unusual and highly localized means that are both valuable and hidden (Apter 2005, 95).

All of this hyperattention to the viola contrasts sharply with the way that the guitar is treated onstage. The guitar is not mentioned in música caipira. It is not only considered easier to tune, play, and govern, but it is also the musical workhorse, providing a kind of "rhythm section" for the viola by giving background chords and keeping the beat. The guitar does the heavy lifting, so to speak, so that the viola can soar and sing.

Pig 1: When Things *Are* What They Seem

Throughout the evening's music and stories, the brothers alternate between two approaches to the production of locality: earnest and wryly removed. Revisiting the story of the pig treated in chapter 2 allows us to consider the way in which traditional rural performance mediates these two possibilities.[15] "Pig 1" represents the earnest face of this production of locality, wherein tradition stands for social identity in an unproblematic fashion. "Pig 2" uses self-reflexive humor to problematize pig 1. With respect to "Pig 2," Zé and his brother call attention to the fact that they are inhabiting hillbilly roles by self-deprecating and donning the same wide-eyed approach to social phenomena that allowed Pires's caipira narrators to comment on urban transition in the early twentieth century. The alignment of footings across interactive space, or the structure of voicing that characterizes this second pig, involves the hick's ability to see through what is inevitably urban overconfidence in its own knowledge, while calling attention to the absurdity of the very hickishness that permits such lucidity.

By framing the evening's proceedings within the context of the spotless pig and his necktie (pig 1), Zé Mulato and Cassiano elevate themselves to defenders of tradition, willing to sacrifice themselves for the cause. They simply are what they are and cannot *be* anything else. The record companies made a mistake way back in the early 1980s by trying to change them. The traditional aspects of their performance are to be read, here, as indexes of their rootedness in Central-Southern locality. The country is figured as the space in which things can simply be what they are meant to be, while in the city, things are forced to take on multiple valences.

According to this aspect of localizing rurality, if the country is natural, the city is not, and numerous songs throughout the evening reinforce the impossibility of integrating the two. If one's roots are in nature, a move to the city constitutes an uprooting. Two songs are narrated by a country-born speaker who tries to live in the city and fails.

In the first, "Ground of Minas," the city is incompatible with the narrator's emotional and spiritual nature. Note that the viola, in these lyrics, points the way back home through its song, and, like the symbol of a Christian cross, has the virtue required to exorcise undesirable feelings:

> This longing is killing me
> I can't stay here anymore.
> I'm going back to my homeland—
> The ground of Minas Gerais.
> Please help me—my viola
> Because I want to sing it right
> Only you have enough virtue
> To cure passion and spite.
> Always being in love
> Is my main fault.
> I make a cross with my body—[16]
> Across my chest—
> To exorcise passion
> True temptation.[17] (Zé Mulato and Cassiano 1999)

The difficulties involved in integrating country and city rest on a negative notion of the city and, importantly, the idea that one who is born in the country is out of his element in an urban setting.

Throughout the evening, daily life in nature is presented as simpler and lacking the complications of living in an urban context. Nature was a place where you had time, you walked instead of driving, you caught your own dinner instead of buying it, you were surrounded by familiar plants and animals. Things were as they seemed. Change came slowly. You had time. But nature was also a place where a reading of surfaces was sufficient, and the necessity to delve into the complexities of things simply disappeared. In this sense, nature is central to a perceptual theory where the meaning of objects, people, and events is immediately evident rather than secret or hidden. As we saw in chapter two, the idea is that as a world of meaning, the country is a place without layers, where things *are* what they seem.

This narrative returns us to the polarizing discourse first put in place by Jeca's sadness. Here, as in all rural genres, there are two distinct Brazils which are in tension with one another (country/city, poor/rich, past/present, rural/urban). This tension is reflected in a theory about time in the life of the fictive speakers. Country is temporalized through the personal narratives of the speakers of the songs. The return to the country is a return to a previous idyllic state. This suggests that Brazilians who were once rural and are now urban live with an irreconcilable tension in their lives. They long for something that necessity tells them they may not attain: a return to their country. Moreover, the tension and difficulty of the way back to an uncomplicated and balanced time and space is projected onto the nation as a whole. If we could just capture this aspect of the way that we were, such songs indicate, we would be more whole as a nation. Urbanization, therefore, is not simply a process in which traditions are lost, although it most certainly *is* that. Urbanization also leads to fragmentation. But even in this most earnest longing for wholeness, a comic remove appears. The announcement of the title of "Caipira's Diary" gets a laugh from the audience. The notion that the simple caipira should keep a diary—a distinctly urbane thing to do, surely—is just too much. Here, the production of rural locality is reflexively reoriented.

Pig 2: Explicit Caipira Metaindexicality

Pig 1 presents locality's production as a largely earnest endeavor. But rurality inevitably introduces an ironic touch—a locality that metaindexically renders preposterous all this countrified posturing. Within this structure of voicing, the two brothers push their hickishness to extremes. They call attention to its inhabitance, problematizing pig 1's earnestness.

Zé tells numerous comic stories which illustrate this point. When he recounts these tales by deepening his already caipira speech, he hardens his /r/ with more force, drops his plurals more frequently, and otherwise calls on the kinds of dialectal features noted in chapter 4. His prosody changes when he does the voices of the characters in these stories, taking on an almost singing cadence that shortens the spaces between his words. The resulting stories are uproariously funny to the audience. In one, he depicts a contest in which two caipiras attempt to prove the validity of their ideas by farting into a sack of flour and seeing which one kicks up a larger cloud. The two find that their strategy presents a problem in that they cannot see behind themselves at the moment of passing gas to verify the size of their own production, and thus must rely on the honesty of their competitor. But caipiras, Zé reports, cannot lie, and when one produces an enormous cloud, the other must grant him his victory. In another story, a caipira takes his sick wife to the city to see a doctor but flees in terror when the doctor proposes an invasive medical exam that will involve scrutiny of her urinary system. "Good God!" the hick exclaims, "she's not *that* sick!" And here is where the hillbilly caricatures himself. The caipira is so naïve that he is unable to recognize the medicalized separation between doctor and patient that would allow him to be comfortable letting the doctor examine his wife's body.

This undercutting of the urgency and inalienable rootedness of caipira essence may be turned to political ends. Comic stories, voiced with a hyper-ignorance that facilitates social criticism, enable commentary on national doings. Pires did this in the 1920s, as did Vargas's critics, then friends, Alvarenga and Ranchinho, in the early 1930s. Toward the end of the evening, Zé speaks of the absurdities of the various economic plans that have been instituted by incoming presidents since the country's return to democracy in 1985 and notes that the common man's fortunes never seem to change whatever the government does. Brazilian governments always seem to promise radical transformation. However, Zé suggests that such promises hide what governments actually do, which is to replicate the existing order. For example, the government may change the currency in association with some ostensibly revolutionary economic plan, and that plan, named after the currency in question, does nothing whatsoever. Such plans keep the rich, rich, and the poor, poor. The brothers point out that there has been a *Plano Cruzado*, a *Plano Cruzado 2*, and a current *Plano Real*.[18] None of these have created the economic recovery they promised. To illustrate, they sing that the common Brazilian is as battered as a boxer in a ring; the parade of currencies continually knocks him down. And here, they deliver their own punch line. The next currency must be better. Instead of names like cruzado or real, it must be called the "knockout," a word Zé and his brother deliver in English, to much applause—a linguistic device I preserve here.

Vou matar essa jogada	I'm going to end this little game
eu vou dar o xeque-mate	I'm going for a checkmate.
Nossa próxima moeda	Our next currency
irá se chamar nocaute.	Will be called the "knockout."

No ringue da economia	In the ring that's the economy
brasileiro perde feio	The Brazilian's getting beaten badly:
O pobre va aprumando	The poor guy gets on his feet
vem o rico e desce o reio	And the rich guy lowers the boom again.
O remédio que nos dão	The antidote they give us
é pior que o veneno	Is much worse than the poison.
Apanhar e passar fome	Getting beaten and going hungry
pra nós é café pequeno	For us—it's child's play.
mudando nosa moeda	Changing our currency
só vai perdendo terreno	Will just lose us ground.
(Zé Mulato and Cassiano 1999)	

This presentation of the common man as the hapless though by no means stupid or unconscious victim of powerful forces directly partakes of Cornélio Pires's voicing structures, though Pires targeted local oligarchies, while Zé Mulato and Cassiano focus more on the consequences of failed liberalization and its incumbent monetary policy. But note that what facilitates this critique is a reflexively emphasized caipira—an ultrahickish hick who nonetheless speaks a little English.

Local Temporalities of Sentiment

The alternation between pig 1 and pig 2 facilitates the country critique in a local mode. But another back-and-forth shapes the production of locality broadly speaking. Central-Southern rurality establishes a specific relationship between language and music as communicative practices. This rural approach adumbrates an epistemology of the body. Participants map the emotional and heartfelt components of communicative practice onto what we might consider the musical aspects of rural song performance. The rational and instrumental components of rural communicative practice reside in a song's language, as evident in the lyrics. This insight encourages us to consider the way in which distinctions between "music" and "language" are instantiated in local practice; they cannot simply be taken for granted. Singing, writing, and playing songs mediate localized distinctions between communicative registers.

The importance of song forms within Central-Southern rural locality requires consideration of the interplay of music and language in caipira song-forms and the way in which this interplay, in turn, enacts distinct forms of "temporalization"(Munn 1992, 116). To elaborate, each song carries its own specific "duration, synchrony, sequence, and rhythm" (Hanks 1996, 270). This tension between musicality and language-as-potential as a way of mapping out temporalities reveals itself in the primacy given to music or language in the emergence of song texts in performance. More specifically, traditional rural musical practice frequently relies on, among other co-occurrent features, a uniform tempo, which in turn structures the way melody and harmony unfold and the way lyrics are sung. Co-occurrent bundles of features also include key signature, time signature, the pace of the singing, parallelism in rhyme and meter (J. Fox 1977; Jakobson 1960), and the quality of the singers' voices (smooth and full-throated as opposed to more clipped and forceful). These features in turn correspond with certain possibilities for subject matter.[19] For instance, the quick tempo and major key of a song said to be played as a batuque (2/4, 85 BPM) call forth statements about the importance of the countryside, tradition, and "pure" rural music. The pagode entails a statement of bold intention on the part of the singer about returning home to the countryside, often having accepted that love has ended. It may also include a criticism of the absurdity of politics, where the caipira (an everyman) gets left out by both the rich and the reformers (see the conclusion). The slower cururú (2/4, 80 BPM) elicits narratives about the pain of trying to live in the city when you're a country person at heart and the need to return to past days of wholeness in love, or innocence in childhood. The minor-keyed but slightly quicker toada (2/4, 70 BPM) involves an even sadder full-throated discourse about the pain of a particular lost love, the importance of tears, and the exquisite beauty of the countryside from the perspective of its absence in the city. And finally, a series of genres in 3/4 time, among them the valseado (3/4, 140 BPM), involve minor keyed and smoothly sung reflections on the way women make men cry.

However, the song form which is frequently spoken of in música caipira as the oldest and most venerable conduit of tradition is the moda de viola, or ten-string guitar song, in which the unfolding of the words drives the tempo. It is essentially recitative, viewed here as a form of musical writing in which the rhythm of the singing matches the delivery of speech. A metronome would be useless in such a song because the pauses between what are here nine, eight, and seven syllable lines, punctuated by strokes on the viola, dictate how the song unfolds. This makes the strict matching of two voices all that much harder. The moda form is strictly narrative from the standpoint of its lyrics, recounting, for instance, the tale of an old man's past losses, the confrontation between a caipira and a stuck-up urbanite in a roadside bar ("The King of Cattle," from chapter 5), or how a man decides it's better to simply be alone because his heart has been broken so badly. Zé Mulato and Cassiano play numerous modas in the course of their show. One of these is "Ruminating on Solitude," which appears here in Portuguese to illustrate its pairing of rhyme with a spoken meter:

Vi um casar de marreco	I saw a pair of mallards
Fazer a volta no ar	Turning in the air
Para descer na lagoa	To descend to the lake
No fundo do meu quintar	At the end of my land.
E bateu um sentimento	It touched something off in me—
Por ver esse lindo par	Seeing that pretty pair,
O tempo do nosso amor	And our time of love
Comecei a recordar	I began to recall.
Esse amor era tão lindo	That love—so beautiful
Que dava inveja de olhar	It made others jealous to see it.
Hoje aqui no sertão	Today—here in the backlands,
Remoendo solidão	Ruminating on solitude
Só tristeza e paixão	Only loneliness and passion
Costumam me acompanhar[a]	Customarily accompany me.
(Zé Mulato and Cassiano 1999)	

In true moda de viola form, the brothers employ recitative from start to finish. But this spoken-sung approach, though characteristic of moda de viola, is not limited to it. Often, songwriters will insert a passage of this recitative at the beginning of a song that moves quickly into a song form governed more uniformly by tempo (such as cururú, or pagode). This means of introducing many songs provides an unspoken clue as to the importance of the form; other song-forms are never inserted into modas.

We can therefore see that the differing relationships between the unfolding of words in relation to musical structure involve temporalities which may be keyed in some places to the musical, or, in other places, to the linguistic—where the relation between both terms requires a localized definition of each. One small example is the way in which the words of the chorus of a song other than a moda provide a certain em-

phasis to linguistic features, or, from another perspective, the catchier
tune of the chorus signals the return of repeated words. Within the
context of these songs that are more patterned by the musical than by
the linguistic (batuque, pagode, cururû, toada, *valseado*), I return once
again to the batuque "Big Nostalgia" with which Zé Mulato and Cassiano opened the evening's festivities. It begins with a chorus that is
repeated three times: "I'm here./ My people, I'm here./ To sing for
missus and mister./ To sing for missus and mister." Like variations on a
theme, this chorus is layered throughout the piece's approximately
three-minute duration, marking the flow from one verse to the next.
Each chorus introduces new content. The song *repeats* certain segments
of text which are parallel blocks of speech underscored by their reappearance, which welds them tightly to the melody. This renders them
easier to remember and sing at the time or after the fact. So the musical
structure maps onto the words at these moments to emphasize them.
Such cyclicality is a way to mark time through the song. The appearance of the second chorus informs listeners that they are approximately in the middle of the song. The last chorus means the song is
coming to an end, and so forth. Moda de viola, by contrast, has no
choruses, so that the alternation between eight-line (or nine-line) verses
and seven-line verses is what marks progress. In terms of musical form
therefore, an evening's performance goes back and forth between one
or the other form of communicative practice, providing the structuring
principle of the passage of time. In one modality, time unfolds according to a prescribed beat throughout the song. In another, the passage of
time unfolds according to the words, with musical pauses and starts
following *from* those words.

 All of these forms are punctuated with frequent use of imagery from
nature. Such references are sometimes explicit, such as singing about
birds, cattle, rivers, waterfalls, and fish. Note, for instance, the final
verse of "Big Nostalgia," where the singers argue for the way in which
the features of the song derive directly from the landscape, which is
held together by the "natural" aspects of the human—a point reinforced by the rhyming of the Portuguese for *brotherhood* and *river bank*:

O compasso e melodia	*The beat and the melody—*
Eu tirei de um ribeirão	*I got from the river bank.*
Juntei raça e harmonia	*Mixed them with race and harmony,*
Á fibra de dois irmão	*In the fiber of brotherhood.*
(Zé Mulato and Cassiano 1999)	

However, in the domain of sound, the viola, or ten-string guitar, is the primary carrier of the natural, and is thus a vital connection with the natural-as-musical aspects of song. In the course of my viola instruction, my teacher informed me that the best way to think about learning to play the viola was to think of crying. The sound was articulate, but only in the limited sense of conveying something very basic about sadness by way of a human voice racked by involuntary sobs and the uneven drawing of breath. When you cry, you are not fully in control of the sounds you make, nor are your sounds articulate in the way that saying "I am sad" might be. The sound of the viola thus edged toward the musical and less expressly articulate. Here was an apparently more *natural* mode of expression than highly structured language. According to a different teacher, another way to think about learning to play the viola was to view it as channeling natural sounds through the instrument itself. The viola should be made to sound like a buzzing mosquito, the call of birds, the motion of cattle, or the pitter-patter of raindrops. Listening to these sounds of the Central-Southern soundscape would help me to play the instrument. In effect, such forms of practice-as-listening would be more useful to me than sitting down and repeating musical figures.

Multiple Musical Localities

I have argued that Zé Mulato and Cassiano's musical performance creates a rural locality. Musicians and listeners participate in semiotic processes which produce their sense of personhood, locate their experience and beliefs with reference to a nation and a world system, and fashion their sense of belonging to a group of people who share beliefs and values. This takes place through the performance's semiotic features: interlocking harmonization, instrumentation, song structure, lyrics, storytelling, dress, humor, sadness, the setting at the Via Roça, the alternation between earnest and reflexive, and the relation between language and musicality. These variables fashion a "local." The creative process involved in this fashioning relies on contrast—such that the local requires the generation of an opposite "global," much as country contrasts with city and natural with artificial.

Part of this discourse involves a historical vision about the way that Brazil has changed in the twentieth century. Within this we can identify a strong critique of the way Brazilians have managed a transformation in the relations between country and city. The assertion is that they have embraced the modern too quickly, forgetting their own history. Whereas in modernist or progress-oriented narratives of the change of urban-rural relations, the urban becomes the center, and the rural, the periphery, these musicians invert this model. Without such an inversion, Zé Mulato and Cassiano and their audience suggest, Brazilians will lose track of what it means to be Brazilian. At the same time, they suggest that the majority of Brazilians have been duped and that it is the brothers' pedagogical responsibility to re-educate residents of the Central-South.

It is essential to understand the argument about cultural distinctness being made in the course of this performance. Central-Southern singers are not nationalist in the way that, for example, the Canadian province of Quebec is sometimes nationalist (Handler 1998); they do not want to form their own nation-state that might someday secede from Brazil. When violeiro Enúbio Queiroz adorns the cover of one of his records with a viola painted with the Brazilian flag and plays a traditional hick version of the Brazilian national anthem, it is not some caipira nation he hopes to play into being (Queiroz 2006). Queiroz and those like him articulate their particular *segment* of Brazil within the context of a series of others and have no objection to other localizing discourses within a larger, multicultural nation. Their nationalism is one of obligatory and didactic plurality. By preserving their own traditions, all of these localities will contribute to the common good of the nation. Thus is the "liberal diaspora" instantiated in this Brazilian context (Povinelli 2002, 5).

Finally, this rural critique portrays a "natural" life as one that revolves around more than simply living in proximity to plants and animals. Living in harmony with nature stipulates various routines for living and relationships to objects and people. These routines and relationships are, it is argued, less mediated and layered than relationships in urban environments. An argument is made for simplicity, such that people are all one way, or all another, rather than mixed. And finally, as Jeca suggested, "nature" involves an approach to sentiment. Brazilian rural genres present emotions as things over which the singing, playing, and listening subject has no control, which brings us to the country cosmopolitan, the topic of the next chapter.

Hicks of the World

THE COUNTRY COSMOPOLITAN

> Cultures cannot be crossed, nor can their crossing be captured,
> simply. Any ethnography refracts. No comparative rep-
> resentation, old or new, develops straightforwardly, however
> political or apolitical its enabling enterprises profess to be.
> —JAMES A. BOON, "Cosmopolitan Moments: Echoey Confes-
> sions of an Ethnographer-Tourist (Echoey 'Cosmomes')"

This book argues that the Brazilian field of rural musical production in
the neoliberal moment is characterized by two mutually reinforcing
sets of practices. One, treated in the last chapter, concerns the production of locality. We saw the way in which rural locality is preoccupied
with what are deemed traditional or folkloric aspects of the countryside. Various semiotic media are laminated together in performance
in order to tie participants strongly to the here and now, or, more
precisely, to the here and now that is simultaneously a "then," and also
a "there" which nonetheless lies close by. You can *point* to those hills
where you were born, your eyes now full of tears, your throat choked up
with a sad song.

This chapter concerns a different face of the rural musical coin: the
international outreach and modernization of rural Brazilian sound. Our
guiding concern here will be the investigation of rurality's progressive
bent, grounded in the intention to take part, by way of "country," in
what participants frame as a transnational sphere of rural cultural production. Whereas in the last chapter we focused to a great extent on
a single performance, this chapter samples from a series of musical
encounters.

It should be clear by now that several labels have already been applied
to the phenomena this chapter treats, among them "cultural imperialism" and "cultural subservience." As I have argued elsewhere (2005),
such responses to commercial rural public culture form part of the field

itself, fostering a dialogic relationship between tradition and commerciality characteristic of neoliberal Brazil. The tremendous importance of the concepts of imperialism and subservience to maintaining the dynamic intimacy of position-takings in the field of rural musical production, however, makes such notions suspect as analytical categories. Instead of beginning by reducing musical participation to materially derived and arithmetically accruing rubrics and assuming that production dictates consumption, accounting for this striving to be *internationally* rural must begin with precisely that: the striving.

It is here that the concept of cosmopolitanism becomes important. I frame cosmopolitanism as a set of practices with critical possibilities which are sometimes subaltern ones (Babha 2001). However, I argue here that this notion of cosmopolitanism requires a developed understanding of cultural intimacy. Cosmopolitanisms most frequently criticize without framing that criticism in earnest and conventionally political modes, unlike most "identity politics." Instead of a cosmopolitanism aimed at the explicitly political, we may thus think more broadly of "rooted" (Appiah 2007) cosmopolitanisms that desire to "project a new world beyond the expected" (Goodale 2006, 641). And rather than employing distinctly global sorts of categories, cosmopolitanisms engage in this outward projection the same way that any projection takes place, by way of culturally embedded modes of understanding. In other words, the cosmopolitan is often transnational in its focus while instantiating highly localized ways of thinking and doing (Goodale 2006, 641).

The historical specificity of this projecting "beyond the expected" needs to be spelled out in more detail. The pan-Americanism of José Martí and his ilk, who ardently wished a kind of cross-spatial and cross-temporal unity for North and South Americas, is not the same thing as Andean hip-hop in twenty-first-century Peru. Yet both "project beyond the expected." The Kayapó approach to those they judged to be outsiders before their "pacification" beginning in the mid-1930s (Turner 1997) is not the same as the current popularity of Korean "boy" bands in China. All cultures project. Our task here is to determine the way in which the Brazilian country cosmopolitan's form of projection fashions distinct subjectivities. What we require for grappling with this present cosmopolitanism is a means of investigating the historical specificity of this projecting. The key will be to analyze the discursive means by which cosmopolitanism fashions itself and its worlds. In other words, we require an approach to the concept that will reveal the ways in which participants orient certain forms of social production *outward*.

It is important to understand that speaking of this cosmopolitan gesturing in terms of projection alone is to miss an important aspect of its process. Cosmopolitanism is not only an outward push. It also revolves around the inwardly focused collecting of bits and pieces from cultural contexts deemed "different"—bits and pieces which must appear to have come from elsewhere. In other words, cosmopolitanism gathers practices, symbols, and positionalities unto itself, which it then fashions into a simultaneously coherent and deliberately conflicted whole. It incorporates just as much as it projects. The moves link.

Some resultant, often overlooked, details follow. First, in terms of the critical stance that cosmopolitanism establishes, it seeks to set itself up in relation to other sets of practices deemed insular, isolated, or old-fashioned. There is always at least a touch of the au courant in the cosmopolitan. Its employment seeks to establish an "us" that is in some sense in the know, as opposed to a "them" that isn't. In this country case in Brazil, this aspect of the country cosmopolitan provides impetus to its cultural intimacy. As mentioned in chapter 3, this is a cosmopolitanism of quite the wrong sort—not a cosmopolitanism that sips jazz, classical music, and high fashion, but one that guzzles mariachi, ten-gallon hats, and Wrangler jeans. In moments in which those who sometimes identify with the country cosmopolitan also revile it, it becomes a kind of cosmopolitanism gone wrong, an ignorant misfire, the critical superiority of which appears temporarily absurd. At such moments, that country could claim to be au courant seems laughable.

An important feature of cosmopolitanism is that part and parcel of its critical stance in relation to other insularities requires that it sample from practices perceived to lie far afield from the place in which that borrowing grounds itself. Consequently, cosmopolitanism cultivates *crossing*—of oceans, cultures, and historical periods. That's its point. Thus the spaces into which cosmopolitanism projects itself and from which it incorporates must seem to be at least somewhat unlikely from the perspectives of its users. This quite deliberate incongruity is part of the way those employing cosmopolitan orientations to the world establish that it might be, in some sense, cutting-edge. In order to capture these faces of cosmopolitanism in this Brazilian context, I offer not just one, but several examples, in cosmopolitan fashion.

Transcendent Hick-Talk

Just because Brazilian commercial country music sometimes imitates North American country, its local valences should not therefore be reduced to the cultural imperialism of the United States and/or Brazil's subservience. The ability of the United States to impose its own cultural products onto the desires of locales deemed not-American is not always as pronounced as some have assumed. We do not live in a world so simple as to be neatly divided between acquiescence and "resistance" (Sahlins 1998). Indeed, those who believe that public cultural texts must be either entirely pure and free of Americanisms, or polluted by them, would seem to be the most dominated of all. Analysis of Brazilian covers of American country songs reveals that, when viewed in terms of their actually occurring entextualizations and contextualizations, Brazilian versions of Nashville country songs both entail and presuppose rather different messages from their North American counterparts, calling different social worlds into being. In the Brazilian case, the cultural intimacies surrounding gender relations, the modes by which subjectivity splits, the constitution of the past, and a countryside that is chronotopically longed for by way of brother siblingship, index Brazilian twentieth-century history and culture. Currently, songs from parts of the world other than the United States, chiefly Latin America and Spain, get covered in the Brazilian field of rural musical production too. Mexican mariachi horns so popular within música sertaneja in the 1960s and 1970s still find their way into música sertaneja songs. But these non-U.S. borrowings do not add up to what has been culled from the United States in the last twenty years if you count by songs. In effect, there has recently been a preponderance of drawing upon Nashville within the field of rural musical production. Why?

We should begin our treatment of this American musical presence in Brazilian commercial country by recognizing that it does not involve strict adherence to the details of what gets borrowed. Rather, it is only in an extremely general sense that what is being called upon may be thought of as North American. The nitty-gritty drops decidedly into the background. This was made clear to me for what must have been the tenth time at the Americana Rodeo of 2006. As I was sitting in the stands recording and taking notes on the rodeo events, a woman leaned over and asked what I was doing. I explained that I was researching a book on Brazilian country music and rodeo. She became excited and suggested that since Edson and Hudson were playing, I was in for a great evening; Edson and Hudson "do a really good show." She wondered if I knew that Edson and Hudson had just collaborated with an American country singer? The American singer was extremely famous, she noted; I'd know his name right away if I heard it. The resulting collaboration was not her favorite song on Edson and Hudson's recent record, mind you. She had simply mentioned it because she thought I, as a North American, might be interested in the *relationship* between Brazilian country and its American counterpart. So I asked if she knew who the American singer was. She looked embarrassed and then pensive. I waited while she consulted with her friends whom she described as "super-fans" of Edson and Hudson, and therefore surefire sources for the necessary information. They spoke among themselves for a few moments, and then she leaned over to me: "King Jagger," she stated confidently, and sat back, watching me, waiting for the full effect. Instead of the hoped-for recognition, however, I looked confused. "*Mick* Jagger?" I asked, incredulous. It struck me as unlikely. No, no, she corrected, seeming to have anticipated my confusing him with another important singer, a British rock 'n' roller that she *did*, in fact, know. It was "King," she assured me. And what was the title of the English-language version of the song, I wondered? That, she and her friends definitely did *not* know. Nor did they seem much to care. The titles, melodies, and words of the actual radio hits from the album were instantly available to them, but this English-language song remained obscure, except in its Brazilian form.

As it turns out, the singer was Kenny Rogers, and the song was "I Can't Unlove You," a single from Rogers's record *Water and Bridges* from 2003 that topped country charts in the United States. But the point is not so much to map the "origins" of the Brazilian cover. Indeed, to attempt to fix something resembling origins runs precisely counter to the point here. Rather, these details about song title and artist simply had not been relevant to this particular listener and her friends, just as they had been irrelevant to countless others I questioned in similar circumstances. Neither she nor her "super-fan" friends were poring over the liner notes of Edson's and Hudson's record to find the identity of "that American singer."

We visit these details not to downplay the significance of the fact that a borrowing took place; the purpose is not to say that the fact that an

American had sung on the track went unnoticed. It is merely to note the *shape* that borrowing takes. Here, fans were not particularly engaged with the details of the American portions of the song. The question then became what they *were* doing as they listened to and discussed the song, while acknowledging its clearly present North American absence. Sitting there in Americana, in the interior of the state of São Paulo, what did the "American" in "North American country singer" *mean*, and what was its relationship to Brazilian rurality? Clearly we were *not*, of course, in Nashville. But we were not entirely *distant* from it either. So where, in fact, *were* we?

Teixeira's Hick-Texan

The answer is that we were in the domain of a Brazilian transnational rurality. To elaborate on the contours of this zone, I turn next to a show by Renato Teixeira. On November 19, 1999, singer-songwriter Teixeira performed to a crowded concert hall with a capacity of five hundred in downtown Campinas. He arrived onstage with an electric-bass player and a lead guitarist, wearing an acoustic guitar. This was not to be a show in *dupla* form, but rather involved a rurally inflected singer-songwriter with a small band. Teixeira is an interstitial figure in the domain of rural music. He does not perform with a brother or partner, nor does he play the *viola* like Almir Sater, one of his frequent collaborators. However, he has written or co-written several songs that are considered to be classics in the current rural musical repertoire, particularly among those interested in the traditional. He has also performed frequently with other artists whose rural profiles are easier to spot, such as Pena Branca and Xavatinho. Indeed, his *Live in Piracicaba* album, recorded with these two brothers, remains one of the best-selling folkloric rural music records of all time and was the best-selling record in the "regional" category in 2000.

On this evening in Campinas, Teixeira's show began with none of the ceremony that characterized Zé Mulato and Cassiano's opening declamation. Teixeira simply arrived onstage and began playing, leaving little by way of a break between each song and saying nothing. In fact, Teixeira engaged in no stage-banter whatsoever until he had played for almost an hour, at which point he began to discuss the Central-Southern hick, or *caipira*. He noted that these days, people were beginning to value the hick more and more because they were beginning to realize that caipira culture was not only music, but also included painting, sculpture, literature, and even dance. Teixeira was thus proposing that the Central-Southern hick might be said to have capital "C" culture after all. He suggested that the fact that many people were coming to this realization meant that things were getting better for Jeca.

Teixeira then leapt into language. Where once upon a time the caipira was discriminated against for his hard /r/, these days that /r/ was less disparaged. This, Teixeira noted, somewhat tongue-in-cheek, was in part because people were realizing that the caipira's hard /r/ sounded a lot like the hard /r/ of North American English, and rural English in particular—the kind of /r/ you might find, for instance, in Texas. So, when Brazilians were intent upon valuing American clothing, electronics, software, and even politics, the hick would seem to have privileged access to at least a small piece of that sought-after Americanness. Perhaps the Central-Southern hillbilly was not as provincial as many once thought.

Then Teixeira went further. Learning English presents tremendous difficulties for many Brazilians, he noted. But the caipira has a much easier time because the way he speaks Portuguese gives him a "natural" advantage. Pushing phonology into grammar, semantics, and pragmatics, he continued. When a caipira runs into some unfortunate Texan with a flat tire by the side of a road, he can communicate with said Texan much more easily than a Brazilian from another part of the nation. *Porta* (Portuguese for door), Teixeira continued, no longer *ought* (from the perspective of those adhering to Standard) to be pronounced with the softer fricative /r/ found, say, in Rio de Janeiro. Now, by that roadside, that hardened /r/ *helps*. Teixeira demonstrates the English word "door," lingering over the final /r/ to hilarious effect. Handicap becomes advantage, and the caipira hasn't had to change a thing.

Teixeira then deepened his analysis of translation. The Central-Southern hick accent, he tells us, *sounds*, naturally, like English. There's no forcing this, of course; it's just the way the Brazilian hick *talks*. So the hick doesn't actually have to learn English sounds. When the hick assures his North American counterpart that he will help him out, the hick simply translates the Portuguese words *directly* into English. The literal translations refract (cosmomically—see Boon 1999), cueing off the mispronunciations of Portuguese terms from the standpoint of

Monoglot Standard Portuguese (examples to follow). We never find out if the Texan understands, though Teixeira's calm rendition of the hick's confident delivery suggests that this hick has tried this before and it worked OK. Consequently, the *rurality* of this Central-Southern Brazilian subject allows for the seamless translation of Portuguese into the English of a rural Southwestern North American, which might otherwise prove challenging. Thus, the rurality that might, in the past, have indexed insularity, and which in turn, might have made cross-cultural communication more difficult, has instead facilitated it.

All this takes time to unfold onstage. On first listening, the hick's statement to the stranded American sounds much like gobbledygook to the audience that night in Campinas. No one seems entirely clear what Teixeira is *up* to. In his thick Brazilian accent, Teixeira speaks the hillbilly's lines in some sort of English: "Tea with me, my good hand, I book your face." No one laughs, and Teixeira appears to have expected this. Either the joke has not worked, or we have not yet heard the punch line. Then, Teixeira delivers what the Portuguese sentence *would* have been before the caipira "translated" it from his hick-pronounced Portuguese into his rural English: "Xa comigo, meu irmão. Eu livro sua cara."[1] A nonliteral translation of this sentence would be: "You're with me, my brother. I'll save your butt." But note that the caipira's Texan-keyed translation derives from what at first seems to be a *misrecognition* emerging from the *sound* of the informal Portuguese lexicon, translated directly into English. Put differently, the translations from Portuguese are not purely incorrect; they simply employ what at first seems to be the incorrect *sense* of each term, garnered sonically. Thus, the "mão" gets pulled out of "irmão" (brother) by our involuntarily but brilliantly polyglot hillbilly. Stripped of its initial /ir/, it becomes "hand." "Livro," the verb "to liberate" conjugated in the first person, switches to its noun-form: the word for book. And "cara," which ought to be "guy," sheds its figurative connotation and becomes, literally, "face," (translated by me, here, as "butt," to preserve Teixeira's sense). The figurative possibilities of the slang fall away in the translation in favor of their more common, literal senses. Is this some Brazilian student of English hacking away at a phrase with a Portuguese-English dictionary and little comprehension of how context shapes the actual use of lexical items? What could the Texan possibly *make* of this?

Whatever the answer to that question, it is instantly clear what we, the audience, are to make of it; the laughter continues for some time. And note that audience members must have some fluency in English in order for the joke to be funny. The audience must "know" that in this sentence, *livro* should not be "book," but rather ought to be "I'll free."

But Teixeira leaves us hanging because the joke ends precisely with our own laughter, not the Texan's. Indeed, the Texan does *not* throw up his hands in incomprehension, invalidating what might have been the hick's gaffe. Indeed, perhaps our North American with the flat tire gets it after all. The fluidity with which our caipira speaks his rural Portuguese-to-English leaves room for the possibility that the joke is actually on us and the translation was, in fact, effective. In this way, Teixeira questions conventional thinking that the rural is backward and isolationist; there may well be a hick lingua franca. But Teixeira also problematizes this contention through the seeming "wrongness" of the translation; the lingua franca's means of bridging linguistic worlds would seem to involve the same mistakes any student of language unable to master vocabulary might make. Both possibilities remain in play. That the translation is meant to be simultaneously ridiculed by the audience *and* treated with some respect leaves in motion the fact that one of the primary ways that it functions is through its literalness, which is a fundamental aspect of the country cosmopolitan and a feature of "pig 1," in the last chapter. Surfaces are sufficient in the countryside, and this translation emphasizes this. It is the mispronounced sonic surfaces of the words that ground the translation and suffice. And note that the hick's newfound comprehensibility has nothing to do with his *intention* to change himself into something more international. This is not a joke in which hicks have made a concerted effort to learn English. It is simply one in which transforming circumstances make what hicks always did suddenly connect to a broader domain than the strictly circumscribed Brazilian rural one.

This discussion of caipira serves to introduce one of Teixeira's songs. He advises the audience that he is going to sing about the way caipiras talk using "Portrait of a Caipira Kid," mentioned in chapter 4 when I discussed the hard hick /r/ (Teixeira). Teixeira notes that since he is in Campinas, the song will probably not amuse anyone, because his pronunciation of the /r/s in the song won't differ from the pronunciation that he might *normally* hear on the street right outside the concert hall. Teixeira's "*que m'impoRta?*" of the chorus ("what does it matter?") might sound funny in other parts of Brazil, but here, the singer wryly asserts, no one will even notice. Of course, this serves to make the audience notice all the more, and the first chorus gets precisely the laugh Teixeira surely hoped for.

In the middle of the song, he pauses, and his band stops with him. The lyric that should come next is that when the caipira lad gets frustrated by people's making fun of his accent, he just jumps into his pickup truck, in Portuguese, a transliteration of the English "pickup" (*pacupe*), and drives off into the distance. This transliteration of the English term "pickup" itself gets a chuckle. But Teixeira suggests that the rural world is subject to change, too. Since the environmental movement is now so important (as indexed by pressure to save the Brazilian rain forest and to reduce emissions in cities such as São Paulo) and the gas mileage of pickups is so awful, he has changed the lyric so that the caipira simply jumps onto his old horse to ride away in frustration. The rusticity of the horse suddenly becomes modern. Note the multiple inversions. The pickup, once a sign of Brazilian rural imitativeness (where that derivativeness is sonically indexed by the Portuguese transliteration of the English lexical item used to point to it) was once thought by the hick to be a sign of progress. But now, the hick, by returning to the way he has always done things, displays a kind of unconscious responsiveness to international movements. The retrograde becomes progressive.

What Teixeira accomplished that night in Campinas was to call the audience's attention to a relationship between Brazil and the United States on rural terms. Rurality became a potential means of overcoming language barriers (one he simultaneously problematized) and a way of rendering ridiculous the changing fashions of global movements. In all cases, as the audience laughs about the ostensible backwardness of the Central-Southern hillbilly, the hick is permitted a last laugh too. Instead of the digression so typical for the American hillbilly (A. Fox 2004, 101), we have a self-deprecating hillbilly whose slowness, through no conscious choice of his own, somehow makes him appear wise in relation to urban and/or American bluster. Throughout, recall that the hick has not changed. He talks the way he always has. He still rides his horse. Hickness, here, is still synonymous with an inability to change, but the humor emerges from the way in which precisely this inability to change makes the hick suddenly quite au courant.

Inescapable Hearts

We next move to analyzing a space which might not, at first, appear rural to the same extent as other spaces we have so far considered.

What we will see is that commercially successful rurality ceases to revolve so much around birds, trees, water, and fire. Much commercially successful rural music continues to do so, of course. But in some rural music, rurality plays out in an emotional topography reliant upon male/female gender distinctions and defined by the rural subject's submission to his own overpowering emotions. Though these qualities have always existed in *música caipira*, drawing them out and emphasizing them, as commercial country has done since redemocratization, is believed, by country cosmopolitans such as Chitãozinho and Xororó, to have made the music "modern," as I will explain. By emphasizing gender distinctions and the inhabitance of emotionally precipitated disempowerment, commercial rural musical practitioners believe they are partaking of a discussion that stretches more easily across geographical, cultural, and historical boundaries. In other words, by singing and talking more about romantic love, these singers believe their music can reach more people in Brazil and around the world. The performances I analyze to clarify these points took place on November 11, 1999, and December 5, 1999, when Zezé di Camargo and Luciano played the Olympia concert hall in São Paulo. These two nights were renditions of the same overall "show." It was titled after a song called "God Save America," which the brothers had included in their 1998 album entitled *In Order Not to Think of You* (Zezé di Camargo and Luciano 1998).[2]

A chapter on the country cosmopolitan requires treatment of this dupla in part because it is one of the best-selling rural musical duplas in Brazil. As a rural musical act, its winter schedule of rodeo shows is one of the best attended. Furthermore, the film that tells the rags-to-riches story of the dupla's rise to fame from humble country origins formed the substance of a best-selling Brazilian film in 2005: *Francisco's Two Sons*. However, in addition to its more evident rural indicators, this dupla is of special interest because of the way in which it has so strongly developed elements of the country cosmopolitan that revolve around love, desperation, and lack of control.

Cursory analysis of their act in 1999 may suggest that there is little that is easily recognizable as rural taking place onstage, something which has not always been the case. Zezé and his brother have partaken of much explicitly rural iconography in the past. A little over a decade ago, for instance, they proudly wore the "mullet" haircut Billy Ray Cyrus wore while making the country song "Achy Breaky Heart" so famous in the early 1990s. So did Chitãozinho and Xororó, which earned the haircut, consisting of a short top and sides with a long back, its Brazilian moniker of "Chitão Hair." Many other rural musical acts sported this haircut during the early and mid-1990s in the United States and Brazil. Such was the country cosmopolitan at that time.

Nowadays, however, Zezé and his brother wear their hair short, like many duplas, and their flat-fronted low-cut slacks, tight-fitting t-shirts, and buttoned dress shirts are made of light-colored synthetic fabrics. Despite how much time these two spend *playing* at rodeos, they do not, in their lyrics, *sing* much about bulls and cowboys; only one of the tunes during these two shows I attended in 1999 had explicitly rural content. In effect, they have employed much less of the rural imagery that so many duplas have adhered to, especially Chitãozinho and Xororó, and Leandro and Leonardo, with whom, as noted, Zezé di Camargo and Luciano form the occasional rural musical touring group The Friends.

Their show nonetheless fundamentally fashions current Brazilian rurality. Instead of grounding itself in explicit references to the countryside, in a Zezé di Camargo and Luciano concert, rurality exists in the way sentiment is handled. Rurality here emphasizes the radical disempowerment that strong emotions bring about. The subject of each song is split between rational-changeable and passionate-immutable halves. In rigorously inculcating this split and then celebrating its latter half, Zezé di Camargo and Luciano are every bit as "rural" as duplas that prioritize cattle and wide open plains. They have simply moved rurality more thoroughly into a state of urgency, inevitability, and perpetuity, resulting from an emergency of the heart. These qualities find expression through the oscillation between hierarchical and egalitarian poses inherent to the brother form itself, and through the way in which these poses are increasingly imbued with gendered connotations. The rurality of a Zezé di Camargo and Luciano show is also brought about by the production values inherent in each show, which simultaneously point *outward* toward other parts of a rural world and absorb inward, collecting *from* that world. This transformation of the spatiality of the rural into something that requires little pointing to a geographical countryside and instead entails a countryside of the heart is the central feature of the country cosmopolitan.

To begin to unpack this face of the rural, we return to the centrality of the dupla form. The shows under consideration here were structured entirely around the dupla as the single most important principle of the evening. The strength of the bond between the two brothers was em-

phasized throughout. They kidded each other about their personal pref-
erences in soccer and food. They stood and sang together, arm in arm.
When they were at opposite parts of the stage, they gazed at each other
as they sang. As in all rural music, the togetherness of their voices was
one of the central ways fans argued for their quality.

The hierarchical nature of their relationship appears every bit as much
as the equality evident in well-tuned singing and in the sharing of their
bond as brothers. Whenever Zezé took front-and-center stage, Luciano
stood to his right, just behind him, singing over his shoulder. Zezé
would be the one to vary the established order of songs if it was to be
altered at all. This was a rare occurrence, but one he nevertheless con-
trolled while Luciano followed. Zezé was the one who played guitar, and
he writes the songs. He is the more experienced musician, the older of
the two by ten years, and he carries the melody. Here, then, is the
hierarchy with egalitarianism that encapsulates the brother form first
outlined in chapter 2.

However, within the context of the country cosmopolitan, the dupla
form imbues hierarchy with a slightly different meaning from the one it
carries in the production of locality. In Zé Mulato and Cassiano's show
on February 12, 2000, the brothers displayed their knowledge of each
other too. They made jokes about each other's personal tastes and
showed that they knew each other's speech rhythms. But in commercial
country music, the tension between equality and hierarchy is managed
somewhat differently. First, the affectionate aspects of the brother bond
are pushed harder and further. But there are additional differences. At
the Via Roça, Zé Mulato and Cassiano faced forward, playing their
instruments and singing directly into microphones on stands. By contrast, in their shows at the Olympia, Zezé di Camargo and Luciano
moved around a great deal, taking advantage of wireless microphones.
They gazed intently at each other through many of the songs, and they
were frequently in physical contact, arms around waists and shoulders.
The fact that neither of them played instruments (with the exception of
a brief interlude of four songs where Zezé played guitar) freed their
hands for just this sort of manually rendered affection. They sang as
though they were one voice, to each other, about love, almost categorically about the love of a woman. For one song, they walked slowly
toward each other as they sang (the moves were repeated through both
shows, a fact to which I will return), delivering the final chorus face to
face, each one placing his hand on the other's chest.[3] In both shows,

toward the end of the evening, Luciano temporarily goes offstage to get two white towels. He returns to the stage and first wipes his own face off, throwing the towel into a crowd suddenly filled with hands hungrily reaching for it. Then he towels off his brother's face. This takes just seconds, and Luciano's motions are businesslike rather than slow and gentle. But the crowd responds strongly. Members of the audience scream, and when Luciano throws the towel into the crowd, a scrum takes place where it lands.

At this point, the inequality, long characteristic of the dupla form, becomes strongly gendered, where Zezé inhabits the male role, and Luciano, the female one. Aspects of their relationship begin to resemble a romance between a man and a woman. The injection of romantic love into this brotherly context is reinforced, not just by actions such as toweling, but also by offstage pronouncements, such as the cover notes of their live album of 2000, *Zezé di Camargo and Luciano Live*, recorded at the Olympia. The last page of the liner notes reveals a letter from Luciano to "Zezé," which is clearly aimed not so much at his brother but at the CD's buyers. Luciano begins by saying to Zezé, "how special you are in my life." He tells Zezé that Zezé is a book where "each page is a new lesson . . . each chapter is a new surprise." Luciano goes on to note that it was his brother who "found" him and gave him the opportunity to begin performing:

> It was on December 23, 1989 that you discovered me, pushed me out into this world so filled with magic in which illusion becomes real. And from there to here, the stage opened up. Not only in dividing the stage with you, but in growing each day. At the difficult moments, you were always by my side, even when my emotion yelled louder and made me lose reason.

Zezé has placed Luciano in a spot where the stuff of dreams can become reality. Not only may he share the stage with his accomplished and talented brother, but doing so provides him with opportunities for personal growth. Furthermore, Zezé furnishes a kind of container for Luciano's potential explosivity, which is, once again, gendered. Of course, rural singers frequently sing about their emotions. But in this case the female-gendered brother, Luciano, is the one that loses control, while Zezé reins in his brother's hysteria. And throughout, we see the importance of Zezé as the teacher and Luciano as the eager student. At the end, there is a heartfelt declaration: "As the old poet said, 'I knew I would love you my whole life'."

In this dupla, the gendering of the hierarchical aspects of the duo form provides the discursive terrain from which to voice the intensely experienced emotions surrounding the romantic love that populates the brothers' songs. This is cosmopolitan outreach. Commercial rural music draws upon the strongly gendered aspects of música sertaneja in order to address the idea that naturally, the world is divided into male and female roles. So fans and practitioners of this commercially successful rural music believe that in more clearly dividing the world between the two genders, they are making their music available to a broader range of listeners; the idea is that love between a man and a woman is universal.

By retreating from the iconic indexes of "country" in favor of a topography of gendered "human" emotions, the brothers project their rurality outward. Everyone has a countryside of the heart, a space of desperation, of heartache, of passion, of mysterious but most importantly inevitable longing. The belief is that this kind of country music requires no translation, as love's ineluctability becomes universal. Here, in this ruralized urban space of a concert hall in São Paulo, amidst the highest production values, the rurality of this performance moves fully into an emotional topology of rural subjectivity. To return to the last chapter's analysis of Connerton's ritual memory, love is *inscribed* in the lyrics and *incorporated* via inescapability and the way the two brothers relate to one another onstage. Consider these distillations of the songs the brothers perform on this particular evening:

1) I've had you once, and now I'm obsessed and *must* have you not just again, but forever

2) The madness of desire is like fire; I want you *so* much

3) I am listless without you

4) I obsess over you

5) The memory of you haunts me

6) You are everything to me

7) I can't be alone—can't be without you

8) Your betrayals are killing me

9) Your indifference is hurting us

10) We will complete each other, without fear

11) Somehow, I am back loving you, despite the madness of our past

12) I'm the best one for you—your one and only

13) This intense memory brings you back to me

14) My heart is in pieces without you

15) I can't disguise how I feel, though I try

16) You have the power to save my heart

17) I am the victim of a serious affliction

18) These memories torture me

19) I try to trick passion in order not to think of you, but it's useless

20) I am trapped in this room, thinking of you without end

21) Our love *exploded* within me

22) I wasn't expecting this, it just hit me so hard

23) This makes no sense, but I can't deny it—as hard as I try

These lyrics, condensed and translated here, deliver the message that love's intensity entraps. And just as one can't escape from the reality of the blood of brotherhood, the speaker in each of these songs can't change, can't escape, and can't do without. The rural involves an inhabitance of disempowerment that derives from the desperation of the lyrics. The country cosmopolitan becomes a paradoxically simultaneous despatialization of musico-emotional practice that makes ten-gallon hats somewhat gratuitous, instead emphasizing sentimentality's inevitability. As a result, the rural embodies a terrain that participants believe transcends the geopolitical while, as we shall see, addressing itself to broader "American" and international spaces, of which Brazil is merely one part.

Here, in the domain of the country cosmopolitan, the fact that it is men delivering this message becomes attenuated. The music is a kind of intimate revelation of the interior, wounded, and often childlike emotional state of masculinity which is frequently covered by a façade of chauvinism. Participants do not necessarily take these songs literally, of course. They *know* that men are not necessarily expressive in this fashion, precisely because they are not *supposed* to be expressive in this way in public. But there is a belief that part of the aspiration to modernity in this form of rural music lies in the fact that men *ought* to learn to be more communicative about emotions linked to love. In this way, men might participate in what is perceived to be an international transformation of masculinity into something more nuanced and less based on force. In her work on the transformation of love in neoliberal northeastern Brazil, Linda-Anne Rebhun (1999) notes that women work hard to extract statements of love from men. And men feel at a loss as to how to "communicate," a requirement once deemed intensely feminine. We need to read the mutual applicability of música sertaneja to both genders in the context of a striving to make men communicative in matters of love. The romantic aspects of the interaction between the brothers appear as a kind of training ground on which males may experience a new emotional palette. At the same time, part of the sadness of the music lies, once again, in its disempowerment. This *makes* the music rural at the same time as it questions whether men ever *could* learn to be more communicative.

The "Production" of Emotion

As in the case of the Via Roça in the last chapter, a variety of social actors collaborate in order for this production of the country cosmopolitan to occur. The hall in which "God Save America" took place, the Olympia, first opened its doors in 1988 and is located in a middle-class district of São Paulo called Lapa, which is near the northwest part of the city. In contrast with the Country Roads of the last chapter, the Olympia is an urban venue that sports neoclassical touches such as columns outlined in gold leaf and black paneling. It is long and thin, holding up to 4,000 for a standing show. On the evenings in question, however, the sold-out performances held 2,700 people because the bottom floor had been set with tables, which required more space per spectator.

The Olympia itself is managed according to a cosmopolitan set of musical principles. It caters to numerous genres, from rock to romantic, from *samba* to música sertaneja. It hosts musicals such as *The Phantom of the Opera*, as well as nonmusical events such as conferences, conventions, product launchings, and lectures. Its promotional materials stress the hall's "quality," its "safety," and its "professionalism."

The Olympia's cosmopolitanism is also reflected in its construction, which enables it to adjust to the broad sampling of music and other events which take place within it. For instance, the hall's modular insides reflect the practices of those booking the shows and allow the space to be reconfigured according to the particular genre being presented. Hard-driving national or international rock plays to standing crowds that dance. British musicals get theater-style seating. Conferences or banquets require dividing the hall up into sections for different activities. Rural music, traditional samba, jazz, and sometimes classical music often see guests seated at tables. The ability to reconfigure the space speaks to its flexibility in being able to address generically appropriate concepts of audience completeness (Kuipers 1998).

In the late 1980s, música sertaneja shows could not book halls like this. Rural music was not perceived to be worthy of inclusion in the list of other possible genres that might play at such locations. Thus, when Chitãozinho and Xororó were finally able to book high-profile halls such as the Olympia for the first time, they had the sense of having "arrived." From a historical standpoint, it is significant that most performers and some fans now deem rural music to be worthy of "respect" from a broad listening public; it is a genre that "people" now "value." This means that having a show in a hall of this sort, with its mixture of musical genres, business activities, and international clients, represents a certain cultural capital for rural musical performers.

"The Show" itself was an extremely produced affair and appears distant from Zé Mulato and Cassiano in several ways. For Zé Mulato and his brother, simple amplification of the acoustic instruments by way of under-the-saddle guitar pickups and microphones for the singers sufficed; indeed, this simplicity, which was always contrasted with música sertaneja's production, was the point. Volume levels were low enough that conversation was possible during the songs. By contrast, for Zezé di Camargo and Luciano, the show was loud. Any talking had to be shouted directly into an interlocutor's ear. In addition, minimal "reverb" (or echo effect) was applied to Zé Mulato and Cassiano's voices. On the other hand, Zezé di Camargo and Luciano's voices were drenched with reverb, producing a substantial echo that actually increased the sustaining of notes past when the brothers had stopped singing and withdrawn the microphones from in front of their mouths.

Production is another crucial means by which the country cosmopolitan takes shape in this show at the Olympia. What may be glossed as

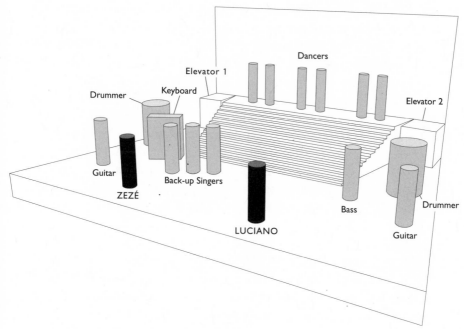

Figure 5. Zezé di Camargo's and Luciano's Stage.

the "production" of the show refers to a confluence of overlapping variables. The setup of the stage is intricate, involving lights, special effects such as artificial smoke, multiple dancers who change costumes, visible elevators to carry the brothers up to the top of a stairway at the center of the stage, and a moveable metal circle of tightly stretched fabric on which lights may be shone and videos projected. Numerous musicians, each one capable of playing several instruments, populate the stage in support of the brothers' efforts (see figure 5). Far from *violeiros* who purport to play only one cantankerous instrument requiring special attention, these instrumentalists switch constantly and are expected to fit seamlessly into the music. There are certainly no extended moments in which someone takes minutes to tune, telling stories about his instrument as he does so. Instead, the keyboard player simply picks up a saxophone and starts playing at the appointed time. And in the domain of preplanning, attendants hand out the set list to ticket holders as they enter the hall, indicating that the order in which songs will be played has been established.

These are just a few of the production features involved in the evening's music. They demonstrate that the level of preparation, the coordination of numerous social actors, each with defined roles, and the emphasis on sound and lighting equipment, all play a vital role in what takes place onstage. These things are not supplemental to the music. Rather, planning, coordination, and equipment provide three axes on which the show spins. Promotional materials for many duplas call attention to the "quality" and "professionalism" of "their show" (note the overlap with the promotional materials for the hall itself). The complexity of this particular evening and other shows within commercial country music is quite to the point and inverts conventional arguments about country music. The message is that música sertaneja is not improvised, technologically backward, and unscheduled. The long wait in evidence at the Via Roça so that everyone who was delayed by wet roads might have time to show up would be unthinkable here. Every aspect of the show points instead to the hyperemployment of production values deemed "modern." Here, the importance of dispelling any notion that country is technically lesser than other genres motivates the performance. By stressing "production," música sertaneja fans and performers feel themselves to be participating in an international musical conversation with other genres that also command these routines; such are the genres that play at the Olympia.

One of the ways to hone in on what is meant by production is to consider three axes of the show: planning, coordination, and equipment. The way in which these are put to the forefront of activity in the service of dupla singing distinguishes this as production in a rural mold. As we discuss these three axes, note that there is a paradox at the center of the country cosmopolitan. It propounds uncontrollable emotions in its lyrics, as evidenced by such frequent confessions of love's "explosions," while proffering a highly orchestrated stage. Thus we have unbridled feelings in a container. This, once again, shows the polarizing action of rural performativity with which this book began and to which we have returned throughout. The country cosmopolitan enacts a contrast between emotion and rationality and then produces this onstage such that the emotional appears in the lyrics, the music, and the relations between the brothers, while the rational is represented most obviously by the production. Just as, in the last chapter, language as a register of communicative practice put the emotional aspects of musicality to "work," so, too, does the emotion of commercial country lyrics get harnessed to the rigors of production.

Predetermination

There is little that the producers of this show leave to chance. Every detail of the evening's events has been planned down to the split second. The set list is preestablished and submitted to us as we walk in. We know what songs we will be hearing and in what order. The fixity of this order was reinforced during the second show when a fan from the upper balcony repeatedly screamed a request and was finally silenced by Luciano when he informed her directly that the song she had asked for was "not on the list." Other details of preshow planning appear below. Complex preshow planning is, of course, the case in many kinds of musical productions around the world. Perhaps no shows are more complex than the musicals of the Andrew Lloyd Weber variety so popular in London, New York, and Chicago, which require that set and costume changes and the layering of musical parts be arranged well in advance. However, rural music must manage the paradox of its rurality with respect to this coordination. Ostensibly, the countryside lacks artifice. Now, rural music has pushed its production levels way past many other musical genres such as MPB, which frequently aspires to minimal lighting and effects. But at a commercial country music show, you are meant to *notice* how well laid out the evening's activities are. This is "updating" the countryside for many rural musical fans and performers. Recall Xororó's statement that now, in the backcountry, people are surfing the Internet and trading cattle in American dollars. The music should reflect this.

Coordination

While the Zé Mulato and Cassiano show involved a single sound control center (called a "board") that was adjusted at the outset of the performance and then simply left on that initial setting, this show required a technical team to coordinate activities, from the sound board to lighting. Many people had to know precisely what they were doing at precisely the right moment. Though much of the lighting was locked in to the songs by way of computer, someone had to *watch* that computer to make sure it didn't go astray.

One of this show's central attributes was the sheer number of people required to put it on. A sizeable technical crew that travels with the brothers must be present to put up, take down, and monitor the equipment used in the course of the evening. This scale and form of involvement also applies to what takes place in the hall itself. The hall supplies many staff, differentiated according to uniform and, to some extent, gender. In fact, the show enacts a kind of Durkheimian division of labor, where the people responsible for putting on the show become the component parts of a larger organism (Durkheim 1933). The security-related tasks are undertaken by males, while promotional activities are handled by females, whose conventional prettiness suggests that they must have been handpicked for their appearance. Staff responsibilities are color coded. Some take tickets from those entering the concert (men dressed in grey pants, white shirts, and blue blazers), look through all bags for recording devices, keep people from storming the stage, police drunkenness, and seat ticket holders at tables. Men wearing black pants and white shirts, as well as women in black skirts and white shirts, bring customers drinks for moderately high prices. Staff also give out advertisements for cars (women in dark blue pantsuits), a furniture store (women in bright blue outfits with miniskirts trimmed with yellow and sporting blue Stetsons with yellow bands), and condensed milk (women in blue and white flowing dresses).

For this show, the way in which the audience was configured called for a large staff. On both nights the hall was divided into table seating, with six seats to a table, and balcony VIP boxes, with fixed, theater-style seats for the high-paying patrons, the famous, and fan-club members. For all involved, the show differed dramatically from the kind of concert where one stands and perhaps dances. During this show, one might wave to a waiter from one's seated position to order drinks as one would at a restaurant, creating a tab that had to be settled before departure. The waitstaff hovered, attentively.

Equipment and the Elasticity of Space

The adaptability of the Olympia's staging facilities was also a part of the show's production. It made use of the latest gadgetry. The brothers seemed to be transported up to a second level of the stage through elevators, and a set of stairs extended from this top level so that they could walk down onto the main stage, singing their opening number. The lights contained various focal possibilities such that they could be sprayed over a wide area or focused to a fine point. They were used so that the visual environment of the hall could be keyed to music. It was common, for instance, that as a song ended in a note held dramatically by the brothers, the lights swept from backstage out into the audience, moving the emphasis from singers to listeners. Artificial smoke was used together with lighting to create walls of a kind. When light hit smoke, whole sections of the stage suddenly became opaque and were shut off from other sections. Thus, without the benefit of physical partitions, zones could be closed and opened simply by means of light and smoke. The result was to create a sense of movement and change. This elasticity of the space received continual emphasis, contrasting starkly with a fixed stage. The landscape employed by Zezé and his brother was therefore reconfigurable. Technology seemed to transcend the conventional rules of matter, transporting, enclosing, and releasing the brothers in the course of their show.

Zones of Projection and Absorption

So far, we have considered several ways in which the brothers seek a cosmopolitan projection outward and a gathering inward. These include the attenuation of the desperate elements of rural sentimentality, a deepening of the treatment of romantic love, the gendering of the hierarchical aspects of the dupla form, the search for mainstream acceptance through playing at halls where other genres with international ties play, and the employment of production standards deemed worldly and sophisticated. All of these come to bear as commercial rural musical acts seek to stretch out to a broader audience. Now let us turn to the show's most important song as an illustration of another way in which Brazilian rurality addresses itself, not just to Brazil, but to a larger space.

The show lasted for over two hours on each occasion, and each time the brothers played their song "God Save America" about three quarters of the way through, right before the show's energy began to wind down. My aim in treating this song in detail is to consider the way in which the simultaneous projection outward and inward absorption of cosmopolitanism can be found in the delineation of the broad social problem that the song lays out. At the same time we can detect a certain kind of cosmopolitanism in the solution proposed. The song has been referred to by music columnists as one of two "political" songs from the dupla's record from 1998—In Order Not to Think of You. It addresses the destruction of the environment, but its politics are not directly engaged with specific leaders, institutions, or events. We do not hear of the melting of the polar ice cap here. Indeed, the very abstractness of the song's statement of the problem aims toward a broader circulation than locality.

To specify the song's central problem, the brothers sing that when they were "out walking," they saw "so much beauty in our America." They elaborate briefly on this beauty: "The people are good / The land is good / Pretty rivers and forests." But then they enumerate the conundrum. How, they wonder, "could these riches / that are part of a history / be the stage for such sadness?"

> *Where there are no glories?*
> *We lack equality, lack union,*
> *We lack people with more heart*
> *Men who believe*
> *In their country*
> *We lack people of courage and race*
> *To change all this.*

The nation, here, is not so much Brazil as nations broadly speaking. These problems are presented in terms of a lack of even-handed social status, of togetherness, of people with sufficient faith in their nations, and of people with the force of will to enact the transformations that might make things better. Here, "race" is used in the sense of distinction, as in—the world lacks people of character and achievement. "Race" can also refer to determination and force. In any case, the message is clear enough: America lacks people of sufficient character to make the changes that might reduce the sadness that the brothers feel.

In the next verse, the brothers return to their consideration of the central problem. "It is so difficult for people to see and to accept / such an absurdity," they begin. God has given us everything, they propose:

> *If God has given*
> *The sky, the earth, and the sea—*
> *He gave us the world!!!*
> *Like a child's dream*
> *All is happiness.*

And along with this gift of everything, we are permitted to believe that all is fine.

But all is not fine. Disillusion accompanies maturity. What will soon become a veiled indictment of corporate pollution and lack of environmental care does not begin with rapacious capitalist extraction, or even alienation, but with something much less specific: growing up. In the process of becoming adults, people hurt each other: "But the child grows up one day / Becomes a man, and hurts," (hurting here is employed as something done to someone else rather than as pain experienced). From here, the problems come fast and furious: "nature is dying / Our animals—my God—what pain / The entire human race is suffering." Once again note that the problems are not cited as specific to Brazil alone. The human race suffers not because Brazil's president has failed to redistribute land in the countryside, but rather, it suffers "for lack of love."

The song's video underscores the scope of the problem. The deficiencies of faith in country and courage clearly touch North America as well as Brazil. There are only scenes of nature, which enact the sort of typical rural musical preoccupation with landscape and animals one might see on motivational posters. But these carefully shot scenes derive from both Brazilian and North American locations and portray mountain streams, eagles soaring above granite cliffs, a family of orangutans moving through the jungle, and sand blowing over worn rocks in some desert. These are shots meant to celebrate the intrinsic beauty of nature, in which the colors of sunsets and trees have been made brighter and deeper. This, presumably, is the beauty with which the song began, the beauty that our collective "hurting" and lack of "race" jeopardize.

The song is not without hope, however. The brothers entreat us to "teach our children" of the beauty of the world as one corrective measure. And then, naturally enough, the love that might make us love one another can be found within each of us, accessible through appeals to a higher power:

God Save America
I see a light that comes
In our direction
God Save America
I feel a love that exists
In our hearts.

In this way, perhaps, we can collectively remedy the problems that the song lays out, problems existing in this "America."

As mentioned above, the video focuses on natural beauty, but in the stage show, characters are important. During the second chorus, where the brothers begin to conceive of a light somewhere, dancers emerge onto the raised back portion of the stage in costume. In all but one case, their outfits point specifically: Carmen Miranda, Fidel Castro, Ayrton Senna, Madonna, Che Guevara, Marilyn Monroe, Pelé, and, somewhat more amorphously, a North American Indian.

This is an inspirational cast in whom the audience is meant to see the right reasons for saving America. Carmen Miranda was a Portuguese-born Brazilian samba singer who became one of the most popular female movie stars in Hollywood in the 1940s. Her departure to the United States and caricaturing of Latinas in her films led to considerable Brazilian criticism, though her work continues to receive praise from prominent musicians such as Caetano Veloso. Cuban revolutionary and president Fidel Castro requires little introduction. After overthrowing Batista in 1959, Castro became Cuba's leader and an eloquent critic of the hegemony of the United States throughout Latin America. Ayrton Senna was a Brazilian three-time Formula One world champion, and by many estimates, one of the finest race-car drivers of all time. Tragically, he died following an accident at the San Marino Grand Prix in 1994, and his Brazilian funeral drew tremendous crowds. Michigan-born Madonna has not stopped selling records since the explosive 1984 release of *Like a Virgin*. She has continued to do so, but has also distinguished herself in the production of ornate stage shows to support her albums. Argentine physician and revolutionary Che Guevara led guerilla movements against tyrannical rule in Cuba, Congo-Kinshasa, and Bolivia in the 1950s and 1960s. He was captured and executed by the CIA-supported Bolivian army in 1967. The popularity of prominent model, singer, and film actress Marilyn Monroe reached its peak during the 1950s and stretched into the early 1960s. Her early suicide ended a career filled with high expectations. "The King," Pelé, began playing soccer at fifteen in Brazil and quickly established himself as one of the most talented players in the game. He is thought by many to have been the greatest soccer player of all time, having been part of three World Cup teams. He lives in Brazil, where he mostly works for charities. The Native American appears in an entirely essentialized form—not as, say, Sitting Bull—but as the embodiment of environmental preservation—objectified.

In this lineup, there are three Americans—one actress, one entertainer, and an indigene. There are three Brazilians—a race-car driver, a soccer player, and a singer. There is a Cuban and an Argentine. All of them hail from America broadly speaking. Several reek of tragedy: Monroe, Senna, and Guevara. One, Miranda, was once a Brazilian sweetheart, but was cast out upon beginning to make movies in the United States.[4] Two heroes have essentially retired while maintaining some news-media visibility: Castro and Pelé. Guevara and Castro had the courage to transform their circumstances, as painful as it was to do so. For the most part, these are notables from the *past* (the Madonna portrayed here sports the lacy leggings look of her *Like a Virgin* years). Native Americans become an endangered species, like those seen in the video. In this way, the presentation of characters continues música sertaneja's fixation on a past where things were once better.

Emerging as they do at the chorus, during the moment at which the brothers are singing that they see a light, these figures arrive to inspire nostalgia. Furthermore, note the inescapably local nature of the politics of this cosmopolitan collection. Fidel Castro and Che Guevara are heroes in many quarters in Brazil, and thus can represent what is best about America right beside Marilyn Monroe. Madonna dances beside an uncannily still Indian. Current critics of Brazilian commercial country music claim that it is "Americanized," but this notion is belied by the way in which this song portrays its "America" in a way that would not function at all in the United States. Cosmopolitanisms are always "rooted" (Appiah 2007) at the very moment that they reach out.

Global Rodeo and the Cosmopolitan

The brothers play halls like the Olympia quite rarely, focusing much of their energy on rodeos. And while their show at the Olympia serves to emphasize important aspects of their country cosmopolitanism, rodeo, too, stretches out to things deemed global, gathering the far-flung at the same time. Rodeos fashion themselves not simply as rural spaces in relation to the city, and not merely as Brazilian spaces, but sometimes, as international ones. While studying Barretos in 2004, I interviewed participants in the youth rodeo competition. I started to ask one announcer-in-training how he reacted to a criticism sometimes leveled at Brazilian rodeo: that it imitates the United States too much. As I moved to elaborate on the criticism, he stopped me. He had heard

efore, he noted, and the arguments always confused him.
st like school, and plenty of schools had exchange pro-
rodeo should focus on what he called "*intercâmbio*" (an
rogram) struck him as every bit as much of a good idea as
cusing on it in school. The term he used was precisely the
used for international educational exchange programs.

Forms of rural internationalism surfaced throughout the Americana Rodeo of 2006, which happened to coincide with the World Cup of soccer. For instance, it is conventional for a part of the ceremonies at the beginning of the night of rodeo activity to contain a segment in which riders carry local, state, and national flags, as well as the flags of sponsors. One particular evening during the World Cup of 2006 was no exception, except that there were also the flags of the countries that remained in play in the final rounds of soccer. This group included Germany, Ecuador, England, Sweden, Argentina, the Netherlands, Portugal, Mexico, Italy, Ghana, Brazil, Australia, Switzerland, France, Spain, and the Ukraine. The rodeo thus sought to include itself in an international sphere of participation with local import. It brought the "world" cup down into the arena, projecting the desire for Brazil's victory outward.

This chapter has argued that rural cosmopolitanism entails both a projection outward and an absorption inward. It portrays itself to be cutting edge because it samples from places far afield. Across the various spaces examined in this chapter, we see that the rural is thought of as a kind of "contact zone" (Lomnitz 2001), characterized by a paradoxically progressive backward glance that celebrates emotional disempowerment. Here, where the hierarchical relation between brothers is transformed into a cross-gendered interaction of romance, unbridled sentiments are tempered by meticulous production. This grounds a reaching out and pulling in that indexes the past and the international at the same time, partaking of a hierarchy which, in turn, manufactures distinction. Cosmopolitanism thus reveals itself to be locality's other face in the neoliberal field of rural musical production.

Conclusion

POSTAUTHORITARIAN MEMORY AND RURALITY

> I must own that I could have assured any questioner that Combray did include other scenes and did exist at other hours than these. But since the facts which I should then have recalled would have been prompted only by voluntary memory, the memory of the intellect, and since the pictures which that kind of memory shows us preserve nothing of the past itself, I should never have had any wish to ponder over this residue of Combray.—MARCEL PROUST, "Swann's Way"

This analysis of one of modernity's primary musicalities has sought to contribute to the ethnography of performativity and neoliberalism. It should be clear by now that rurality is not simply a spatial index of country people, though it is sometimes called to this role. More broadly, rurality should be thought of as a form of social identification akin to race, gender, and social class, which is of particular importance in the neoliberal period both in Latin America and elsewhere (Fox and Yano forthcoming). As we have seen, however, Brazilian rurality is a form of social identification with particular entailments and presuppositions. In order to review these, we conclude with the dialogic relation between *música caipira*'s locality and *música sertaneja*'s cosmopolitanism. We are now in a position to see the way in which Central-Southern rural performativity relies upon an elastic space between old-fashioned and commercial. Like all public culture, rural music emerges "interdiscursively" (Agha 2005; Bauman 2005, 146) in layers that both participants in the moment and analysts after the fact may peel away or leave undisturbed. Examination of mediatized forms of communicative practice, in particular, must attend to this layering, recognizing that any given "text" (Hanks 1989) operates in many places at once.

Scrutiny of the relationship between *caipira* and sertanejo returns us

to the embeddedness of musical practice in fields of cultural production. The productive tension between elements within fields, parsed
according to actors, institutions, and genres, underscores the systematicity of human interaction, broadly speaking. Within such systems,
such as the Brazilian field of musical production, elements are bound
up with one another, and motion in one quadrant creates motion in the
others. So when two genres get cozy or fall out, this transforms not just
those genres themselves, but also their compatriots. Dialogic processes
of approximation and distancing thus transform fields over time.

Intergeneric fields reveal how communicative practice relies upon the
interrelation of the indexical and the meta-indexical (Lee 1997, 164), or
the pointing *to*, of the pointing to. This means that performativity's
meta-indexicality makes it relentlessly comparative. Moreover, in its
insistence on the inevitability of comparison, the performance of, in
this case, rural genres bears a resemblance to ethnography's comparative bent (G. Urban 1999). Both anthropologist and singer must
monitor their interdiscursive relation to other genres, actors, and institutions in an emergent fashion at the moment of singing, playing,
speaking, interviewing, writing notes or chapters, and listening. In
illustrating how these projects unfold, this work contributes to the
anthropology of performativity, which is central not just in circumstances involving what might be narrowly defined as "the arts," but
also in politics, economics, and religion.

The book also contributes to the ethnography of Brazil in the period
problematically classifiable as "neoliberal." I say problematically because we must be cautious about overselling neoliberalism's novelties.
Such enthusiasm can be made to trot politely alongside triumphalist
accounts of democracy's link to free markets (Friedman 1962) or pan-
icky indictments of the "commodified" evils of an oppressive present.
But both perspectives tread a predetermined path where ambiguity falls
away. The former reading ignores the growing inequality of income
distribution in Brazil, while the latter elides the efficaciousness of new
grassroots activism. Instead of such economistic thinking, this study
shows the way in which public culture under neoliberalism mixes novelty with throwback. So far as rural music in Brazil is concerned, the
brother form has deep roots in gendered migration patterns, even as it
is put to new use in the celebration of the powerlessness that love
brings. The *viola* takes on new importance as a way of connecting with
the past, while its students apply themselves to arcane rhythms by way

of digital recording. The local implications of "country" music in a global perspective thus provide a means through which to examine continuities and transformations in present-day Brazil. Rurality has become a way to interpret new developments using long-standing pre-occupations, such as aggravated boundaries between social classes, marked along financial, racial, and gendered lines. Contrary to what Fredric Jameson (2003) has suggested, modernity's premodern "temporality" shows no sign of disappearing any time soon.

Indeed, rural music grew so much after the return to democracy in 1985 not simply because larger numbers of people viewed it as an exclusive badge of identity, though this is certainly the case (Carvalho 1993; Reily 1992). More significantly, the answer to rurality's post-authoritarian popularity in Brazil lies in the way it increasingly provides a position that people may inhabit with varying durations and intensities. I encountered some people residing in both country and city spaces who considered themselves rural through and through, listening to música caipira and música sertaneja exclusively. But I met more who owned rural music CDs and went to rodeos while enjoying other genres as well. In studying forms of public culture such as popular music, we must account for these other modalities of participation as much as we account for those who find a given genre in every fiber of their being. "Publics" form through multiple levels of attention (Warner 2002). Inhabitance of the country critique may be long, short, all-encompassing, or halfhearted.

The increasing importance of the agricultural production of the Central-South to national economic matters both has been facilitated by, and it has facilitated, rural music. This, in turn, increased rurality's visibility. The growing capital generated by agriculture has flowed into rodeo, which further augments rurality's profile. Framed by this rural presence in public space, people, mostly from cities, watch, by way of the news media, the unfolding of an increasingly fraught contest over rural landscapes. The fight is between the conservative forces of the likes of the UDR (The Democratic Ruralist Union) and the left-wing MST (The Rural Landless Worker's Movement). The UDR argues for the preservation of private property, which they judge to be under threat by sinister socialists, while the MST wishes to take possession of fallow lands owned by barons.

Rural music plays a complex role in this standoff, where both sides mediate their positions musically through both caipira and sertanejo.

Both factions draw succor from the way in which rural genres pine for the good old days in which life was better, more honest, and more whole. The MST gives workshops in traditional viola playing as a way of strengthening the traditional knowledge of its participants; it believes that understanding folkloric "roots" will eventually aid in acts of possessing, planting, and harvesting. But MST's viola workshop attendees are not exclusively traditional types. Many follow the rise to fame of the latest música sertaneja *dupla* (lately, the brothers César Menotti and Fabiano). They buy and listen to its records, feeling their heartstrings tugged by the poignant union of words with melody, while sensing that life used to be easier. Meanwhile, César Menotti and Fabiano's record sits beside self-consciously old-fashioned música caipira and solo viola music by Enúbio Queiroz in the CD changer that animates a party I attended at a rich farmer's house. He extols the beauty of the melodies in *sertanejo* as well as the instrumental virtuosity of caipira while complaining that under the dictatorship, when politicians were corrupt, at least they had the grace to keep it *hidden*. Nowadays, under democracy, the scoundrels rob "right out in the open." Back in the good old days, things were better. Both political orientations therefore find that rural music provides resources for the construction of opinions.

The country critique is not just tied up with explicitly rural space, however. I have argued that it also applies in a much broader sense to the dynamics of memory and to the neoliberal period's treatment of change in relation to that of the dictatorship. The widening reach of the country critique in the late twentieth and early twenty-first centuries is in part due to the fact that it presents an antidote to progress hunger of the sort documented by Marvin Harris when he studied the relations between town and country in the interior of the Northeastern state of Bahia in 1971:

> The people of Minas Velhas are ready to accept radical cultural changes, especially as these pertain to technological innovations. Far from presenting any ideological resistance to technological progress, they desperately desire it in all forms, from automobiles and electric power, to modern housing and miracle drugs. Modernity is well-nigh a passion with them and the new is valued over the old in almost all situations where the townspeople are presented with a choice. (Harris 1971, 288)

So powerful an appetite in part maintained the dictatorship by naturalizing the industrialization on which it rested. Progress narratives continue to play a major role in national self-figuring in the democratic era, often fed by an economic discourse whereby "BRIC countries" (Brazil, Russia, India, and China) are expected to shape the future of the world system (2007). Brazil, the sleeping giant, finally stirs to take its rightful place among the nations.

But as we have seen, this sort of talk creates tensions. Brazilians in the locations I studied continue to experience discomfort over the speed of change, as well as the forms it takes. On the one hand, they feel that a propensity for unlikely mixtures makes them inherently suited to absorb the latest innovation. On the other, fears of an imminent loss of selfhood circulate widely. Rural genres are one form in which these fears emerge. Suspicion of change forms part of the "intimate" quality of rural music. Being against linear progress is clearly not "the nation" putting its best foot forward (Herzfeld 1996).

Recent work on Latin American postdictatorial public culture has considered some of its less "intimate" forms and has suggested that they play a significant role in the way in which authoritarian regimes are currently being remembered through forgetting. For instance, Idelber Avelar (1999) has argued that Latin American fiction in the redemocratized period evidences a letting-go of the dictatorship that has been necessary for mourning to take place. Rural genres both support and trouble this claim. Rural music would seem, at first listen, to skip over the dictatorial period, perhaps inculcating forgetting by remembering a past *beyond* 1964–85. These are not songs about torture, disappearances, and censorship, but about lost loves, homes, and hearts, all set in an idealized country past. But at the same time, the country past that rural genres seek to emphasize continually criticizes the progress narratives so central to the dictatorships' coercive economic "miracles." In this sense, the authoritarian years are an ever-present absence, and the loss of innocence so central to rural performativity's split subject may well be the authoritarian bureaucratic years themselves. Perhaps the dictatorship is what brings about leaving home, love, and wholeness in rural songs.

Understanding the loss of innocence that rural music reinforces and partakes of requires grappling with its multiple drifts. Brazilian musical rurality treats the past in two distinct ways at the same time. First, it argues for the necessity of bringing the past forward into the present, and for the real possibility of doing so. But at the same time it obsessively ruminates on the *impossibility* of the past's presence in the here and now. The alternation between these two epistemological modes becomes audible in this book's last dance, a discussion of the song "Pagode em Brasília" (Blowout in Brasília).

Blowout in Brasília—A Cross-temporal Performance

"Pagode em Brasília" illustrates the arguments I have made above. It reveals the multiple layering, meta-indexicality, and embeddedness of performances within fields of cultural production. It illustrates the way in which rurality engages in an ambiguous way within modernity, seeking sometimes to counteract it, sometimes to encompass portions of it, and at other times simply to accept it. The song outlines the way in which neoliberal public culture in Latin America is frequently characterized by a dialogic relation between the traditional and the commercial. It suggests how rurality fashions Brazilian experience as simultaneously peripheral and central with respect to a world system. And finally, by emphasizing the increasing importance of the brother form, the song reveals the way in which the historical inversion on which rurality depends takes shape by way of a reversal of conventional expectations for Latin American "masculinities" (Fonseca 2003; Gutman 2003).

To elaborate: "Pagode em Brasília" was one of the hit songs of the Barretos Peon's Festival in 1999. This favorite, written in the late 1950s and made famous by the dupla composed of the late Tião Carreiro (b. 1934, d. 1993) and his singing partner Pardinho, was performed at the rodeo by current brother dupla Chitãozinho and Xororó and, in a somewhat different modality, by Tião Carreiro and Pardinho themselves. The pairing would have struck rodeo goers as moderately unusual, since caipira duplas (represented here by Tião Carreiro and Pardinho)[1] and sertanejo ones (represented here by the brothers) infrequently mix in performance, particularly when one of the members, Tião in this case, has passed away. But other factors made the pairing noteworthy. Critics and musicians often describe Tião Carreiro and Pardinho as one of the most "refined" roots duplas of recent memory (see, for example, Faria 1993). By contrast, Chitãozinho and Xororó are megastars squarely in the commercial country vein.

With respect to the title of the song that brought them all into the same musical space, *pagode* refers to a spontaneous party, or "blowout," often an informal one that includes ample food, drink, and banter.[2] In the Central-South, *pagode* also connotes a complex rhythm for strumming the strings of the viola. Listeners argue that the animated timing beat out by the *violeiro*'s right hand indexes the animation of pagode-as-party.[3] Pagode-as-rhythm musically both presupposes and entails the fun that may be had at social gatherings in which such music plays. Stories abound among disc jockeys, journalists, performers, and fans as to how the rhythm was created. What seems most likely is that Tião Carreiro fashioned it in 1959 by experimenting with an older and more established Central-Southern folkloric rhythm; apparently, he was always looking for new ways to play. These days, this once innovative rhythm stands as the sonic instantiation of caipira: the most folkloric Central-Southern sound bite imaginable.

In the first recording of "Blowout in Brasília" from the 1960s, the novelty of this new rhythm lauded another novelty. The song's writers, Lourival dos Santos and Teddy Vieira, conceived of it as a celebration of the new national capital, Brasília, which had been moved from Rio de Janeiro to the interior in April of 1960. Tião Carreiro and Pardinho's performance of the song attracted the attention of president Juscelino Kubitschek, who was mainly responsible for spearheading the plan to create Brasília. And the building of Brasília itself was a long time in the making. Since the eighteenth century (Holston 1989, 16), scholars and politicians had suggested that one of the sources of Brazil's economic and political troubles was that it had focused too much of its economic and political power near its coast, in cities such as Rio de Janeiro, Recife, Salvador, and the slightly inland São Paulo (Lima 1999). The argument was that this "coastalism" left the vast rural interior in a slumber. The construction of the capital in the middle of the country would wake it up.

The late 1950s was just the moment for such a scheme. Kubitschek had campaigned on the saying "fifty years' progress in five" (Skidmore 1967, 164). The progress he had in mind focused on the rapid expansion of industrialization. The building of Brasília played an important role in his efforts to develop the interior since it required the mobilization of capital, labor, and materials to the largely rural state of Goiás. A design competition yielded a high modernist city in the middle of the *sertão*: a capital poured almost entirely out of concrete, shaped from an aerial viewpoint like that ultimate symbol of progress at the time, the airplane. As ethnographer James Holston (1989) notes in his analysis of the execution of Brasília, planners also hoped that its construction would address the divide between rich and poor by having them live side by side.

Vieira and Santos's song partook of this enthusiasm in a decidedly rural mode. "Blowout in Brasília" set the construction of the capital into the context of typically rural challenges such as making a weed-choked field suitable for planting and getting a stubborn donkey to work. They thus simultaneously acknowledge the construction of Brasília as part of a linear progress narrative intent upon a rupture with the past, while subsuming it within an argument for rural cyclicality. Fields must be cleared and planted *each* year. Donkeys will refuse *again*. But hope for a better future is evident. At the end of the song, listeners were told that the song's sound shook the earth in the state of Goiás where Brasília was being built. The singers eventually took their leave to join the hard labor of building the new city in the hinterland:

> I'm sending my pagode
> To the state of Goiás
> At the Waldomiro bazaar
> In Brasília—the best in town
> That viola lick
> Shakes the ground of Goiás,
> So now, I'm going to play the final bars:
> Bidding farewell to the residents of São Paulo.
> See you later, I'm going
> —'Cus Goiás is calling me.

What has been pining for an abstract rural space in previous rural songs here becomes a desire to participate in ruralized progress.

In 1999, however, the song grappled with a different national-political context than that of the 1960s. This time, it addressed a postauthoritarian and democratic moment in which modernization's continued hegemony seemed tinged with sadness, once again requiring tempering by way of rural performativity. Here, we see the significance of "intimacy" for the management, not just of national self-imagining, but also the politics of gender, the expression of emotion, and the fashioning of subjectivities.

The way in which the song musically and lyrically sought to innovate within a rural mold back in the early 1960s made it available for the kind of generic melding that was required of it when Chitãozinho and Xororó "decontextualized" and then "recontextualized" (Bauman and Briggs 1990) it at Barretos in 1999. The version sung at Barretos in 1999 involved playing the original 1960s recording over the public address system. The lyrics had not changed in the delivery; the 1999 performance still celebrated the construction of an urban space in the rural interior as part of a larger cyclically rural project of cultivating fields for planting. However, listeners in the 1990s had other possibilities on their horizons of interpretation. They knew, for instance, that the original aspirations for the new capital had been overblown. Brazil was still overwhelmingly coastal, and if the interior had woken up, it was not around Brasília, but only further south, in the state of São Paulo. Furthermore, Brasília's attempts to dismantle rifts between social classes had been unsuccessful; the upper middle classes had taken over the ostensibly pan-status apartments, pushing the poor to the city's periphery, just as in most Brazilian cities.

Instead of converting Brasília's rupture with the present into rhythms of field planting and harvesting, the version of the song performed at Barretos in 1999 technologically facilitated movement between old and new. We can think of this as a to-and-fro between the song's older version and its newer one: past anticipation and current disappointment. And the *accomplishment* of such an oscillation in 1999 took the place of Tião's fancy right hand in the 1960s. The computer technology involved in pitch-shifting and tempo maintenance of two different versions became a central feature of the rendition. The resulting juxtaposition of the original song with modern performance characteristics enabled the mingling of a past dupla with a current one. Since Tião had passed away six years before, the rodeo's producers required digital sleight of hand in the form of a computer program that could change the key signature without altering its tempo. Tião Carreiro and Pardinho sang in a lower pitch than Chitãozinho and Xororó, which required a transition upward in the present. This sonic feat had hitherto been impossible since the only way to raise or lower the pitch of a recorded piece was to speed up the tape, or slow it down (respectively), thereby altering its key. Not so at fin-de-siècle Barretos. In the opening verse, the original recording played. For the next verse, live viola and regular six-string guitar cut in, modulating the tune up to a higher key to accommodate the higher live voices of Chitãozinho and Xororó, though without changing the tempo. As the tempo of the original recording continued, Chitãozinho and Xororó sang the next two verses live to the new instrumental accompaniment, layered over the old version that still played, pushed somewhat into the background. For the last verse, the original vocal track with Tião Carreiro and Pardinho blended back into the mix, shifted in pitch such that all four voices could finish together.

This song and its mediatized cross-temporality sought two conjoined effects. First, the song resuscitated the ruralist argument for Brasília as part of the cycle of growth and death, carried by the link between lyrics about a brand new rural capital city and an innovative rhythm. At the same time, this could be treated with suspicion in the present because of the failings of the project. But the late twentieth-century "country" innovation was not simply the ability to relive this message at one of the largest rodeos in the world, something that could have been facilitated simply by playing the older song over the public address system. Rather, the innovation lay in being able to *combine* a performance from the past with one from the present, providing a kind of tracking shot of Central-Southern rural music in which the commercial and tremendously successful Chitãozinho and Xororó could co-participate with their now-lauded caipira "roots" in the form of Tião Carreiro and Pardinho's recording.

The new version of the song flagged the capacity to create a certain kind of cross-temporal text. The song promulgated two distinct approaches to history by way of a movement backward and forward between the voices of the past and those of the present, tradition alternating with the contemporary, caipira with sertanejo. Approach to history number one existed in the ending to the song, when all four voices sang together. This suggested that the sometimes distinct practices of caipira and sertanejo could fuse in the same space and time. Past and present could collapse into one another through the melding of the two musical genres. However, the harmonious ending did not mean that the song could be reduced to arguing exclusively for the togetherness of then and now. In this markedly dialogic performance, the genre associated with the past is just as often *not* reducible to the genre associated with the present in the act of singing and playing for an audience. Indeed, in order for there to be a sense of alternation in the first place, there must be two entities which, in some sense, remain distinct. Thus, according to the second approach to history promulgated by the performance in 1999, the past is gone; caipira can never fully return because it has become sertanejo. It has modernized.

These two positions alternate within this instance of rural performativity. The dissolution of the past into the present—their blending—frames caipira and sertanejo in terms of their "affinities" (see Boon 1990, x, 12). The irreducibility of the past—its existence side by side with the present without overlapping with it—frames their "extremes" (ibid.). One of the messages of present-day Brazilian rurality is that these two historicities must struggle with one another. Rurality therefore entails a dialogue between modes of remembrance, and the continual split between them, and within the listening subject. In this way, rural performativity maintains a relentlessly polarizing action. The discursive play between these poles is the way in which these two modes give substance to each other in acts of playing, singing, and listening. At one moment, the past could well be brought forward for scrutiny. In the other, it must fall away forever, as Jeca weeps, "like water t' the sea."

~ↄℯↄ

Notes

Introduction

Epigraph is from Lévi-Strauss 1969, 14.

1. I use "rurality" here to capture a state and process of indexing country. Terms such as "rural" and "peasant," by themselves, simply reinforce the materially instantiated belief in an unproblematic urban/rural dichotomy that this book seeks to analyze.

2. For statistical purposes, the states within the Central-South often find themselves in three different regions: the "Southeast" includes São Paulo, Minas Gerais, Espírito Santo, and Rio de Janeiro; a "Central-West" includes Goiás, Mato Grosso do Sul, and Mato Grosso; and a "Southern" region includes Rio Grande do Sul, Paraná, and Santa Catarina. Such conventional definitions are used by geography texts on Brazil (see, for example, Poppino 1968), and also by the IBGE—the Brazilian Institute of Geography and Statistics (2003).

3. These rurally themed soap operas date almost precisely from redemocratization, beginning with a *novela* entitled *Pantanal*, set in the swamps of the western portion of the Central-Southern region, then *The King of Cattle* which takes a *música sertaneja* hit from the 1960s for its title, and finally, *América*, which revolves around contemporary rodeo.

4. Before his recent death, Bandido resided on a farm in the interior of São Paulo, where he awaited challenges from rodeo cowboys like 2004 world champion Edinei Caminhas, who failed to remain on the bull's back for the required eight seconds at Barretos that year. When he was not at rodeos, he spent his time being filmed for the TV show at home, traveling to Rio for shoots, and appearing at rodeos such as The Americana Peon's Festival of 2006. He has now been cloned.

5. From an economic standpoint, neoliberalism refers to a specific set of policies in Latin America often spoken of as "liberalization." Among these are the reduction of tariffs on foreign goods, the increasing penetration of foreign capital in national enterprises, the selling-off of national corporations to private interests abroad, the loosening of credit, and, significantly for Brazil, the rigorous maintenance of the integrity of the new currency (the *real*, as of 1994). This last measure has largely stemmed the wildfire inflation characteristic of Brazil's immediate return to democracy. Also included in

Brazilian liberalization is the policing of the strict fiscal responsibility of government, as well as adherence to the policy stipulations of the International Monetary Fund (IMF) and the World Bank. On a social level, neoliberalism is associated with the promulgation of regimes of individuated consumption, an ethos of private enterprise, and the belief in something deemed "personal choice" as the chief structuring principle of human action. Also of paramount importance is the notion that something called free and open "competition" should govern social life, an idea that rurality tackles head-on. Several scholars have proposed an anthropology of neoliberalism, among them, the various authors in the edited volume by J. Comaroff and J. L. Comaroff (2001b), and, about Brazil, O'Dougherty (2002).

6. For an analysis of the social category of the *caboclo* in a different context, suggesting that the term applies more to civilized Indians, see Chernela (2004).

7. This is not precisely the same thing as the discourse of "whiteness" some have claimed plays an important role in North American country music (see Fox 2004). Brazilian country's racialized identity politics still stresses mixture. It simply stresses a different *form* of mixture.

8. For an extended treatment of rural classifiers, see Brandão (1983, 7–11).

9. Two prominent exceptions to this are Sandy, of *dupla* Sandy and Júnior, and Roberta Miranda. I will address their exceptionalism, and the role of gender more broadly, in chapter 2.

10. Note that the capital of Brazil moved from Rio de Janeiro to Brasília in 1960.

11. I discuss this *dupla* in more detail in chapter 2.

12. "Gringo" is usually a less derogatory term in Brazil than it is in Mexico.

13. Lopes (2000) discusses this famous player's funeral.

14. Here, I take social class to be one's position within society as derived from one's level of control over culturally and historically defined means of production. In more detail, Turner (1984, 2003) follows Marx in arguing that social class may be thought of as a social grouping or category that plays a particular role within the relations of production (1984, 6).

15. The song, currently spelled "Chitãozinho and Xororó" but originally appearing as "Chitãnzinho and Chororó," was written by Serrinha and Athos Campos in 1947. The titles are nonetheless pronounced the same.

16. *Música caipira* is also sometimes referred to as *música sertaneja raíz*, although the caipira label is rapidly becoming the most common designation. R. Corrêa (2000) distinguishes between two forms of música caipira: duo-style and *viola*-style.

17. I classify this dupla as *caipira* with full knowledge that this classification will irk those who claim to practice "true" *música sertaneja*; in their heyday, brothers Tonico and Tinoco referred to themselves as practitioners

of música sertaneja. The necessity that some feel to describe them today as música caipira will be addressed in chapter 7.

18. Population figures are from the Instituto Brasileiro de Geografia e Estatísticas (IBGE—The Brazilian Institute of Geography and Statistics) and are available from their web site. All figures are rounded to the nearest thousand and are from 1996.

19. José Manuel dos Santos is a pseudonym.

1 What Counts as "Country"?

Epigraph placed before the section "Two Brazils, One Ruefully Proud" is from Lambert 1967. My italics.

1. Other scholarly analyses of the song do not necessarily agree. For example, in a brilliant and enigmatic treatise on *caipira* music, journalist and professor of communications Romildo Sant'Anna (2000) finds this song to be a middle-class lampoon of what he deems to be "true" caipira musicality. However, Sant'Anna's concern is to establish what "real" caipira music is. My preoccupation here is more with practice itself and with how actual users understand the song. It is thus the song's memorialization by most traditionalists and commercial musicians alike that concerns me. I will address genre-policing tactics like those practiced by Sant'Anna in chapters 3 and 4.

2. I include the original text here. The original contains attempts to mark the text as *caipira* by way of what might, in other contexts, be considered "errors" of Standard Portuguese. I have attempted to preserve these moments in the English. "Já num posso mais cantá [in Standard, *cantar*] / pois o jeca quando cantá / tem vontade de chorá [in Standard, *chorar*] / e o choro que vai saindo / devagá [*devagar*] vai se sumindo / como a água vai pro má [*mar*]." For more on caipira usage, see chapter 3.

3. An interior town in São Paulo. See map 2.

4. The SESC cultural space in Campinas is part of a national network of governmentally funded performance spaces which hold programming deemed "cultural" for children and adults.

5. See Nísia Trindade Lima's adept *Um sertão chamado Brasil* (1999) for a treatment of the durability of this dichotomous approach to Brazil in the social sciences.

6. Emilia Viotti da Costa (2000, 172) suggests that the durability of the distinction between town and country in the Brazilian social sciences results from using "models of interpretation" from "the 'central' areas of the capitalist world." But wherever this polarizing model may be said to have "originated," at this point town and country have taken on distinctively Brazilian attributes.

7. The concept of privative marking emerges from Jakobson and Pomorska (1995), such that within an opposition, one term is defined by what it lacks with respect to the other. See also Hanks (1996, 105).

8. As I use the term *poetry*, I underline Herzfeld's point, which anyone familiar with his approach to poetry already understands. This is that poetics applies to all domains of communicative practice, not just poetry.

9. An abridged sample from this list includes the magazines *Country Music Brasil*, *Revista Rodeio*, and *Rodeio—Mundo Valente*, as well as web sites Os Independents (The Independents), Festa do Peão de Americana (The Americana Rodeo), Cowboy do Asfalto (Asphalt Cowboy), Movimento Country (Country Movement), and Planeta Rodeio (Planet Rodeo).

10. Most of the web sites devoted to Barretos Rodeo, also known as the Barretos Peon's Festival, suggest that attendance was closer to 2 million. See p. 100.

11. I will treat this and other song-forms in more detail in chapter 7. For the present purpose, the *toada* is considered a traditional song-form practiced in many regions of Brazil. The *toada caipira* is in 2/4 time, played with a slow tempo (R. Corrêa 2000, 177–80). The melody is often sad, and the subject matter, as in this case, pertains to sadness, frequently through treatment of a lost or unattainable love (Marcondes 1998, 776).

12. I include the Portuguese text of this song here because of the importance of the *toada* form, which, as noted, I will discuss in more detail in chapter 7. Notice, here, the cadence and rhyming structure of the Portuguese: "Quando amanheço sensível / com os olhos rasos d'água / É que a saudade no peito / fez enchente, fez represa / E a lágrima e o ladrão / que dá vazão à tristeza / Se não chorar, esse açude / vai explodir no certeza / Cada lágrima ceu cai, / portanto é nossa defesa."

13. The rhyming scheme of the song gives poetic equivalence, in Jakobsonian terms, to the line-endings; this does not emerge in my English version. I call attention to this by quoting from the Portuguese after the ellipsis: "E assim vou vivendo / Sofrendo e querendo / Esse amor doentio / Mas se falto pra ela / Meu mundo sem ela / Também é vazio."

14. Though there are, of course, numerous sambas that end on a less upbeat note, most *sambistas* have this sort of tune in their repertoires. *Música sertaneja* singers don't.

2 Country Brothers

Epigraph at start of section "Kinship as Country Epistemology and Sociology" is from Bakhtin 1981, 250. My annotation. Epigraph at start of section "Heading Out Together" is from DaMatta 1979, 69.

1. The Portuguese suggests an equivalence by way of rhyme across the words brother, heart (embedded in the middle of my English line), and bread: "Não importa de onde venhas me irmão / Nossa casa será tua, será teu meu coração / Tomarás do nosso vinho e comerás do nosso pão."

2. For a detailed analysis of the importance of audience "completeness" for performative efficacy, see Kuipers (1998, chap. 4).

3. Parallel harmony describes the maintenance of a fixed interval between harmonic and melodic parts throughout the piece. This contrasts with harmonic singing in most other contexts, where the interval between singing voices varies. In the case of rural musical genres, brothers most often maintain parallel thirds or sixths. I will treat the significance of this parallelism below.

4. Practitioners of Brazilian country music would not be the first to posit the prediscursivity of kin relations. Evolutionary paradigms often take it for granted. One intriguing example is that of Aubrun (1999), who proposes that what he terms "non-rational knowing" as evidenced in aesthetic perception derives from kin recognition—biologically determined, of course.

5. My meaning here is that there is a sense that the conventional relationship often acknowledged to exist between a symbol and what it stands for is suspended. Instead, there is the notion that blood brothers are related by something deeper than convention.

6. As Munn has noted, the notion that kinship has an inevitable temporal component is hardly new. Treatments of "lineages" in part depend on it (Munn 1992, 97).

7. This version of the song is taken from Tonico's and Tinoco's dual biography, From the Bank of the Creek to the Municipal Theater: Tonico and Tinoco—The Dupla Closest to Brazil's Heart (Tonico and Tinoco 1984, 73–74). It is worth noting that the words of the Portuguese text are written in such a way as to preserve the brothers' hick pronunciation, a point to which we will return in chapter 4: "Cada vez que me alembro / Do amigo Chico Mineiro, / Das viage que nóis fazia / Era ele meu companheiro. / Sinto uma tristeza, / Uma vontade de chorá / Alembrando daqueles tempo / Que não hai mais de vortá. / Apesá de sê patrão, / Eu tinha no coração / O amigo Chico Mineiro, / Cabocro bão, decidido, / Na viola era delorido / E era o peão dos boiadeiro."

8. For a staunchly Marxian analysis of this song, where music is not quite able to escape its role as superstructure, see the superbly researched work of José de Souza Martins (1975, 161).

9. Bakhtin was not referring to Homer's Odyssey as a Greek Romance.

10. Much analysis of family structure over time in Brazil has emphasized a movement from extended, patriarchal families to nuclear, conjugal ones. Some have claimed that this notion may be due to the fact that analysts have more closely scrutinized the transformation of wealthier families, while poorer ones, which had long been conjugal, were ignored. Thus, the importance accorded to this extended-to-nuclear transformation may, in part, be due to an overemphasis in the history of families on the dominant classes. There nonetheless appears to be suggestive overlap between these extended families in the seventeenth and eighteenth centuries and much more current migratory patterns, even among poor farmers turned migrants in the mid-to-late twentieth century (Durham 1984, 62).

11. The importance of brothers migrating together in the present was also

reinforced to me by Brazilian anthropologist Flávia Maria Galizoni. Personal correspondence.

12. Interview of Liu and his brother, Zico, August 20, 2004. The dupla Liu and Leu is made up of Lincoln Paulino da Costa (Liu) and Walter Paulino da Costa (Leu). They were born in the 1930s and moved to São Paulo in 1957. They recorded their first 78 RPM record in 1959, and their first LP in 1962. They continued to record and achieved substantial success—though never quite as much as their brothers Zico and Zeca (Antônio Bernardes da Costa and Domingos Paulino da Costa, respectively). All four brothers started their own recording company in 1978, which they eventually sold. Both duplas constitute two of the most respected duplas in the history of Brazilian rural musical genres.

13. Though the periodicity is somewhat different, the contours of the story of Zezé di Camargo and Luciano, and Chitãozinho and Xororó resemble this story.

14. See Reily (2002).

15. I extend thanks to Jaelson Bitran Trindade for clarification of these points.

16. Note that Carreirinho described his success with Zé Carreiro as being due to the fact that their voices were like the voices of brothers. They eventually split up because Zé Carreiro started to have difficulty with his voice and hearing.

17. Noteworthy in this respect are Alisson and Alessandro, and Otávio Augusto and Gabriel.

18. The berimbau is the central instrument of capoeira, providing much of the rhythm and tonality for the "game." It looks much like a bow with a metal string and a resonating gourd at one end.

19. Probably the most successful of the sister teams was the Galvão sisters. The husband and wife team, whose music some fans of música caipira label as pop, was Cascatinha and Inhana.

20. For more on the simultaneity of hierarchy and egalitarianism in Brazilian society, see DaMatta (1979, chap. 4, 137–97).

21. In the dupla Edson and Hudson, both are instrumentalists. Edson sings melody and plays acoustic guitar, while Hudson sings harmony and plays accomplished lead electric guitar. This does not so much neutralize hierarchy as divide it between melody and instrumental virtuosity. Where the dominant position lies onstage, then, simply circulates more briskly than in most duplas.

22. Some commercial rural music (música sertaneja) allows for soloing of one voice. However, in many cases, brothers alternate solo roles, and in any case, when the harmony is present, it is still of the fixed-interval variety. Furthermore, in terms of the spatial placement of brothers onstage, both brothers are pushed out from the rest of the musicians, even while one might briefly solo.

3 Mixture, Sadness, and Intimacy

The first epigraph at the start of the chapter is from M. d. Andrade 1991. The essay from which this quotation is taken was originally published in 1939. The second epigraph at the start of the chapter is from O. d. Andrade 1970. The epigraph at the start of the section "Mixture as Sadness and as Historicity" is taken from Prado 1962.

1. Benjamin Lee Whorf (1956) described the process of analogical patterning by way of Standard Average European (SAE) languages' approaches to time. He argued that these languages quantified time as though it could be poured into cups or tied into bundles and that this profoundly influenced the way SAE's speakers approached the subject.

2. See Ana Maria Ochoa's *Between Desires and Rights* (*Entre los deseos e los derechos*) (2003a) for treatment of the multiple drifts of "popular" in Latin America.

3. See the discussion of these institutions in Cabral (1974).

4. I refer, here, to many analyses of composers. In the Brazilian case see, for example, copious writing on composer Heitor Villa-Lobos, who is presented as utterly revolutionary in a way that obviates his social context (Horta 1987; Machado 1987; Mariz 1967; Marx 1939).

5. This record received little praise from traditionalists. Despite the duo's selection of esteemed pieces from the repertoire, their arrangements relied on keyboards and digital voice enhancements, which disqualified their recording from serious consideration by traditionalists.

6. Jesuit priest Antônio Nóbrega's letter to the pope (1552) details the Jesuit use of music, though not the presence of the *viola*, in colonial Brazil (Mills et al. 2002). The use of music was later criticized (1553) by a Catholic bishop sent by the pope to oversee the Jesuit conversion of Indians (Mills et al. 2002).

7. A digital delay is a device, in this case, a foot pedal, that may be attached to a guitar. It records some short piece of sound and then plays that piece back after a demarcated period of time. It essentially recreates the effect of a repetition of the initial sound, which can often sound like an echo with varying degrees of intensity.

8. *Nueva canción* is a mixed love song, chronicle of events, and political critique, sung by a solo singer-songwriter accompanying himself or herself on the guitar. The genre rose to prominence as a form of political protest, chiefly in Argentina and Chile in the late 1960s and early 1970s (Broughton, Ellingham, Muddyman, and Trillo 1994, 569–577).

9. I provide the names of the performers who made these songs famous rather than their authors, who are Don Von Tress, Darrell Brown and Radney Foster, and Frank Meyers and Gary Baker, respectively.

10. In the Brazilian press, there is some debate over whether current

Brazilian commercial country music is, in fact, simply "pop" music. I contend that it is not. Pop music in Brazil may be characterized by using some of the same descriptive terms applied to it in other contexts. Employing the music of Elton John to characterize the sounds of "pop," British musicologist Simon Frith (2001, 95) describes John as "slippery" because his music is "so familiar, so easily used." He continues that those making pop music orient it toward a broad public: it "is designed to appeal to everyone" (Frith 2001, 95). Indeed, domestically produced pop accounts for the largest segment of licit market sales in Brazil. Sonically, North Americans might compare Brazil's local pop to the music of Julio Iglesias. Best-selling Brazilian examples include ex-rocker Roberto Carlos and Amado Batista. These artists deal overwhelmingly with "romantic" subject matter, which is to say that their lyrics revolve around heterosexual love from its early stages to its poignant end, and all phases of elation and desperation between. Pop's "soft" sound is here defined by light drum-kit technique, de-emphasized electric guitar, bass, and keyboards providing most melodic leads. But *música sertaneja* differs from Brazilian pop in important ways. In most blurry cases where rural genres might begin to resemble pop, one can distinguish between the two because música sertaneja overwhelmingly preserves the *dupla*. Furthermore, though some música sertaneja may sound very much like pop in instrumentation, melodic line, and topicality, its frequent treatment of rural subject matter preserves its distinctness, despite charges by critics that it has lost all specificity. Duplas appear in the press speaking on rural matters, or working and vacationing on their farms in the "interior," where they are pictured on horseback, herding cattle. Leonardo has several farms. Chitãozinho finds cattle to be a more secure investment than stocks: "I don't trust the financial markets much," Chitãozinho told the *Folha de São Paulo* in an interview in 1999. "I even run away from savings accounts," Xororó seconded (França and Nascimento 1999).

Both genres may be classified as distinctly intimate because of the way in which their singers publicly display their feelings; indeed, it might be more accurate to say that singers of both genres fail to control their emotions. However, música sertaneja differs from Brazilian pop in its emphasis on the desperation and extent of its expressiveness about love. We will explore love as a dire and inevitable experience that pushes men to the natural extreme of their affective possibilities when we consider the country cosmopolitan in chapter 8.

4 Hick Dialogics

The first epigraph at the start of the chapter is taken from G. Urban 1993, 24. The second epigraph is from Lee 1997, 321.

1. The arrival of the American style of riding in Brazil, a style characterized by a single rope that the cowboy holds with only one hand, is debated.

The most credible claim seems to be from a cowboy named Tião Procopi, who competed in the United States in the early 1980s and brought the new technology back with him to supplant the older two-handed metal device that had been used in Brazil up to that time.

2. Precisely which rodeo is the largest in the world is not simple to determine. The Houston Livestock Show and Rodeo (one million spectators) as well as Cheyenne Frontier Days ("hundreds of thousands") both claim the distinction. Those making such claims in the United States have not heard much about the attendance figures in Brazil, nor do they seem to attend to claims made in Canada about the Calgary Stampede. Wooden and Ehringer (1996) consider the growth of rodeo, but the sport has grown so rapidly in the years since this publication that their treatment requires updating. One of the chief transformations in the rodeo field has been the success of the Professional Bull Riders (PBR), which has managed to bring the sport to a mainstream audience.

3. I heard the English word "performance" used in numerous contexts in Brazil. Its employment here cannot be tied directly to this rural context.

4. The organizers experienced no dissonance in folding contemporary categories into this old-fashioned competition. When I asked the director if cowboys would, for example, have been "hygienic" in quite the same way, I received an emphatic "clearly, yes."

5. This was the last time anyone tried to ride Bandido, who was subsequently incorporated in 2005 into one of the most successful soap operas, *América*, as one of the main characters. The bull's difficulty is said to reside not in the unpredictability of his bucking patterns—his twisting and turning—but in the fact that he becomes so "angry" if he has not dislodged his rider after a second or two that he flings himself on the ground, often crushing some part of the cowboy. He also "goes after" his riders once he has unseated them, sometimes tossing them into the air. Though he failed on Bandido, Ednei Caminhas won the world bull-riding championship in 2002 in Las Vegas.

6. For elaboration of this understanding of a "text" see Hanks (1989), and Silverstein and Urban (1998).

7. This is essentially the argument of Ferdinand de Saussure (1983).

8. Such oppositional strategies exist in other times and places. Just think of the elaborate discontent associated with championing "real" country music over industry "garbage." In Lockhart, Texas, for instance, fans of an older and less rock 'n' roll-influenced form of country music performed by the likes of George Jones and Johnny Cash deride the slicker productions of Garth Brooks and Shania Twain (A. Fox 2004). Or, in another domain altogether, consider purporting to address "real" issues instead of just spinning a "message" in American political discourse (Silverstein 2003, 17).

9. It is indeed the case that much *música sertaneja* produced during this period contains the accordion. Nonetheless, the contention that the accordion formed an integral part of the *sertanejo* sound is increasingly rare. These

days commentators interested in such historical issues argue for *viola* and guitar as the essential instruments of the genre.

10. Borges cites Skidmore for this point, and notes that Skidmore, in turn, owes his understanding of Lobato's shift to Dante Moreira Leite's *O carater nacional brasileiro*.

11. Nísia Trindade Lima (1999) treats the extent to which the interior was thought to be a place of illness.

12. See chapter 6 for a full account of Pires's first recordings of rural genres.

13. Chantecler was one of the most prolific *música sertaneja* labels during this period and has since been bought by Warner Entertainment.

14. Once again, for Rosa, the chief means of creating rural space was through language in rigorously documented stories, lexicons, word contractions, and speech rhythms of the backlands of his home state of Minas Gerais. Indeed, his attention to such matters has earned him comparisons to the James Joyce of *Finnegan's Wake*.

15. The Portuguese term "education" here really points not so much to schooling as to good manners. Notice, also, that, in virtuosic fashion, the lines *all* rhyme in Portuguese, a feature not preserved in my English: "A enxada respondeu: que bateu vivo no chão, / Pra poder dar o que comer e vestir o seu patrão / Eu vim no mundo primeiro quase no tempo de adão / Se não fosse o meu sustento não tinha instrução. / Vai-te caneta orgulhosa, vergonha da geração / A tua alta nobreza não passa de pretensão / Você diz que escreve tudo, tem uma coisa que não / É a palavra bonita que se chama. . . . educação!"

5 Teleologies of Rural Disappearance

Epigraph is from Kearney 1996, 59. His italics.

1. José Manuel dos Santos is a pseudonym.

2. Sater is often credited with being one of the first to popularize the *viola* in the mid-1980s (see, for example, Nepomuceno 1999). He did this, it is claimed, by appearing in these highly watched *novelas* as a Central-Southern musician. In one called "O Rei do Gado," or "The King of Cattle," Sater starred with another country singer, Sérgio Reis, as a *dupla*, and several episodes involved the two performing rural songs.

3. Ariovaldo eventually became one of the most important lyricists and radio-show hosts of Central-Southern music through the 1940s, 1950s, and 1960s, under the stage name Captain Swindled (*Capitão Furtado*).

4. Individual performers used a different pseudonym for each label. Luminary Raul Torres, for example, used both his actual name, and the moniker *Bico Doce*, or Sweet Beak, "beak" here being a colloquialism for mouth.

5. As we shall see in a moment, Martins (1975) takes an opposite tack, placing the act of mediation at the center of his argument for the commodification and downfall of the genuinely *caipira*.

6. In Brazil, the distribution of record players was undertaken through a joint agreement between the American Victor Talking Machine and the British Phon-O-Gram companies, both of whom sold virtually identical machines for similar prices. This dual selling arrangement makes the establishment of the total number of machines in this part of Brazil at the time complicated. I am grateful to Paul Edie of the Victrola Museum in St. Louis for this information.

7. The song is in a form known as *moda de viola*, or "viola song," which I will discuss in chapter 7. For now, I simply note that such songs are more spoken than sung. I quote a portion of the Portuguese to give a sense of the text's original rhythm: "Com um modo bem cortês / Respondeu o peão pra rapaziada / 'Essa riqueza não me assusta / Topo em aposta qualquer parada / Cada pé deste café / Eu amarro um boi da minha envernada / E pra encerrar o assunto eu garanto / Que ainda me sobra uma boiada'."

8. Import substitution industrialization was an economic technique whereby the Latin American governments attempted to substitute locally made goods for foreign ones (Skidmore and Smith 1997, 54). In this Brazilian case, the Vargas government hoped that this substitution would jumpstart Brazilian manufacturing (Skidmore 1967, 43–47).

9. Tinhorão is most famous for his harsh criticism of bossa nova and *tropicália*, both celebrated by many as emblematically Brazilian musical genres. Instead, he decries both as little more than Brazilian subservience to American cultural imperialism.

10. Note, here, that critics and advocates alike sometimes use the English word *country* instead of the Portuguese *sertanejo*, or "of the backlands" (*sertão*).

11. This group was founded during redemocratization in 1985, with the aim of lobbying against land reform in Brazil. The group was funded by large landholders and transformed into a political party in 1989, forwarding its leader, Ronaldo Caiado, as a candidate for the presidency. The group was not active between 1994 and 1996, but has since returned to its previous lobbying activities.

12. Note that, in support of ex-president Fernando Henrique Cardoso's argument for considering associated-dependent development in its specifically Latin American context (Cardoso 1989), England's urban population reached the three-quarter mark by the end of the nineteenth century (R. Williams 1973, 217). Brazil cannot, in any meaningful sense, be said to be going through the exact same process of "development" as Europe.

6 Digital Droplets and Analogue Flames

1. The acquisitions and mergers that characterized the 1980s and 1990s have continued to shift this list of companies. However, the largest players in Brazil and throughout the world, are Sony, Universal, BMG, EMI, and AOL/Time Warner.

2. McCann (2004, in particular, chap. 2) notes that this enshrining of samba often existed in a "contrapuntal" relationship with its own critique.

3. Soccer, not previously central to *brasilidade*, was eventually included as a focus of national definition in the mid-1930s. This took place, in part, as a result of the writings of Gilberto Freyre (Bellos 2002, 36).

4. The informal economy in music plays a substantial role in Brazilian musical production and consumption. Though Brazil began to experience moderate levels of piracy when cassettes became cheaply available in the 1970s, the explosive growth of the production of contraband music can be linked most directly to the substantial investment in plant infrastructure in the Free Trade Zone of Manaus. The informal musical economy in Brazil revolves almost entirely around the circulation of inexpensive digital copies of nationally available acts produced by the big five record labels. If the ABPDs figures are correct, fully 52 percent of the CDs sold in Brazil in 2001 were illegally copied CDs purchased at *camelô*, which are small stands located in the squares, parks, and bus and train stations of every city or town in Brazil, for about one third to one quarter of what one might pay at a "legitimate" record store.

5. The *real* was what economists call "artificially inflated" during this time. Essentially, this meant that then-president Fernando Henrique Cardoso used Brazil's considerable cash reserves to protect the currency from speculators. In August of 1998, when an economic crisis hit in Asia and several Latin American countries looked like they might fall next, speculation on the real began in earnest.

6. The Free Trade Zone of Manaus is located in the Northern state of Amazonas and was created by the military dictatorship in 1967 as a way to create an incentive for foreign companies to invest in manufacturing. The zone was ratified by the constitution of 1988, and despite Collor's attempts to dismantle it in the early 1990s, it remains the second-largest manufacturing zone in the country after São Paulo. Every CD I purchased or examined in Brazil indicated that it was made in Manaus.

7. The prevalence of television is in part a legacy from the years of dictatorship (particularly 1968–74), during which the military government sought to place one in every home (Skidmore 1988, 111). Brazil achieved one of the most effective networks of terrestrial broadcast coverage in Latin America through the 1960s (Galperin 2000).

8. The CIA reported 71 million radios in 1997, and 1,365 AM, 296 FM, and 161 shortwave radio stations in 1999.

9. In 2000, the number of households with at least one player was 25 percent, though many of these households had more than one (IFPI 2001, 119). My experience suggested that this number was far too low, as most of the households I entered, regardless of social class, had at least one CD player. My guess as to why this official number is so low is because it does not take CD players purchased at unofficial electronics stands into account, focusing only on official, or licit, stores selling mainstream brands.

10. The state of São Paulo contains approximately 20 percent of the nation's population, the city itself, approximately 11 percent.

11. Marinho is a pseudonym.

12. Marinho's version of the song suggests a rhyming confluence of the words *past*, *fire*, and *forest*: "Quando ainda era criança, / numa noite do passado / Eu vi um clarão de fogo / lá na mata do cerrado." The rhyming scheme thus paradigmatically draws these items together. Those curious about other attributes of the Portuguese rendition of this song should visit www.riveroftearsbrazil.com.

13. For more on the history of bribes for airtime in the United States, see Doerkson (2002).

7 Producing Rural Locality

Epigraph is from Oliven 1992. Oliven's book was translated in 1996 as *Tradition Matters: Modern Gaúcho Identity in Brazil*. However I have translated this passage myself from his Portuguese.

1. The Prêmio Sharp is a kind of Brazilian Grammy. To contextualize: Caetano Veloso did not attend the Grammy Awards on the night in 2000 on which he was to receive the award for Best World Music record in the United States. He did not think the award should be particularly important to Brazilians and did not wish to be seen as being overly excited about an award simply because it was North American. Those who sympathized with Veloso do not feel the same way about the Prêmio Sharp, a homegrown honor.

2. During extremely crowded performances, eating was not possible. The waitstaff were unable to navigate the crowded performance space with its rows of chairs and standing listeners, and the kitchen could not process the necessary quantity of food because it contained just one wood-burning stove.

3. These include: Pena Branca and Xavatinho, Pena Branca solo, Luiz Faria and Silva Neto, Ivan Vilela, Paulo Freire, Pereira da Viola, Chico Lobo, João Ormond, Vinícius Alves, Inezita Barroso, and Almir Sater. Folkloric musicians from the Northeast of Brazil have also figured prominently in the calendar of events, among them Elomar and Xangai. Finally local traditionally inflected singer-songwriters who consider themselves to be producers of MPB more than *música caipira* or *música de viola* also perform there.

4. In the fall of 1999, Fifa eventually secured some loads of gravel and a

front loader for an afternoon, a feat that has made the approach on a rainy evening somewhat less treacherous and time-consuming, but only in the immediate vicinity of the site; the roads leaving Campinas are as rutted as ever in 2007. As of 2008, she has stopped hosting musical performances and is selling the restaurant—hoping to retire.

5. I often had the same feeling I had as a child at Disneyland's ride "Pirates of the Caribbean," in the sense that I was in a space which was built to seem old and haphazard, but was clearly made of new materials and designed with care.

6. This is late by any standards. It is no doubt true that shows of many different genres in many countries begin much later than stated. Indeed, in North America, one often speaks of "musician's time" as the players begin to set up their instruments when the show is due to begin. But in my experience, delays of longer than an hour are unheard of. In this case, lateness didn't matter much. People ate, drank, and talked. This not mattering much was part of the country point of things.

7. Note that "sir" or "mister" (*senhor*) would normally be written as *senhor* in Standard Portuguese. Though the lyric sheet for their CD writes "*senhora*," their pronunciation of the word sounds much more like the equivalent of the way they both write *and* pronounce *senhô*—which is to say, senhâ: "Aqui estou. / Minha gente—Aqui estou. / Pra cantá pra senh[ora] e pro senhô—/ Pra cantá pra senhora e pro senhô."

8. The brothers in fact worked with several companies in their early years: Xororó, Tocantins, and Warner/Rodeio.

9. There are at least three types of viola in Brazil, the *viola caipira*, the *viola nordestina*, and the *viola de cocho*, the first two with metal strings. The first is small and has a thin waist (which is to say that it has a pronounced hourglass shape), giving it a more piercing tone than the larger and more gently sloped viola nordestina, which tends to be the same size as a guitar. The viola nordestina is also often tuned differently. This, together with its lower tone, gives it a different sound. The viola de cocho is a much smaller and simpler instrument, often with no sound hole, and only four strings. This last instrument is rarely used in *música caipira* performed in *dupla*, though certain revivalists, particularly Corrêa, feature it prominently in solo performance.

10. Such "open" tunings are also common in blues guitar playing, particularly in slide techniques where a bottleneck or small piece of pipe placed over one of the fingers of the left hand rather than simply the fingers is used to change the length of the strings.

11. The most common tuning is *cebolão* (the big onion), which is often in D: the lowest pair of strings are octaves of A, the next pair, moving down the fretboard, are octaves of D, then unison F♯, unison A, and unison D. Another common tuning is *rio abaixo*, or downriver. Rio abaixo is tuned as follows: G, D, G, B, D.

12. Such notions are, of course, not limited to the playing of the Brazilian

ten-string guitar. Blues great Robert Johnson, who disappeared for a year after having made his neighbors and friends miserable with his attempts to play and then returned as the best "slide" player in the world, was rumored to have made a pact with the devil.

13. Paulo Freire (2000) recounts one pact story. Roberto Corrêa (1994, 1998, 1989) recounts others. Almir Sater states his affection for these tales in an interview on a *viola* website (1999).

14. Snakes are thought to provide power in domains other than learning. Many *violeiros* keep a rattlesnake rattle inside their instrument in order to inoculate them against their own jealousy of other violeiros.

15. I am indebted to John Pemberton for spotting pig 2, which arrived greased and initially escaped my attention. This, of course, is pig 2's *point*.

16. Here, Zé means that by holding a *viola* across his chest he is making the shape of the cross. As Reily (2002, 73) notes, the viola is often held in a manner that is described as "sacred" in some *folia de reis* traditions, that is, up high, close to the player's neck.

17. The song's form is called *a pagode de viola*. The pagode is sometimes said to be the most difficult right-hand technique in rural music. Indeed, in his recent viola method, Roberto Corrêa (2000, 179, 213–17) calls it "without question" the most difficult rhythm, and whereas he devoted a page or two to rhythms such as the *toada* or the *moda de viola*, he devotes four to the pagode. We will treat this rhythm in more detail in the conclusion.

18. Most of these plans are named for the currency that they ushered in. Thus, the *Plano Cruzado*, or Cruzado Plan was associated with Brazil's currency at the time, the cruzado, and was launched by President Sarney in 1986. Nine months later, Sarney shifted to a Cruzado Plan 2. The next administration, that of Collor (see chapter 2), proposed yet another currency, the *cruzeiro*.

19. Note that this is not the same thing as saying that these "musical" features provide a "setting" for the words. Indeed, such a pat distinction between music and words is precisely what I am writing against here.

8 Hicks of the World

Epigraph is from Boon 1999.

1. Millôr Fernandes (1988) contains a version of this translation-joke.

2. The song was actually written by Fauze and Jamil.

3. The iconography of record covers and posters reinforces this. When *dupla* members are not actually pictured together, two pictures of them in identical lighting are brought together, and they often face each other.

4. The criticism Miranda was subjected to is identical to that applied to *música sertaneja*, and thus her presence here may be read as a reprimand to such indictments.

Conclusion

Epigraph is from Proust 1981.

1. Note that at their moment of greatest popularity, Tião Carreiro and Pardinho presented themselves as practitioners of *música sertaneja*. It is only from today's position, where some older practitioners of música sertaneja are now seeking to distance themselves from current commercial rurality, that it is possible to classify them as *música caipira*.

2. The term *pagode* is more commonly associated with a commercially successful form of speeded-up samba. The prevalence of samba pagode is credited by some with the commercial revitalization of samba starting in the 1970s and intensifying in the 1980s.

3. The right hand most often strums, plucks, or hits the strings of guitar-styled instruments over the instrument's sound hole, while the left hand adjusts the length of the strings—and hence the resulting pitch—usually through the use of fixed intervals on the instrument's neck, referred to as frets.

Musical Works Cited

Chico Lobo. 1997. *No Braço dessa Viola*. Kuarup Discos.

Chitãozinho and Xororó. 1982. *Somos Apaixonados*. Copacabana.

Edson and Hudson. 2005. *Galera Coração*. EMI.

Gino and Geno. 1981. *Os Xonados*. Copacabana.

Leandro and Leonardo. 1985. *Leandro & Leonardo—Vol. 1*. WEA.

Leandro and Leonardo. 1998. *Sonho por Sonho*. WEA International.

Luiz Faria and Silva Neto. 2002. *Rio Formoso*. R. Farath Records.

Pena Branca. 2000. *Semente Caipira*. Kuarup.

Pena Branca and Xavatinho, and Renato Teixeira. 1999. *Ao Vivo em Tatuí*. Kuarup Discos.

Pereira da Viola. 1998. *Viola Cósmica*. Lapa Discos.

Querioz, E. 2006. *Raízes Brasileiras*. Viola Caipira Vol. 4. Discos Arlequin.

R. Corrêa. 1994. *Uróboro*. Viola Corrêa Produções Artisticas.

R. Corrêa. 1998. *Sertão Ponteado*. Viola Corrêa Produções Artisticas.

Tião Carreiro and Pardinho. 2002. *Vol 2.—Pagodes*. WEA.

Tonico and Tinoco. 1968. *As 12 mais de Tonico e Tinoco*. Continental.

Various Artists. 1999. *Tributo a Leandro*. BMG International.

Zé Mulato and Cassiano. 1997. *Meu Ceu*. Velas.

Zé Mulato and Cassiano. 1999. *Navegante das Gerais*. Velas.

Zé Mulato and Cassiano. 2003. *Sangue Novo*. Viola Brasileira Shows Produções.

Zezé di Camargo and Luciano. 1991. *Zezé di Camargo & Luciano*. Sony BMG/Columbia.

Zezé di Camargo and Luciano. 1998. *Pra Não Pensar em Voçê*. Sony BMG/Columbia.

Zico and Zeca. 2004. *Zico & Zeca*. EMI International.

Bibliography

ABPD. 2002. Associação Brasileiro de Produtores de Disco. http://www
.abpd.org.br/

Abu-Lughod, L. 2002. "The Objects of Soap Opera: Egyptian Television and
the Cultural Politics of Modernity." In The Anthropology of Media: A Reader,
K. Askew and R. Wilk, eds., 376–93. Malden, Mass.: Blackwell.

Adorno, T. 1938. "On the Fetish Character in Music and the Regression of
Listening." In The Essential Frankfurt School Reader, ed. A. A. a. E. Gephart,
270–99. New York: Continuum.

———. 1989. "Perennial Fashion—Jazz." In Critical Theory and Society, S. Bron-
ner and D. Kellner, eds., 199–209. New York: Routledge.

Agha, A. 2005. "Introduction: Semiosis across Encounters." Journal of Linguistic Anthropology 15 (1): 1–5.

Alves, L. R. 1997. "Políticas de cultura e comunicação na urbanidade." Estudos avançados 11 (30): 293–307.

Amaral, A. 1982. O dialeto caipira—gramática, vocabulário. São Paulo: Editora
Hucitec.

Andrade, M. d. 1972. Ensaio sobre a música brasileira. São Paulo: Livraria Martins Editora S.A.

———. 1989. Dicionário musical brasileiro. Belo Horizonte: Editora Itatiaia Limit-
dada.

———. 1991. Aspectos da música brasileira. Rio de Janeiro: Villa Rica.

Andrade, O. d. 1970. Obras completas—Oswald de Andrade. Rio de Janeiro: Civilização Brasileira.

Appadurai, A. 1996. Modernity at Large: Cultural Dimensions of Globalization.
Minneapolis: University of Minnesota Press.

———. 1998. "Dead Certainty: Ethnic Violence in the Era of Globalization."
Public Culture 10 (2): 225–47.

Appiah, K. A. 2007. The Ethics of Identity. Princeton: Princeton University
Press.

Apter, A. 2005. "Griaule's Legacy: Rethinking 'la parole claire' in Dogon Studies." Cahiers d'études africaines 45 (1): 95–129.

Araujo, S. 1988. "Brega: Music and Conflict in Urban Brazil." Latin American
Music Review 9: 50–89.

Askew, K. 2002. Performing the Nation: Swahili Music and Cultural Politics in
Tanzania. Chicago: University of Chicago Press.

Assunção, M. R. 2004. Capoeira: The History of an Afro-Brazilian Art. London:
Routledge.

Aubrun, A. 1999. "The Aesthetics of Kin Recognition." *Journal of the Royal Anthropological Institute* 5 (2): 211–27.

Austin, J. L. 1962. *How to Do Things with Words.* Cambridge, Mass.: Harvard University Press.

Avelar, I. 1999. *The Untimely Present: Postdictatorial Latin American Fiction and the Task of Mourning.* Durham, N.C.: Duke University Press.

——. 2001. "Defeated Rallies, Mournful Anthems, and the Origins of Brazilian Heavy Metal." In *Brazilian Popular Music and Globalization,* C. Dunn and C. Perrone, eds., 123–35. New York: Routledge.

Avritzer, L. 2002. *Democracy and the Public Space in Latin America.* Princeton: Princeton University Press.

Babha, H. 2001. "Unsatisfied: Notes on Vernacular Cosmopolitanism." In *Postcolonial Discourses: An Anthology,* ed. G. Castle, 38–53. Oxford: Blackwell.

Bacellar, C. d. A. P. 1991. *Família, herança e poder em São Paulo: 1765–1855.* São Paulo: Centro de Estudos de Demografia Histórica da América Latina— CEDHAL.

——. 1997. *Os senhores da terra: Família e sistema sucessório entre os senhores de engenho do Oeste Paulista, 1765–1855.* Campinas: Centro de Memória— UNICAMP.

Bakhtin, M. M. 1981. "Forms of Time and of the Chronotope in the Novel: Notes Towards a Historical Poetics." In *The Dialogic Imagination,* ed. M. Holquist, 84–258. Austin: University of Texas Press.

——. 1986. *Speech Genres and Other Late Essays.* Austin: University of Texas Press.

Bauman, R. 2001. "Genre." In *Key Terms in Language and Culture,* ed. A. Duranti, 79–82. Malden, Mass.: Blackwell Publishers.

——. 2005. "Commentary—Indirect Indexicality, Identity, Performance: Dialogic Observations." *Journal of Linguistic Anthropology* 15 (1): 145–50.

Bauman, R., and C. Briggs. 1990. "Poetics and Performance as Critical Perspectives on Language and Social Life." *Annual Review of Anthropology* 19: 59–88.

——. 1992. "Genre, Intertextuality, and Social Power." *Journal of Linguistic Anthropology* 2 (2): 131–72.

Bellos, A. 2002. *Futebol: Soccer, the Brazilian Way.* New York: Bloomsbury.

Benjamin, W. 1968. "Theses on the Philosophy of History." In *Illuminations: Essays and Reflections,* ed. H. Arendt, 253–64. New York: Schocken Books.

Bernstein, B. 1977. *Class, Codes and Control.* London: Routledge.

Bohlman, P. 1992. *The World Centre for Jewish Music in Palestine, 1936–1940: Jewish Musical Life on the Eve of World War II.* Oxford: Oxford University Press.

Boon, J. A. 1990. *Affinities and Extremes: Crisscrossing the Bittersweet Ethnology of East Indies History, Hindu-Balinese Culture, and Indo-European Allure.* Chicago: University of Chicago Press.

———. 1999. *Verging on Extra-Vagance: Anthropology, History, Religion, Literature, Arts . . . Showbiz.* Chicago: University of Chicago Press.

Borges, D. 1993. " 'Puffy, Ugly, Slothful and Inert': Degeneration in Brazilian Social Thought, 1880–1940." *Journal of Latin American Studies* 25: 235–56.

Bourdieu, P. 1977. *Outline of a Theory of Practice.* Cambridge: Cambridge University Press.

———. 1984. *Distinction: A Social Critique of the Judgment of Pure Taste.* Cambridge, Mass.: Harvard University Press.

———. 1993a. *The Field of Cultural Production, or, The Economic World Reversed.* New York: Columbia University Press.

———. 1993b. "Manet and the Institutionalization of Anomie." In *The Field of Cultural Production,* ed. R. Johnson, 238–54. New York: Columbia University Press.

Brandão, C. R. 1983. *Os caipiras de São Paulo.* São Paulo: Editora Brasiliense.

"Brazil: Land of Promise." 2007. *Economist.*

Broughton, S., M. Ellingham, D. Muddyman, and R. Trillo. 1994. *World Music: The Rough Guide.* The Rough Guides. London: Penguin Books.

Browning, B. 1996. *Samba: Resistance in Motion.* Bloomington: Indiana University Press.

Cabral, S. 1974. *As escolas de samba do Rio de Janeiro.* Rio de Janeiro: Editora Luminar.

Caldas, W. 1977. *Acorde na aurora: Música sertaneja e a indústria cultural.* São Paulo: Companhia Editora Nacional.

———. 1987. *O que é música sertaneja.* São Paulo: Editora Brasiliense S.A.

Canclini, N. G. 1992. "Cultural Reconversion." In *On Edge: The Crisis of Contemporary Latin American Culture,* G. Yúdice, J. Franco, and J. Flores, eds., 29–43. Minneapolis: University of Minnesota Press.

Cândido, A. 1956. "Possíveis raízes indígenas de uma dança popular." *Revista de Antropologia* 4 (1): 1–23.

———. 1976. "Preface." In *Cornélio Pires: Criação e riso,* ed. M. Dantas, 11–12. São Paulo: Livraria Duas Cidades.

———. 1979. *Os parceiros do Rio Bonito.* São Paulo: Livraria Duas Cidades.

Cardoso, F. H. 1989. "Associated-Dependent Development and Democratic Theory." In *Democratizing Brazil: Problems of Transition and Consolidation,* ed. A. Stepan, 299–326. New York: Oxford University Press.

———. 2001. *Charting a New Course: The Politics of Globalization and Social Transformation.* Lanham, Md.: Rowman and Littlefield.

Carvalho, M. d. U. 1991. " 'Música Popular' in Montes Claros, Minas Gerais, Brazil: A Study of Middle Class Popular Music Aesthetics in the 1980s." Ph.D. diss. Ithaca, N.Y.: Cornell University.

———. 1993. "Musical Style, Migration, and Urbanization: Some Consideration on Brazilian 'Musica Sertaneja'." *Studies in Latin American Popular Culture* 12: 75–94.

Chacur, F. 1999. "Tribuna—Democracia e tolerância são o caminho." *Country Music Brasil.* March 1.

Chernela, J. 2004. "Constructing a Supernatural Landscape through Talk: Creation and Recreation in the Central Amazon of Brazil." *Journal of Latin American Lore* 22 (1): 83–106.

Chernoff, J. M. 1979. *African Rhythm and African Sensibility.* Chicago: University of Chicago Press.

Ching, B. 2001. *Wrong's What I Do Best: Hard Country Music and Contemporary Culture.* New York: Oxford University Press.

Comaroff, J. 1987. "Sui Genderis: Feminism, Kinship Theory, and Structural 'Domains'." In *Gender and Kinship: Essays Toward a Unified Analysis,* J. F. Collier and S. J. Yanagisako, eds., 53–85. Stanford: Stanford University Press.

Comaroff, J., and J. L. Comaroff. 1991. *Of Revelation and Revolution: Christianity, Colonialism, and Consciousness in South Africa.* Chicago: University of Chicago Press.

——. 2001a. "Millennial Capitalism: First Thoughts on a Second Coming." In *Millennial Capitalism and the Culture of Neoliberalism,* J. Comaroff and J. L. Comaroff, eds., 1–56. Durham, N.C.: Duke University Press.

——, eds. 2001b. *Millennial Capitalism and the Culture of Neoliberalism.* Durham, N.C.: Duke University Press.

Comaroff, J. L., and J. Comaroff. 1992. "The Madman and the Migrant." In *Ethnography and the Historical Imagination,* J. L. Comaroff and J. Comaroff, eds., 155–78. Boulder, Colo.: Westview Press.

Connerton, P. 1989. *How Societies Remember.* Cambridge: Cambridge University Press.

"Cornélio Pires." 1999. *Jangada Brasil—Almanaque: Suplemento de Variedades* 15. Rio de Janeiro.

Corrêa, R. N. 1989. *Viola caipira.* Viola Corrêa Produçãoes Artísticas.

——. 2000. *A Arte de Pontear Viola.* Brasília: Projeto Três Américas—Associação Cultural.

Costa, E. V. d. 2000. *The Brazilian Empire: Myths and Histories.* Chapel Hill: University of North Carolina Press.

Costa, S., and J. Brener. 1997. "Coronelismo electrônico: O governo Fernando Henrique e o novo capítulo de uma velha história." *Comunicação and Política* 4 (2): 29–53.

da Cunha, E. 1944. *Rebellion in the Backlands.* Chicago: University of Chicago Press.

DaMatta, R. 1979. *Carnivals, Rogues, and Heroes: An Interpretation of the Brazilian Dilemma.* Notre Dame: University of Notre Dame Press.

——. 1982. "Esporte na sociedade: Um ensaio sobre o futebol Brasileiro." In *Universo do futebol: Esporte e sociedad Brasileira,* R. DaMatta, L. F. B. N. Flores, S. L. Guedes, and A. Vogel, eds., 19–42. Rio de Janeiro: Ediçãoes Pinakotheke.

——. 1984. "On Carnival, Informality, and Magic: A Point of View from Brazil." In *Text, Play, and Story,* ed. R. Bruner, 230–46. Washington: American Ethnological Society.

Dantas, M. 1976. *Cornélio Pires: Criaçá e riso.* São Paulo: Livraria Duas Cidades.

Dent, A. S. 2003. "Country Critics: *Música Caipira* and the Production of Locality in Brazil." Ph.D. diss. Chicago: University of Chicago.

———. 2005. "Cross-Cultural 'Countries': Covers, Conjuncture, and the Whiff of Nashville in Brazilian Country Music (*Música sertaneja*)." *Popular Music and Society* 28 (2): 207–29.

Doerksen, C. 2002. "Same Old Song and Dance." *Chicago Reader.* October 11.

Downey, G. 2005. *Learning Capoeira: Lessons in Cunning from an Afro-Brazilian Art.* New York: Oxford University Press.

Dunn, C. 2001. *Brutality Garden: Tropicália and the Emergence of a Brazilian Counterculture.* Chapel Hill: University of North Carolina Press.

Dunn, C., and C. Perrone, eds. 2001. *Brazilian Popular Music and Globalization.* Gainesville: University Press of Florida.

Durham, E. R. 1984. *A caminho da cidade: A vida e a migracão para São Paulo.* São Paulo: Editora Perspectiva.

Durkheim, E. 1933. *The Division of Labor in Society.* New York: W. W. Norton.

Eakin, M. 1998. *Brazil: The Once and Future Country.* New York: Palgrave.

Erlmann, V. 1996. *Nightsong: Performance, Power, and Practice in South Africa.* Chicago: University of Chicago Press.

Faria, L. 1993. "Homenagem: Tião Carreiro." *Correio Popular* (Campinas, SP). October 20.

Fausto, B. 1994. *História do Brasil.* São Paulo: Editora da Universidade de São Paulo.

Feld, S. 1989. *Sound and Sentiment: Birds, Weeping, Poetics, and Song in Kaluli Expression.* Philadelphia: University of Pennsylvania Press.

Ferguson, J. 1992. "The Country and the City in the Copperbelt." *Cultural Anthropology* 7 (1): 80–92.

Fernandez, Millôr. 1988. *The Cow Went to the Swamp.* Rio de Janeiro: Editora Record.

Ferrete, J. L. 1985. *Capitão furtado: Viola caipira ou sertaneja?* Rio de Janeiro: FUNARTE—Instituto Nacional de Música, Divisão de Música Popular.

FNRC. 1999. "Rodeio com status de esporte." Federação Nacional do Rodeio Completo. 2003. Mission statement.

Fonseca, C. 2003. "Philanderers, Cuckolds, and Wily Women: Reexamining Gender Relations in a Brazilian Working-Class Neighborhood." *Men and Masculinities in Latin America,* ed. M. Gutmann, 61–83. Durham, N.C.: Duke University Press.

Fox, A. 1992. "The Jukebox of History: Narratives of Loss and Desire in the Discourse of Country Music." *Popular Music* 11(1): 53–72.

———. 1994. "The Poetics of Irony and the Ethnography of Class Culture." *Anthropology and Humanism* 19 (1): 61–66.

———. 2004. *Real Country: Music and Language in Working Class Culture.* Durham, N.C.: Duke University Press.

Fox, A., and C. Yano, eds. Forthcoming. *Global Country.*

Fox, E., and S. Waisbord, eds. 2002. *Latin Politics, Global Media.* Austin: University of Texas Press.

Fox, J. 1977. "Roman Jakobson and the Comparative Study of Parallelism." In *Roman Jakobson: Echoes of His Scholarship*, C. H. van Schooneveld and D. Armstrong, eds., 59–90. Lisse, Netherlands: Peter de Ridder Press.

França, R., and S. Nascimento. 1999. "Dupla sertaneja investe sua fortuna na criação de gado: Chitãozinho and Xororó acham boi gordo mais seguro que aplicações." *Folha de São Paulo*. March 15.

Freire, P. 1996. *Eu nasci naquela serra: A história de Angelino de Oliveira, Raul Torres e Serrinha*. São Paulo: Paulicéia.

———. 2000. *Lambe lambe*. São Paulo: Casa Amarela.

Freyre, G. 1933. *Casa Grande e Senzala: Formação da família Brasileira sob o regime da economia patriarcal*. Rio de Janeiro: Editora Record.

———. 1986. *Order and Progress: Brazil from Monarchy to Republic*. Berkeley: University of California Press.

Friedman, M. 1962. *Capitalism and Freedom*. Chicago: University of Chicago Press.

Frith, S. 2001. "Pop Music." In *The Cambridge Companion to Pop and Rock*, S. Frith, W. Straw, and J. Street, eds., 93–109. Cambridge: Cambridge University Press.

Fry, P. 1982. *Para Inglês ver: Identidade e politica na cultura Brasileira*. Rio de Janeiro: Zahar Editores.

Gal, S. 1995. "Language and the Arts of Resistance." *Cultural Anthropology* 10 (3): 407–24.

Galizoni, F. M. 2000. *Migrações, família e terra no alto Jequitinhonha, Minas Gerais*. Seminário sobre a Economia Mineira 9.

Galperin, H. 2000. "Regulatory Reform in the Broadcasting Industries of Brazil and Argentina in the 1990s." *Journal of Communication* 50 (4): 176–91.

Gaonkar, D. P., and E. Povinelli. 2003. "Technologies of Public Forms: Circulation, Transfiguration, Recognition." *Public Culture* 15 (3): 385–97.

Gasperin, E. 2000. "Nação de todos os sons: O projeto música do Brasil, que estréia em março na MTV, mostra que este não e só o pais do samba, mas também do cururu, do siriri, do caroço, do carimbó, do marabaixo, do . . ." SHOWBiZZ 15 (2): 28–35.

Geertz, C. 1973a. "Deep Play: Notes on the Balinese Cockfight." In *The Interpretation of Cultures*, 412–53. New York: Basic Books.

———. 1973b. "Thick Description: Toward an Interpretive Theory of Culture." In *The Interpretation of Cultures*, 3–30. New York: Basic Books.

Goffman, I. 1979. "Footing." *Semiotica* 25 (1/2): 1–29.

Goodale, M. 2006. "Reclaiming Modernity: Indigenous Cosmopolitanism and the Coming of the Second Revolution in Bolivia." *American Ethnologist* 33 (4): 634–49.

Gordon, L. 2001. *Brazil's Second Chance: En Route toward the First World*. Washington: Brookings Institution Press.

Graeber, D. 2001. *Toward an Anthropological Theory of Value*. New York: Palgrave.

Gupta, A. 1992. "The Song of the Nonaligned World: Transnational Identities and the Reinscription of Space in Late Capitalism." *Cultural Anthropology* 7 (1): 63–79.

Gutman, M. 2003. "Introduction: Discarding Manly Dichotomies in Latin America." In *Changing Men and Masculinities in Latin America*, ed. M. Gutman, 1–26. Durham, N.C.: Duke University Press.

Habermas, J. 1991. *The Structural Transformation of the Public Sphere*. Cambridge, Mass.: MIT Press.

Hacking, I. 2006. *The Emergence of Probability: A Philosophical Study of Early Ideas about Probability, Induction, and Statistical Inference*. Cambridge: Cambridge University Press.

Hale, C. R. 1997. "Cultural Politics of Identity in Latin America." *Annual Review of Anthropology* 26: 567–90.

Hall, K. 2001. "Performativity." In *Key Terms in Language and Culture*, ed. A. Duranti, 180–83. Malden, Mass.: Blackwell.

Hanchard, M. G. 1998. *Orpheus and Power: The Movimento Negro of Rio de Janeiro and São Paulo, Brazil, 1945–1988*. Princeton: Princeton University Press.

Handler, R. 1998. *Nationalism and the Politics of Culture in Quebec*. Madison: University of Wisconsin Press.

Hanks, W. 1987. "Discourse Genres in a Theory of Practice." *American Ethnologist* 14 (4): 668–92.

——. 1989. "Text and Textuality." *Annual Review of Anthropology* 18: 95–127.

——. 1996. *Language and Communicative Practices*. Boulder, Colo.: Westview Press.

——. 2001. "Indexicality." In *Key Terms in Language and Culture*, ed. A. Duranti, 119–22. Malden, Mass.: Blackwell.

Harris, M. 1971. *Town and Country in Brazil*. New York: W. W. Norton.

Herzfeld, M. 1985. *The Poetics of Manhood*. Princeton: Princeton University Press.

——. 1996. *Cultural Intimacy: Social Poetics in the Nation State*. London: Routledge.

——. 2007. "Global Kinship: Anthropology and the Politics of Knowing." *Anthropological Quarterly* 80 (2): 313–23.

Holanda, S. B. d. 1995. *Raízes do Brasil*. São Paulo: Companhia das Letras.

Holquist, M., and C. Emerson. 1981. "Glossary." In *The Dialogic Imagination: Four Essays by M. M. Bakhtin*, ed. M. Holquist, 423–34. Austin: University of Texas Press.

Holston, J. 1989. *The Modernist City*. Chicago: University of Chicago Press.

Holtzman, J. 2006. "Food and Memory." *Annual Review of Anthropology* 35: 361–78.

Horowitz, A. 2003. "Brazil: It's a Sleeping Giant with a Tradition of High-Quality Software." *Computer World*. September 15.

Horta, L. P. 1987. *Villa-Lobos: Uma introdução*. Rio de Janeiro: Jorge Zahar Editor.

Hymes, D. 2001. "Poetry." In *Key Terms in Language and Culture*, ed. A. Duranti, 187–89. Malden, Mass.: Blackwell.

IBGE. 2003. Instituto Brasileiro de Geografia e Estatistica. Web site accessed 2003. http://www.ibge.gov.br/

IFPI. 2001. *2001: The Recording Industry in Numbers*. London: International Federation of the Phonographic Industry.

Irvine, J. 2004. "Say When: Temporalities in Language Ideology." *Journal of Linguistic Anthropology* 14 (1): 99–109.

Ivy, M. 1995. *Discourses of the Vanishing: Modernity, Phantasm, Japan*. Chicago: University of Chicago.

Izique, C. 2000. "O novo rural Brasileiro." In *Pesquisa FAPESP*, 48–55. Sao Paulo: FAPESP.

Jakobson, R. 1960. "Closing Statement: Linguistics and Poetics." In *Style in Language*, ed. T. A. Sebeok, 350–77. Cambridge, Mass.: MIT Press.

Jakobson, R., and K. Pomorska. 1995. "The Concept of Mark." In *Style in Language*, ed. T. A. Sebeok, 134–42. Cambridge, Mass.: MIT Press.

Jameson, F. 2003. "The End of Temporality." *Critical Inquiry* 29 (4): 695–718.

Janer, A. 2000. "Brazil: Is the Sleeping Giant Waking Up to Ecotourism?" *International Ecotourism Society Newsletter*. Third Quarter.

Joyce, J. 1997. *A Portrait of the Artist as a Young Man*. New York: NTC/Contemporary Publishing.

Junior, A. C. 1986. *Cornélio Pires: O primeiro produtor independente de discos do Brasil*. Sorcaba, São Paulo: Delegacia Regional da Cultura de Sorocaba: Fundação Ubaldino do Amaral.

Júnior, F. 2000. "Canto do peão—evolução." *Rodeo Country 2000—Canto do Peão* 3 (21).

Kearney, M. 1996. *Reconceptualizing the Peasantry: Anthropology in Global Perspective*. Boulder, Colo.: Westview Press.

Kuipers, J. 1990. *The Power in Performance: The Creation of Textual Authority in Weyewa Ritual Speech*. Pittsburgh: University of Pennsylvania Press.

———. 1998. *Language, Identity, and Marginality in Indonesia: The Changing Nature of Ritual Speech on the Island of Sumba*. Studies in the Social and Cultural Foundations of Language. Cambridge: Cambridge University Press.

Lambert, J. *Os Dois Brasis*. Rio de Janeiro: INEP.

Leavitt, J. 1996. "Meaning and Feeling in the Anthropology of Emotions." *American Ethnologist* 23 (3): 514–39.

Lee, B. 1997. *Talking Heads: Language, Metalanguage, and the Semiotics of Subjectivity*. Durham, N.C.: Duke University Press.

Lever, J. 1999. "Two Essays on Sports: I—National Madness." *The Brazil Reader: History, Culture, Politics*, R. Levine and J. Crocitti, eds., 497–50. Durham, N.C.: Duke University Press.

Lévi-Strauss, C. 1969. *The Raw and the Cooked*. Chicago: University of Chicago Press.

———. 1973. *Tristes Tropiques*. New York: Atheneum Books.

Lewin, L. 1979. "Some Historical Implications of Kinship Organization for Family-Based Politics in the Brazilian Northeast." *Comparative Studies in Society and History* 21 (2): 262–92.

Lima, N. T. 1999. *Um sertão chamado Brasil*. Rio de Janeiro: Revan.

Lipset, D. 2004. "Modernity without Romance? Masculinity and Desire in Courtship Stories Told by Young Papua New Guinean Men." *American Ethnologist* 31 (2): 205–24.

Lobato, M. 1998. *Urupês*. São Paulo: Editora Brasiliense.

Lomnitz, C. 2001. *Deep Mexico, Silent Mexico*. Minneapolis: University of Minnesota Press.

Lopes, J. S. L. 2000. " 'The People's Joy' Vanishes: Considerations on the Death of a Soccer Player." *Journal of Latin American Anthropology* 4 (2): 78–105.

Lucy, J., ed. 1993. *Reflexive Language: Reported Speech and Metapragmatics*. Cambridge: Cambridge University Press.

Machado, M. C. 1987. *Heitor Villa-Lobos: Tradição e renovação na música Brasileira*. Rio de Janeiro: Francisco Alves.

Mankekar, P. 2001. *Screening Culture, Viewing Politics: An Ethnography of Television, Womanhood, and Nation in Postcolonial India*. Durham, N.C.: Duke University Press.

Marcondes, M. A., ed. 1998. *Enciclopédia da música Brasileira: Popular, erudita e folclórica*. São Paulo: PubliFolha.

Mariz, H. 1967. *Hector Villa-Lobos*. Paris: Editions Seghers.

Martins, J. d. S. 1975. *Capitalismo e tradicionalismo: Estudos sobre as contradicões da sociedade agrária no Brasil*. São Paulo: Livraria Pioneira Editora.

Martins, S. 1999. "Beibe, ai lóvi iú: Banidas da MPB por duas décadas, versões voltam a fazer sucesso." *veja*. June 7, 166.

Marx, B. 1939. "Brazilian Portrait—Villa-Lobos." *Modern Music* 17 (1): 10–17.

Matory, L. 2004. "Sexual Secrets: Candomblé, Brazil, and the Multiple Intimacies of the African Diaspora." In *Off Stage/On Display: Intimacy and Ethnography in the Age of Public Culture*, ed. A. Shryock, 157–90. Palo Alto, Calif.: Stanford University Press.

Maxwell, K. 1999. "The Two Brazils." *Wilson Quarterly* 23 (1): 50–60.

Mazzarella, W. T. 2003. *Shoveling Smoke: Advertising and Globalization in Contemporary India*. Durham, N.C.: Duke University Press.

McCann, B. 2004. *Hello, Hello Brazil: Popular Music in the Making of Modern Brazil*. Durham, N.C.: Duke University Press.

McGowan, C., and R. Pessanha. 1998. *The Brazilian Sound: Samba, Bossa Nova, and the Popular Music of Brazil*. Philadelphia: Temple University Press.

McLuhan, M. 2005. *The Medium Is the Message*. Corte Madera, Calif.: Gingko Press.

Meihy, J. C. S. B. 1999. "Two Essays on Sports: II—A National Festival." In *The Brazil Reader: History, Culture, Politics*, R. Levine and J. Crocitti, eds., 501–4. Durham, N.C.: Duke University Press.

Metcalf, A. 2005. *Family and Frontier in Colonial Brazil: Santana de Parnaíba, 1580–1822.* Austin: University of Texas Press.

Mills, K., S. L. Graham, and W. Taylor, eds. 2002. *Colonial Latin America.* Wilmington, Del.: Scholarly Resources.

Mintz, S. 1996. *Tasting Food, Tasting Freedom: Excursions into Eating, Culture, and the Past.* Boston: Beacon Press.

Morse, R. 1996. "The Multiverse of Latin American Identity, c. 1920—c. 1970." *Ideas and Ideologies in Twentieth-Century Latin America,* ed. L. Bethell, 3–129. Cambridge: Cambridge University Press.

Munn, N. 1992. "The Cultural Anthropology of Time: A Critical Essay." *Annual Review of Anthropology* 21: 93–123.

Nassif, L. 1999. "Pena Branca and Xavatinho." *Folha de São Paulo.* October 10, 2/3.

Nazzari, M. 1991. *Disappearance of the Dowry: Women, Families, and Social Change in São Paulo, Brazil, 1600–1900.* Palo Alto, Calif.: Stanford University Press.

Negus, K. 1999. *Music Genres and Corporate Cultures.* London: Routledge.

Nepomuceno, R. 1999. *Música caipira: Da roça ao rodeio.* São Paulo: Editora 34 Ltd.

Neto, J. S., and J. Edward. 1999. "O Brasil que agüenta o tranco: A civilização criada longe dos grandes centros é rica e orgulhosa de seus valores." *veja.* May 19, 122–27.

Ochoa, A. M. 2003a. *Entre los deseos y los derechos: Un ensayo crítico sobre políticas culturales.* Bogotá: ICANH.

———. 2003b. *Musicas locales en tiempos de globalizacion.* Bogotá: Grupo Editorial Norma.

O'Dougherty, M. 2002. *Consumption Intensified: The Politics of Middle-Class Daily Life in Brazil.* Durham, N.C.: Duke University Press.

Oliven, R. G. 1992. *A parte e o todo: A diversidade cultural no Brasil-Nação.* Petrópolis: Editora Vozes.

Ortiz, R. 1999. *A moderna tradição Brasileira: Cultura Brasileira e indústria cultural.* São Paulo: Editora Brasiliense.

Paley, J. 2001. "Making Democracy Count: Opinion Polls and Market Surveys in the Chilean Political Transition." *Cultural Anthropology* 16 (2): 135–64.

———. 2004. "Accountable Democracy: Citizens' Impact on Public Decision Making in Postdictatorship Chile." *American Ethnologist* 31 (4): 497–513.

Pascal, B. 1999. *Penseés and Other Writings.* Oxford: Oxford University Press.

Pecknold, D. 2007. *The Selling Sound: The Rise of the Country Music Industry.* Durham, N.C.: Duke University Press.

Peterson, R. A. 1997. *Creating Country Music: Fabricating Authenticity.* Chicago: University of Chicago Press.

Pires, C. 1927. *Conversas ao pé do fogo: Paginas regionães.* São Paulo: Companhia Editora Nacional.

———. 1985 [1910]. *Musa caipira: Contendo algumas produções em dialeto paulista* and *As aestrambóticas aventuras do Joaquim Bentinho (O Queima-Campo)*. Tietê, São Paulo: Prefeitura Municipal de Tietê.

Polanyi, K. 2001. *The Great Transformation: The Political and Economic Origins of Our Time*. Boston: Beacon Press.

Poovey, M. 1998. *A History of the Modern Fact: Problems of Knowledge in the Sciences of Wealth and Society*. Chicago: University of Chicago Press.

Povinelli, E. 2002. *The Cunning of Recognition: Indigenous Alterities and the Making of Australian Multiculturalism*. Durham, N.C.: Duke University Press.

Power, T. J., and J. T. Roberts. 2000. "A New Brazil: The Changing Sociodemographic Context of Brazilian Democracy." In *Democratic Brazil: Actors, Institutions, and Processes*, P. R. Kingstone and T. J. Power, eds., 236–63. Pittsburgh: University of Pittsburgh Press.

Prado, P. 1962. *Retrato do Brasil: Ensaio sobre a tristeza Brasileira*. Rio de Janeiro: Livraria José Olympio Editora.

Proust, M. 1981. "Swann's Way." In *Remembrance of Things Past*, vol. 1, 3–465. New York: Vintage Books.

Rebhun, L. A. 1999. *The Heart Is Unknown Country: Love in the Changing Economy of Northeast Brazil*. Stanford: Stanford University Press.

Reily, S. A. 1992. "'Música Sertaneja' and Migrant Identity: The Stylistic Development of a Brazilian Genre." *Popular Music* 11 (3): 337–58.

———. 2002. *Voices of the Magi: Enchanted Journeys in Southeast Brazil*. Chicago: University of Chicago Press.

Ribeiro, J. H. 2006. *Música caipira: As 270 maiores modas de todos os tempos*. São Paulo: Editora Globo S.A.

Ripardo, S. 2005. "Crítica: Formiguinhas da globo salvam 'América' do desastre." *Folha Online* (São Paulo). August 2.

Rohter, L. 2002. "Brazil Sets an Example in Computerizing Its National Elections." *New York Times*. October 30.

———. 2003. "Carnival in Rio Is Dancing to More Commercial Beat." *New York Times*. February 24.

———. 2004. "South America Seeks to Fill the World's Table." *New York Times*. December 12.

Rondon, J. E. 2005. "Empresa vai clonar touro bandido, da novela 'América'." *Folha de São Paulo*. August 17.

Rosa, J. G. 1963. *The Devil to Pay in the Backlands: 'The Devil in the Street, in the Middle of the Whirlwind'*. New York: Alfred A. Knopf.

———. 2001. *Sagarana*. Rio de Janeiro: Nova Fronteira.

Rosaldo, M. 1982. "The Things We Do with Words: Ilongot Speech Acts and Speech Act Theory in Philosophy." In *Language in Society*, vol. 2, 203–37. Cambridge: Cambridge University Press.

Sabino, M. 1996. "Jecocentrismo globalizado." *veja*. June 24, 101.

Sader, E. 2006. "Américas Latinas." *Caros Amigos* 10: 42.

Sahlins, M. 1998. "Two or Three Things That I Know about Culture." *Journal of the Royal Anthropological Institute* 5 (3): 399–421.

Saler, M. 2006. "Modernity and Enchantment: A Historiographic Review." *American Historical Review* 111 (3): 692–716.

Sant'Anna, R. 2000. *A mmoda é viola: Ensaio do cantar caipira*. São Paulo: Editora Unimar.

Santos, D. 1999. *Leandro and Leonardo: A vida real da querida dupla sertaneja*. Petropolis: Editora Vozes.

Santos, M. 1993. *A urbanização Brasileira*. São Paulo: Editora Hucitec.

Sarmiento, D. 1998. *Facundo: Or, Civilization and Barbarism*. New York: Penguin Books.

Saul, S. 2005. *Freedom Is, Freedom Ain't: Jazz and the Making of the Sixties*. Cambridge, Mass.: Harvard University Press.

Saussure, F. d. 1983. *Course in General Linguistics*. La Salle, Ill.: Open Court.

Sawaya, A. L., G. M. B. Solymos, T. M. Florêncio, P. Martins. 2003. "Os dois Brasis: quem São, onde estão e como vivem os pobres Brasileiros." *Estudos Avançados* 17 (48): 21–44.

Sebastião, R. F. 1999. "Dupla sertaneja investe sua fortuna na criação de gado." *Folha de São Paulo*. March 15.

Seeger, A. 1987. *Why Suyá Sing: A Musical Anthropology of an Amazonian People*. Cambridge: Cambridge University Press.

Shirley, R. 1971. *The End of a Tradition: Culture Change and Development in the Município of Cunha, São Paulo, Brazil*. New York: Columbia University Press.

Shryock, A. 2004a. "Other Conscious/Self Aware: First Thoughts on Cultural Intimacy and Mass Mediation." In *Off Stage/On Display: Intimacy and Ethnography in the Age of Public Culture*, ed. A. Shryock, 3–30. Palo Alto, Calif.: Stanford University Press.

———, ed. 2004b. *Off Stage/On Display: Intimacy and Ethnography in the Age of Public Culture*. Palo Alto, Calif.: Stanford University Press.

Silverstein, M. 1979. "Language Structure and Linguistic Ideology." Paper presented at the conference The Elements: A Parasession on Linguistic Units and Levels. Chicago: Chicago Linguistic Society.

———. 1981a. "The Limits of Awareness." *Working Papers in Sociolinguistics* 84: 31.

———. 1981b. "Metaforces of Power in Traditional Oratory." Lecture delivered at Yale University, February.

———. 1996. "Monoglot 'Standard' in America: Standardization and Metaphors of Linguistic Hegemony." In *The Matrix of Language*, ed. D. B. a. R. Macaulay, 284–306. Boulder, Colo.: Westview Press.

———. 1998a. "Contemporary Transformations of Local Linguistic Communities." *Annual Review of Anthropology* 27: 403–26.

———. 1998b. "The Uses and Utility of Language Ideology: A Commentary." In *Language Ideologies: Practice and Theory*, K. W. Bambi Schieffelin and Paul Kroskrity, eds., 123–45. New York: Oxford University Press.

———. 1999. "NIMBY Goes Linguistic: Conflicted 'Voicings' from the Culture of Local Language Communities." In *Proceedings from the Panels of the Chicago Linguistic Society's Thirty-Fifth Meeting*, 101–23. Chicago: The Chicago Linguistic Society.

———. 2003. *Talking Politics: The Substance of Style from Abe to 'W'*. Chicago: Prickly Paradigm Press.

———. 2005. "Axes of Evals: Token versus Type Interdiscursivity." *Journal of Linguistic Anthropology* 15 (1): 6–22.

Silverstein, M., and G. Urban. 1998. "The Natural History of Discourse." In *Natural Histories of Discourse*, M. Silverstein and G. Urban, eds., 1–17. Chicago: University of Chicago Press.

Skidmore, T. 1967. *Politics in Brazil, 1930–1964: An Experiment in Democracy*. New York: Oxford University Press.

———. 1988. *The Politics of Military Rule in Brazil, 1964–1985*. New York: Oxford University Press.

Skidmore, T., and P. Smith. 1997. *Modern Latin America*. New York: Oxford University Press.

Souza, O. d. 1999. "Oura na garganta: A riqueza do interior impulsiona as duplas sertanejas na conquista do público das grandes cidades." *veja*. May 19, 132–33.

Spitulnik, D. 1997. "The Social Circulation of Media Discourse and the Mediation of Communities." *Journal of Linguistic Anthropology* 6 (2): 161–87.

———. 2002. "Mobile Machines and Fluid Audiences: Rethinking Reception through Zambian Radio Culture." In *Media Worlds: Anthropology on New Terrain*, F. Ginsburg, L. Abu-Lughod, and B. Larkin, eds., 337–54. Berkeley: University of California Press.

Steedman, C. 1987. *Landscape for a Good Woman: A Story of Two Lives*. New Brunswick, N.J.: Rutgers University Press.

Stepan, A. 1998. "Federalism and Democracy." Democratic Invention Lecture Series, Washington, D.C. November 2.

Stewart, K. 1996. *A Space on the Side of the Road: Cultural Poetics in an "Other" America*. Princeton: Princeton University Press.

Stokes, M. 1992. *The Arabesk Debate: Music and Musicians in Modern Turkey*. Oxford: Clarendon.

Sudnow, D. 1978. *Ways of the Hand: The Organization of Improvised Conduct*. Cambridge, Mass.: Harvard University Press.

Tigre, P. B. 2003. "Brazil in the Age of Electronic Commerce." *The Information Society* 19 (1): 33–43.

Tinhorão, J. R. 1986. *Pequena história da música Brasileira: Da modinha ao tropicalismo*. São Paulo: Art Editora.

Tonico and Tinoco. 1984. *Da beira da tuia ao teatro municipal*. São Paulo: Editora Ática.

Trouillot, M.-R. 1991. "Anthropology and the Savage Slot: The Poetics and Politics of Otherness." In *Recapturing Anthropology*, ed. R. Fox, 18–44. Santa Fe: School of American Research.

Turner, T. 1979. "The Gê and Bororo Societies as Dialectical Systems: A General Model." In *Dialectical Societies: The Gê and Bororo of Central Brazil*, ed. D. Maybury-Lewis, 147–78. Cambridge, Mass.: Harvard University Press.

———. 1984. "Value, Production, and Exploitation in Non-Capitalist Societies." Paper presented at AAA—Symposium on Culture and Historical Materialism, Denver. November.

———. 1992. "Os Mebengokre Kayapo: de communidades autónomas ao sistema inter-etnica." In *Historia dos Indios no Brazil*, ed. M. Carneiro da Cunha, 311–38. São Paulo: Companhia das Letras.

———. 2002. "Representation, Politics, and Cultural Imagination in Indigenous Video: General Points and Kayapo Examples." In *Media Worlds: Anthropology on New Terrain*, F. Ginsburg, L. Abu-Lughod, and B. Larkin, eds., 75–89. Berkeley: University of California Press.

———. 2003. "Class Projects, Social Consciousness, and the Contradictions of 'Globalization'." In *Globalization, the State, and Violence*, ed. J. Friedman, 35–67. Lanham, Md.: Rowman and Littlefield.

Urban, G. 1993. *A Discourse-Centered Approach to Culture: Native South American Myths and Rituals*. Austin: University of Texas Press.

———. 1999. "The Role of Comparison in Light of the Theory of Culture." In *Critical Comparisons in Politics and Culture*, J. Bowen and R. Peterson, eds., 90–109. Cambridge: Cambridge University Press.

Veloso, C. 2002. *Tropical Truth: A Story of Music and Revolution in Brazil*. New York: Alfred A. Knopf.

Vianna, H. 1999. *The Mystery of Samba: Popular Music and National Identity in Brazil*. Chapel Hill, N.C.: University of North Carolina Press.

Vicente, E. 2002. "Música e o Disco no Brasil: A Trajetória da Indústria nas Décadas de 80 e 90." PhD dissertation. School of Communication and the Arts, University of São Paulo.

Viola, B. d. 1992. *A viola caipira: Técnicas para ponteio*. São Paulo: Ricordi.

Waisbord, S. 1998. "The Ties That Still Bind: Media and National Culture in Latin America." *Canadian Journal of Communication* 23: 381–411.

Warner, M. 2002. "Publics and Counterpublics." *Public Culture* 14 (1): 49–90.

Weidman, A. 2006. *Singing the Classical, Voicing the Modern: The Postcolonial Politics of Music in South India*. Durham, N.C.: Duke University Press.

Whorf, B. L. 1956. "The Relation of Habitual Thought and Behavior to Language." In *Language, Thought, and Reality*, ed. J. B. Carroll, 134–60. Cambridge, Mass.: MIT Press.

Wilk, R. 1999. " 'Real Belizean Food': Building Local Identity in the Transnational Caribbean." *American Anthropologist* 101 (2): 244–55.

Williams, G. 2002. *The Other Side of the Popular: Neoliberalism and Subalternity in Latin America*. Durham, N.C.: Duke University Press.

Williams, R. 1973. *The Country and the City*. New York: Oxford University Press.

———. 1977. *Marxism and Literature*. Oxford: Oxford University Press.

Wooden, W. S., and G. Ehringer. 1996. *Rodeo in America: Wranglers, Roughstock, and Paydirt*. Lawrence: University Press of Kansas.

Woolard, K., and B. Schieffelin. 1994. "Language Ideology." *Annual Review of Anthropology* 23: 55–82.

Yeats, W. B. 1996. *The Collected Poems of W. B. Yeats*. New York: Scribner.

Yúdice, G. 1994. "The Funkification of Rio." In *Microphone Fiends: Youth Music and Youth Culture*, A. Ross and T. Rose, eds., 193–217. New York: Routledge.

Yúdice, G., J. Franco, and J. Flores, eds. 1992. *On Edge: The Crisis of Contemporary Latin American Culture*. Cultural Politics. Minneapolis: University of Minnesota Press.

Zan, J. R. 1995. "Da roça a Nashville." *Rua, Campinas* 1: 113–36.

Index

Note: f = figure; m = map; n = note; t = table

ALEXANDER DENT is an assistant professor
of anthropology and international affairs
at The George Washington University.